About Island Press

ISLAND PRESS, a nonprofit organization, publishes, markets, and distributes the most advanced thinking on the conservation of our natural resources—books about soil, land, water, forests, wildlife, and hazardous and toxic wastes. These books are practical tools used by public officials, business and industry leaders, natural resource managers, and concerned citizens working to solve both local and global resource problems.

Founded in 1978, Island Press reorganized in 1984 to meet the increasing demand for substantive books on all resource-related issues. Island Press publishes and distributes under its own imprint and offers these services to other nonprofit organizations.

Support for Island Press is provided by Apple Computers Inc., The Mary Reynolds Babcock Foundation, The Educational Foundation of America, The Charles Engelhard Foundation, The Ford Foundation, The George Gund Foundation, The William and Flora Hewlett Foundation, The Joyce Foundation, The J. M. Kaplan Fund, The John D. and Catherine T. MacArthur Foundation, The Andrew W. Mellon Foundation, The Joyce Mertz-Gilmore Foundation, The New-Land Foundation, Northwest Area Foundation, The Jessie Smith Noyes Foundation, The J. N. Pew, Jr. Charitable Trust, The Rockefeller Brothers Fund, The Florence and John Schumann Foundation, and The Tides Foundation.

SHADING
OUR CITIES

SHADING OUR CITIES

A RESOURCE GUIDE FOR URBAN AND COMMUNITY FORESTS

EDITED BY
Gary Moll and Sara Ebenreck

Introduction by R. Neil Sampson
American Forestry Association

Foreword by F. Dale Robertson
Chief, U.S.D.A. Forest Service

ISLAND PRESS
Washington, D.C. ☐ *Covelo, California*

© 1989 by American Forestry Association

All rights reserved. No part of this book may be reproduced in any form or by any means without permission in writing from the publisher: Island Press, Suite 300, 1718 Connecticut Avenue NW, Washington, D.C. 20009.

Permissions to quote from copyrighted material appear on page 317.

Library of Congress Cataloging-in-Publication Data

Shading our cities.

    Sponsored by the American Forestry Association.
    Includes index.
    1. Urban forestry.   2. Urban forestry—United States.
I. Moll, Gary. II. Ebenreck, Sara. III. American
Forestry Association.
SB436.S49 1989   715'.2'091732   89-15453
ISBN 0-933280-96-3 (alk. paper)
ISBN 0-933280-95-5 (pbk. : alk. paper)

Printed on recycled, acid-free paper

Manufactured in the United States of America

10 9 8 7 6 5 4 3 2 1

Contents

APPENDIXES

Foreword

FOR MANY AMERICANS, the word *forest* brings images of rural lands covered with mile after mile of trees. But it is important to recognize that the nation's forests are not limited to rural America. As cities have become home for more and more of our citizens, awareness of the importance and value of the forests that cover—or should cover—our urban and community areas has grown. We know that the trees of our cities are vitally important for social, economic, and environmental reasons. They also add natural beauty to our urban surroundings, but they do far more than this. They are the lungs, air-conditioners, and natural filters of our cities. They, too, are a national treasure that needs appreciation, conservation, and active management.

Urban trees are in the minds and hearts of many people, and their involvement in urban forestry action projects exemplifies their interest and support. Because, as this book documents, the health problems of our urban forests are so great, an unparalleled opportunity and need exists for citizens and local communities to increase and expand their urban forestry activities. This book provides the information that community leaders, urban forestry professionals, and all citizens need to create stronger programs in places where actions have begun *and* to get new programs under way in places where none exists.

We encourage citizens, communities, and community leaders everywhere to join in renewed efforts to expand and better manage our urban and community forests. These trees are a resource not only for us, but for our children and their children. Our efforts will reward us not only with what we need today, but will also provide a rich legacy for future generations.

F. Dale Robertson, Chief
U.S.D.A. Forest Service

Acknowledgments

THIS BOOK REQUIRED the thoughtful, kind, and prompt attention of many people for its completion. The members of the National Urban Forest Council, by focusing on major gaps in published material about urban forestry, provided the stimulus for many of the articles first published or reprinted here. The board of directors and executive vice president of the American Forestry Association, by their enthusiastic approval for the project, provided the institutional support without which the book could not have been completed. And the interest expressed by Island Press in the potential of this book provided the publishing framework needed to move ahead with it.

Without exception, the authors of articles included here responded with prompt generosity to our requests for new materials, adaptations, and reprint rights. Their spirit of commitment to the future of city and community forests is one strong grounds for the hope that, by the dawning of the twenty-first century, we will indeed see significant positive change in the ways we integrate forests and people in community environments.

As the project moved into its final phase, its timely completion is indebted to the assumption of assistant editorial duties by Robert Dyke, who also acted as photo editor and gave oversight to the final preparation of appendix materials. Rita Rooney gave prompt and capable word processing to large portions of the manuscript. Finally, we would like to acknowledge the work of *American Forests* editors Bill Rooney and Deborah Boerner, who first prepared a number of these manuscripts for their original publication in that magazine; and Island Press editor Barbara Dean and her associated staff, who provided a final polishing of the manuscript.

Gary Moll and Sara Ebenreck

Introduction

R. Neil Sampson

THIS BOOK REPRESENTS a significant milestone for the survival of trees in our cities—what are called our "urban forests"—and the people who care about trees and community. Although a good amount of published information about urban forestry exists, this is the first compilation of articles from a wide spectrum of viewpoints designed for the concerned public as well as for interested professionals. Citizen activists, community leaders, and voices from the inner city and the newly transformed country-side are all included here along with the viewpoints of professionals, many of whom have given decades of service to the cause of urban trees.

At the same time, this book is a harbinger of a renewed, stronger urban ecology movement. Citizens and communities in the United States have only begun to understand the value and significance of their community forests. The current decline in urban forests, combined with mounting pressures on the overall environmental health of our communities, make it vital that more Americans come to see these values more clearly. We think that accessible information is essential to inspiring an even stronger urban forestry effort, both nationally and locally.

Where trees are ill-kept, dying, or diminishing, we often find a community that feels run down, although trees are seldom recognized as either part of the cause or a symptom of the community's woes. But the truth stands clear—trees symbolize permanence and stability. Where they thrive, a community feels good about itself, and that feeling manifests itself in many ways, both socially and economically.

The chapters in this volume demonstrate how communities can both feel better and be made more livable through more attention to their trees. Another of the book's underlying ideas is that improving the condition of today's urban forests can be one positive response to the global threat of climate change. This is not to claim that the world's woes can be solved in any one community, but if each community improves itself a little, the global situation will improve in the process.

This then is a sourcebook for that purpose. Although no single book can provide comprehensive practical information on urban forestry for a nation of such diverse climates you will find a solid selection of practical advice in these pages. This volume will tell you, for example, how to calculate the economic worth of a tree, how to measure the health of your community forest, and how to build a citizen action program. Along with reporting that lack of rooting space is a major cause of health problems in urban trees, this book will explain how a tree's root system works and what both individual homeowners and city planners can do to assure that roots have space to grow. Because these chapters span the distance from vision to practical ideas, we hope they will be read not only by already committed people, but also by city councilmembers, planners, and managers, by county commissioners and state politicians, and by anyone else whose decisions affect the future of our nation's urban forests.

Over the last decade, a special kind of ingenuity and strength has developed among local urban forestry activists in their struggle to develop urban forestry programs. Their stories and original ideas about building better cities are included in these pages along with overviews of programs and new scientific information from experts.

Also important to the entire urban forestry effort, although it is less visible in these pages, is the support provided by the U.S. Department of Agriculture, in particular the Forest Service and Extension Service, which have been strong, supportive partners in the movement. The Forest Service has administered federal grants, coordinated efforts between Washington and the states, and provided the basic financial support to allow a national program to gain a foothold. The National Urban Forest Council, sponsored by the American Forestry Association, has relied heavily on that federal support. The fifty state foresters have taken federal grants that were never very large in terms of dollars and leveraged them to build an increasingly effective cadre of urban forestry professionals in cities and communities across the country.

Without strong friends in Congress, however, there would be no federal urban forestry program. This has always been one of those small programs that are so easily targeted in budget-cutting exercises, and almost every administration budget proposal in the last decade would have eliminated it. That didn't happen largely because citizens from all over the country informed their congressional delegation about the broad range of benefits being achieved with the small budgets of this program. Effective and powerful members of Congress listened, understood, and acted to keep the federal program intact, so that in 1989, $3.2 million in federal funds have been allocated for urban and community forestry programs.

So the fact that urban forestry programs are alive, well, and growing in the United States today is the result of many helping hands. The American

Forestry Association is privileged to have occupied a central role in this emergence of public attention to the trees and forests that occupy our urban and community living spaces. Gary Moll, coeditor of this book, has been a primary source of the energy that has created a strong and growing network of information-sharing and technical support among state and local programs. As a vice president at the American Forestry Association, he and the others you will meet in the following pages exemplify what members and staff of the association have represented since 1875: concerned citizens and professionals willing to expend time, energy, and skills in order that the United States may continue to be blessed with environments graced by healthy, thriving trees and forests.

We at the association hope this book will be a catalyst for even further growth in public consciousness about the importance of trees in the places where we live and work.

PART ONE

URBAN FORESTS: AN OVERVIEW

Trees—some deliberately planted, others volunteer sprouts or stalwart remnants of an earlier forest cover—have been part of most American cities from their very beginnings. Today, changes in climate, the decline of existing urban forests, and a growing awareness of the value of trees tell us it is time to give more attention to how trees and people are getting along in our cities. This section provides an overall look at the urban forest and its issues.

1

Needed: A New Vision for Our Communities

R. Neil Sampson

PEOPLE ARE BY nature forest dwellers. The evidence is all around us—not in some theoretical book about human origins—but in the way we choose to live. From pioneer families moving into sod huts on the prairie to today's young couples anxiously contemplating the enormity of the mortgage on a first home, the same instincts prevail. As soon as possible, just about everyone plants trees around the dwelling place. Shade trees, fruit trees, windbreaks, ornamentals—all are aimed at marking the site as a home, a place where life is pleasant both inside and outside the four walls and where the dwellers feel secure in their environment.

In the past, those who treasured trees the most seemed to be people who settled in areas where trees were not common. Scandinavians settling in Wilton, North Dakota, planted windbreaks and shelterbelts to soften a cold, windy climate. Germans settling in New Braunfels, Texas, planted trees for shade from a harsh sun.

Today, more than ever before, Americans are city dwellers. Gone are many of the original homesteads of the rural countryside (except, in some cases, for the remaining trees), and gone, too, are many rural families who have migrated to the cities in search of better opportunities. Estimates indicate that the 1990 census will find 75 percent of all Americans living

within fifty miles of the nation's coastlines, most of them within the con-
fines or orbits of large urban areas.

At one extreme, this urban environment can be sterile and mechanistic,
made up of concrete, stone, iron, and copper—square buildings, each a lot
like the ones on either side, connected by a complex system of pipes, wires,
tunnels, sidewalks, and streets. Put a dome over the top and introduce
artificial heating, cooling, and light, and you have the space city that has
long captured the imagination of science fiction writers. But when that
same city is softened and buffered by trees, parks, boulevards, flower
beds, curved walkways, and shady river banks, it becomes something
entirely different. The term *habitat* comes to mind. This is a place where
people—and plants, birds and animals—live. This is home.

The challenge, of course, is not to abandon urban design or workable
systems. The challenge is to merge the designed, man-made environment
and the managed, natural environment so that neither is destroyed in the
process.

From Heat Islands to True Habitats

Unfortunately, in most American cities, the downtown area may be from
three to ten degrees hotter than the surrounding region on a summer
day—a fact that has given rise to the phrase "urban heat islands." City air is
almost certain to be polluted, often to the point of being health-
threatening. Water, while readily available, is often heavily chlorinated to
assure reasonable freedom from bacteria and parasites, at the same time
increasing the likelihood that it will contain cancer-causing chloro-organic
compounds. City streets are more likely to be known for crime statistics
than for safety.

Why are we not more successful in creating a better quality of life in
urban areas? It can't be because it doesn't matter; anything that affects the
everyday life of the majority of Americans must matter. It can't be that we
don't know how; each generation has the knowledge of prior generations at
its disposal, and the current generation is the most technologically advanced that ever lived. While we debate the intricacies of Star Wars and
space travel, it seems reasonable that keeping our own nest unfouled
would be a fairly basic achievement.

It may be that the huge size of many urban areas and the enormity of the
problems affecting them paralyze people and overwhelm the institutional
capacity of local governments. But that wouldn't explain why a small town
that has spent decades enjoying the ambience created by its founders
would let that ambience slowly deteriorate.

It may be that American society has become so self-centered and self-
indulgent that there are not enough people willing to pay attention to the

good of the community and to make the individual effort needed to rebuild community institutions. But there are too many examples of excellent community work to make that a general indictment. So that leaves the possibility that if there were more enlightened leadership—appointed and elected officials willing to take risks—and more public education so that people were more skilled in recognizing the slow and steady deterioration of their community, if the technologies involved in repairing that deterioration were more widely available, and if the job were broken down into small segments that individuals and community-sized groups could successfully tackle—the result would be more livable communities.

One area where this communal effort is doable is in our city forests. The quality of the environment is a major factor in establishing the quality of community life, and it is here that individuals and small groups can make a significant difference.

Trees planted around homes, along streets and parking lots, and in urban lots and parks can break up the heat islands that develop around most communities. The decrease in air-conditioning needed would help lower everyone's energy costs and cut energy usage and its consequent pollutants accordingly. Obviously, trees that shade dark surfaces such as streets, buildings, and parking lots are the most valuable, so older, larger trees are more effective than smaller ones. But every tree is of some value as it affects air currents, cools the air through transpiration, and shades the ground from the summer sun.

Researchers have found that recuperating hospital patients placed in rooms with windows facing trees heal significantly faster and require far less pain-killing drugs than those in rooms without such a view. It seems logical to assume that the same benefits might extend to the concept of "wellness," where people who live within constant view of the natural world enjoy better health, although no research to demonstrate that claim has been conducted.

The best time to make a city fit into the natural environment, of course, is during the planning and development phases. Obviously, that time is long gone in many urban areas, but not everywhere. New developments are a constant factor in many communities. Are those new developments being fitted into the environment skillfully, or are they just being "bulldozed in" as quickly as possible?

Are new homebuyers paying premium prices for "wooded homesites," only to discover in a couple of years that the excavation, construction, and landscaping have compacted soils, damaged root systems, and scarred tree trunks to the point where their valued shade trees are simply high-priced firewood? Are streets, sidewalks, and waterways being designed wide enough to provide room for trees to grow and be healthy?

In established communities, are the trees that our parents planted being cared for properly? Are they trimmed before they become a hazard and removed promptly when they die? Are new trees constantly being planted to replace those that are removed or die or to fill open spaces?

The answer, too often, is no. In many communities, the urban forest is deteriorating—and the quality of life of the community is declining with it. For these areas, a new vision is needed. Instead of being content with letting the natural environment be abused and natural elements such as urban forests die, people can decide to rebuild and renew their community.

Renewing the urban forest won't fix everything that's wrong with a community, but it is an excellent place to begin. The growth in community pride and spirit that results from the work of planting and caring for trees, the very real change in appearance that results in only a few short years, and the unseen but very real benefits—such as cooler temperatures and more healthful surroundings—are soon reflected in a variety of other ways.

Efforts to renew downtown and older urban areas can bring a new infusion of community pride to a city's most neglected residents, its inner city dwellers. Here is where we find the poor, the homeless, the elderly. They are more at the mercy of the elements than their more affluent neighbors, yet too often they live in the most exposed portions of the community. Increasing shade trees, greenways, and parks here is not just a matter of beautification. It can mean air that's fit to breathe on a stifling summer day, tolerable temperatures and places to sit in the shade and cool off, and homes and schools with a far lower level of heat-induced stress and social unrest.

So it is important to all city dwellers—and especially those in charge of city government—to envision new possibilities for our communities. When our communities are shady, tree-covered, pleasant places, we can truly say that they have been designed as home—habitat—for all their residents and visitors.

Disturbed Soil to Gypsy Moth: The Obstacles We Face

The urban environment may be improved by a better urban forest, but getting and maintaining that forest are not easy tasks. In too many cities, the space for trees to grow and thrive no longer exists. Streets, sidewalks, and building foundations take up most of the space, channeling available water into storm sewers and providing almost no open soil to take up air and water needed for healthy tree-root growth. Air pollution concentrations are abnormally high and have exceptionally high levels of ozone, one of the major products created in the air as the result of automobile exhaust and a pollutant that has been scientifically linked to tree damage.

So urban trees are almost always facing bad growing conditions. Drought is rampant because of hotter temperatures in midcity and because most of the available rain is channeled off rather than soaking into the soil. Urban soils are largely construction rubble and have little resemblance to normal soil structure. Fertility may be nonexistent when urban soils are badly disturbed and when there is no undergrowth or animal life to help produce nutrients.

Mechanical damage is common as well. Trees may be destroyed by automobiles, trucks, bicycles, or other sources of bruising, such as lawn mowers. A seemingly innocuous bump may produce an opening to the inner bark, which allows disease or fungus to enter, spelling the beginning of the end for the tree. As a result, according to recent surveys, the average city tree lives only thirty-two years and dies just when it is beginning to reach the most valuable stage of its life.

America's urban forests are in trouble—in the average city, about four trees die or are removed for each new one planted. That number can go as high as eight or ten in some cities. The reasons are many. One is that trees have often been allowed to grow old without maintenance or replacement. Suddenly, the city finds itself awash in dead and dying trees. The budget for urban forestry is fully absorbed with cleaning up these problems, and nothing remains for the necessary planting and tree care needed to rebuild a healthy, productive urban forest.

Another problem in recent years has been insect and disease epidemics that have swept through many portions of the country. Dutch elm disease moved through many cities in the 1970s; where the stately elm was used almost exclusively for its wonderful shade properties, the effect was disastrous. Today, few American elms remain in any city, and the rebuilding process has been both slow and expensive. The gypsy moth, eating its way through hardwoods (primarily oaks), and oak wilt are creating similar problems. When such epidemics hit, shady, pleasant communities can be converted almost overnight into barren urban heat islands.

Urban trees, just like forests everywhere, respond to good management. We can extend the lives of urban and community trees from their current average of thirty-two years to something far longer—and in the process double or triple the benefits each tree confers on the community. Good forest management doesn't cost. It pays.

THE GLOBAL CONTEXT AND THE GREENHOUSE EFFECT

As we look at the opportunities and recognize the difficulties of improving our urban habitats, it is important to look beyond the city's boundaries and think of its relationship to the region, the nation, and the world as a whole. Economically and environmentally, a city's influence extends far beyond its boundaries. Cities that produce significant amounts of waste heat or air pollution affect surrounding and downwind environments for many miles. A serious water pollution problem can affect whole river systems and pollute estuarian and ocean habitats far beyond the river's mouth.

Today, more than ever before, we are aware that many of our actions have global consequences. We're also aware that global systems, even though they appear large and complex beyond all human scale, are being adversely affected by human actions. Thus, we come to an important realization: human actions, whether those of one person, one community, or an entire nation, need to be environmentally constructive. People need to make the earth more healthy, not more sick. If humans continue to wage war upon the planet, there is no guarantee that the planet and its systems will not strike back. The evidence that some of that is already happening is compelling and frightening.

During the 1980s, we endured the six hottest years of the century. According to scientists from the National Aeronautics and Science Administration (NASA), the rate of global warming during the past two decades is the highest since records have been kept (for about 130 years), about three times higher than would be anticipated from normal cycles or fluctuations.

What's happening? Has the greenhouse effect finally begun, some one hundred years after it was first predicted? Scientists can't say for sure, but Dr. James Hansen of NASA told Congress in 1988 that he was "99 percent confident" that the current temperatures represent a real warming trend rather than a chance fluctuation.

Scientists agree that carbon dioxide levels have been rising swiftly and steadily for several decades, causing a 30 percent increase in atmospheric concentration over the past twenty years. Many scientists predict a doubling of the gas within forty to fifty more years. There is significant disagreement, however, on the exact effect this could have on the climate.

Some, like NASA's Hansen, use computer models—called *global circulation models*—to predict a continuing rise in average global temperatures, particularly in the northern temperate regions. Others, looking at similar models but making different assumptions, predict a new ice age. Still others look at the current temperature trends as simply part of normal weather cycles that will return to cooler years as usual.

But a growing number of scientists agree on the global warming theory. They point to the rise in carbon dioxide as one of the major culprits. This gas acts like the glass in a greenhouse. The sun's rays penetrate the atmosphere, hit the earth, and are reflected as a longer-wave heat. Layers of carbon dioxide bounce the heat waves back toward the earth, trapping heat that would otherwise radiate back into space from earth. Other gases such ·as chlorofluorocarbons and methane add to this effect, but carbon dioxide is estimated to cause about half the greenhouse effect. If the present rate of carbon dioxide release continues, scientists estimate that atmospheric levels of the gas could double in a few years.

On the basis of global circulation models, these scientists are now convinced that a doubling of carbon dioxide in the atmosphere will be accompanied by a further rise in *average* temperatures in parts of the United States of anywhere from six to twelve degrees Fahrenheit.

Six to twelve degrees may not seem like much if we consider that on a normal autumn day temperatures may zoom up and down over a thirty-degree span. But overall rises of this magnitude in the average global temperature aren't normal. In fact, they've never occurred in recorded history.

The possible effects are far-reaching. Millions of acres of forests could be lost as heat and drought make trees more susceptible to disease, insects, and fire. Droughts could threaten food crop production. Desert conditions could spread in parts of the South and Midwest, and ocean levels could rise by as much as five feet, polluting groundwater supplies with salt and badly damaging low-lying cities and regions. Personal levels of discomfort felt by heat-sensitive people in summer of 1988 may seem minimal compared with such a future. The thought of such disastrous changes has created intense public pressure to find ways to begin slowing down carbon dioxide buildup and reducing the ultimate effect of the greenhouse phenomenon.

None of these changes is inevitable, of course. Scientists who make predictions are only guessing, and there is considerable room for speculation and skepticism. But there is little doubt that the risks are high. If serious climatic changes can be somehow avoided or made less serious, they should be. If people are convinced that scientists have enough evidence to make a credible case, then it is no longer sufficient simply to be concerned. It is time for action.

In the search for places to begin reducing carbon dioxide levels, it is clear that world energy use is the major culprit. In 1987, the world's people burned enough fuel to release about 5.4 billion tons of carbon into the air. The United States alone contributed an estimated 25 percent of that amount. Deforestation is the other major cause, accounting for about 20 percent of the additional carbon dioxide. An estimated 27 million acres of tropical forests are destroyed by land clearing and burning each year. Add to that some 13 million acres logged or used for firewood and the total comes up to some 40 million acres each year. Satellite photographs showing as many as 7,000 fires burning in the Brazilian forest on one day in 1988 gave indications that this estimate may need to be raised.

As forests are cleared and burned, huge amounts of carbon dioxide are released directly to the air. Where forests are replaced by farm crops or pastures, the resulting vegetation is not nearly as effective in converting carbon dioxide to cellulose as a regrowing forest would be. The result is subtraction from the total amount of global plant life working to take carbon dioxide from the air and return it to an earthbound form.

The real key lies in how fast trees grow and add wood to their roots, trunks, and limbs. A tree takes up carbon dioxide in the process of photosynthesis, uses it as a basic building block for new organic compounds, and gives off oxygen in the process. The former carbon dioxide is then stored as cellulose in the tree's wood, or moves on to muscle tissue in an animal that eats leaves, or becomes part of the body of a soil bacterium that feeds on tree roots. It will remain bound to the earth until it is released again through respiration, burning, or some other chemical transformation.

Thus, carbon moves through plants, soils, animals and the air in a continuous cycle of change. Although all plants are important in taking carbon dioxide out of the air and converting it to plant material and oxygen, when it comes to taking the carbon "out of circulation" for a longer period of time, it is forests that are the most critical. Of the total amount of carbon tied up in earthbound forms, it is estimated that 90 percent is contained in the forests of the world.

Clearly, trees and forests are major actors in keeping the carbon cycle balanced. A fast-growing forest tree absorbs up to forty-eight pounds of carbon dioxide a year; that adds up to ten tons per acre of trees—enough to offset the carbon dioxide produced by driving a car 21,000 miles.

The contribution of an urban tree may be even more significant if fast-growing species are given good growing space and favorable light, fertility, and moisture conditions. In addition to its direct benefit from taking up carbon dioxide through photosynthesis, an urban tree may have an indirect effect upon carbon dioxide that is up to fifteen times larger. This will come about because of the energy-conserving value of its shade and the cooling effect of transpiration. That cooling translates into lower energy consumption for air-conditioning, which translates into less coal and oil burning, which in turn means less carbon dioxide buildup in the atmosphere. So planting trees around homes and in communities is one of the best ways to address the greenhouse effect and the global warming problem.

It has been estimated that there are 100 million "tree spaces" available around homes and businesses within American communities. Filling these spaces with mature trees could result in a savings of 500 *trillion kilowatt-hours* of energy and cut as much as 18 million tons of U.S. carbon dioxide production each year. Those trees would reduce the amount of carbon dioxide in the air—and the greenhouse effect—as much as a new forest larger than the state of Connecticut. In addition, there are 60 million open spaces along public roadways that need trees and millions of other open spaces in parks in greenways. Having trees in all these planting places would help to cool urban heat islands.

Compared with total global emission levels, that amount is still small—a good deal less than 1 percent of the total. So it is important not to envision urban and community tree planting as the only approach to global warming issues. If tropical forests continue to be destroyed, for example, the results of our community tree planting would be overwhelmed. But global issues need multiple approaches, and the right niche for any particular citizen or organization is something that can be *done*, not just something they *hope* someone else will do. Tree planting and urban forest improvement have the virtue of being actions that move in the right direction and, at the same time, educate about the fundamental nature of the global issue.

THINK GLOBALLY, ACT LOCALLY: THE VALUE OF SMALL ACTS

The point that is so vitally important to understand is that individual citizens *can make a difference.* Global environmental conditions, despite their enormity, may be out of balance because neglect as well as destructive actions have damaged the natural world. What is needed are constructive actions that are aimed at rebuilding and regenerating natural systems, locally and globally.

Cleveland Division of Forestry

An important step in improving our urban forests: passing our knowledge and commitment to the next generation. Alan Klonowski, systems forester for the Cleveland Electric Illuminating Company, demonstrates to school children how to plant a tree.

In the yards of homes all over the nation, people can begin by planting trees. Working with their neighbors, citizens can bring pressure on city officials to improve community forests and parks. The effect will be a better, more livable community for everyone and a community that does its one small part toward solving a global problem. A really good community forestry program is virtually always backed up by active, involved citizens groups.

Obviously, urban and community trees won't address all the forest problems in this country or the world. National as well as international actions are needed to right the imbalances now leading toward global climate change. In the United States, energy waste needs to be reduced and alternative fuel sources sought out and implemented. Air pollution, which is spewing greenhouse gasses and the chemical ingredients of ozone and acid rain into the air, must be reduced. Research on the changes likely to result in forestry and agriculture from climate changes—and the practices that will be helpful to respond—is in its infancy and needs priority attention. And incentives for improved forest management on both private and public lands must be put in place.

These actions will demand strong national political leadership. But national leadership needs to be backed by national constituencies. Each of us has the chance to multiply our individual effectiveness by exercising our citizenship as well. We need to let our leaders know how we feel. We need to join national organizations that are promoting ideas that we feel are important. The Global ReLeaf effort at the American Forestry Association is one such effort that needs citizen support. Working together, through our conservation organizations and the various levels of government, Americans can accomplish a great deal. We can't fix all the world's problems, but we can fix many of our own and be a model for other countries as they search for their own solutions. One hundred million new trees in America's communities could send a signal worldwide that Americans are not just asking Third World countries to save their tropical forests, but that we are acting to right the balance here in our own country as well.

A happy side effect of such efforts is that they can't go wrong. If, as the skeptics predict, all this talk about global warming is just a scare story that will never become a reality—Americans will have done the right thing anyway. We'll have halted the destruction of one of the world's greatest resources, made our homes and communities more pleasant, livable places, reduced the burning of fossil fuels for energy production, created economically and environmentally beneficial wildlife habitat and ground cover on more of our rural lands, and provided a shade canopy over our cities that our grandchildren will bless us for in the summer of 2020.

The way to start is with the improvement of our common habitat—our own town or city—by renewing the urban forest. The time to start is now.

2

In Search of an Ecological Urban Landscape

Gary Moll

IN 1869, ERNEST HAECKEL, a German scientist known for his ability to popularize science, introduced the world to the concept of ecology. Deriving the new term from the Greek word *oikos,* which means house, Haeckel used *ecology* to explain a concept of evolutionary theory involving the interactions of diverse organisms with their environment. Over the last 130 years, however, the popular use of the concept has steadily expanded its original meaning. Paleontologist and writer Stephen Jay Gould, in his first book, *Ever Since Darwin* (1977), mused: "Ecology [has become] a label for anything good that happens far from cities or anything that does not have synthetic chemicals in it."

Cities and ecology are an odd association, as Gould suggests, because our track record of building cities has nothing to do with understanding how natural organisms relate to their environment. Most of the people who design and build cities have successfully isolated themselves from the natural sciences and make no attempt to cultivate even a superficial relationship. Cities could be considered the "black holes" of the natural landscape because in them the fibers that connect nature's web have been broken. A city is not now the place to discover the complex workings of the natural system where species can develop in the wealth of diversity. It is rather a place where nature is sparse, where plants and wildlife struggle to survive, where growing healthy trees is a challenge as big as downtown skyscrapers.

13

The health and condition of urban trees is in fact a mirror image of the whole community's ecology. Trees are the giants of the plant community; they require large portions of nature's bounty to survive, and under their wings a complex of smaller plants can thrive. Understanding the state of our urban forest is, therefore, one sure way to grasp a sense of the ecological state of our cities. It is a first step in the challenge of reviving—or creating for the first time—a flourishing ecological city.

What Is an Urban Forest?

Urban forests in the United States cover some 70 million acres of municipal land and an uncountable number of acres in suburbia and small towns. They are dispersed over 6,375 urban areas ranging from 2,500 to over 1 million in population. So evaluating the condition of the urban forest is no easy task.

Geographically, urban forests exist in four zones. The *suburban fringe*—that area where an occasional new subdivision can be found—begins at the rural edge. Here tree cover is being removed and topography reshaped to make room for roads and house lots.

Where exactly is the line that separates urban from rural forests? Out at the edge of the suburbs, both forests look alike. You can tell the difference by how the land is used—or not used. Rural forests are valued for products—lumber, firewood, maple syrup, and the like—and for wilderness qualities. The urban forest is valued for house and business sites, urban recreation, and water quality. Planning and zoning boards change land from rural to urban when they create ordinances restricting timber cutting, for example, or when they rezone property for "higher" use. Rezoning property not only allows development there but also increases the value and taxes on neighboring parcels.

The second zone on our way to the city is the *suburbs*, where housing subdivisions are numerous and most of the natural forest has been removed. Patches of trees remain—usually along streams, creeks, and wetlands—but most of the trees in this zone were planted after construction was completed. There are trees in most yards and in public spaces—parks, schools, and along the streets.

Streetside space in this zone can handle medium to large trees, depending on the size of the "tree lawn" and restrictions such as overhead wires. Large trees like the oaks, ash, and American elm graphically demonstrate the potential for creating forestlike conditions along street corridors. The average suburban homeowner has about three trees.

The *city residential* zone features individual homes and townhouses on small lots. It starts at about the city limits and stretches inbound to the commercial district. The existing space for trees in this zone is about half

American Forestry Association

Not all cities can boast of an urban forest such as this one, but sound forestry practices can make our city trees live longer, healthier, more productive lives.

that in the suburbs, which restricts the numbers and sizes of trees. Larger trees or groupings grow in occasional parks, while smaller trees stand in lines in the narrow strips of grass next to the streets. Carefully tended trees grace some of the small yards. Yards and open spaces are small, but soil can be found everywhere.

In the *city center*—the inner reaches of the urban forest—trees grow in pots, in holes in the sidewalk, in vacant lots, and even on buildings. Almost every tree has to be "engineered" into this zone or a space cut out of the concrete if the planners neglect to allot one.

In the city center, people outnumber the trees by a large margin, and life for trees is difficult and usually short. In fact, in many cities the urban forest doesn't exist. The late Marvin Black, a distinguished spokesman for trees in Seattle, Washington, described this unfortunate situation as the urban forest doughnut. The city center is the discarded hole that has been forgotten in the rush to progress.

STATE OF THE URBAN FOREST

Considered overall, we know that urban trees in any of these four zones are most valuable to a community during the middle part of their growing cycle—from the time they are about five inches in diameter until they're almost thirty years old. Generally, the condition of the urban forest can be measured by the average age of its trees (the longer trees live, the healthier the forest), by the density of its tree cover (every stand has an optimum tree cover), by the ratio of trees planted to trees dying, and by the quality of the wildlife that can survive in the forest. All these factors are important in determining urban forest health, and no single method is considered a standard because data is limited and urban forests cover such a wide range.

By late-1980s estimates, the average city has a 30 percent tree cover, and many can boast some sort of thriving wildlife. Birds and squirrels have adapted well to cities where trees are abundant, while rats and mice dominate those with little or no vegetation.

For the purpose of evaluating its health, the established segment of the urban forest can be divided into street trees, park trees, yards, and greenways. About a third of the trees within the city limits are street trees. They are the most widely understood because they are officially maintained by the city governments in most communities. In the interior of the city, experienced tree managers select specific sizes, shapes, and cultivars of trees for planting. Planting space and tree size tend to increase in the suburbs. Here, large trees are planted about forty feet apart, and branches often reach over the streets and walks to form a canopy. Because these trees are publicly owned, their care is the responsibility of the city.

Parks offer a great variety of space for trees. Large spreading trees have room to grow in all but the tiny vest-pocket parks. We estimate the number of trees in city parks also to be about one-third of the urban forest. Park trees tend to live longer than street trees and have better growing conditions. However, the trend in park management in the 1970s and early 1980s was toward active recreation rather than emphasis on landscaping. Park trees may outlive street trees, but a large percentage are old and in need of care or replacement.

Yard trees make up the last third of the total trees in the urban forest. Trees in older residential areas tend to appear better off than many of the trees in newer neighborhoods. Construction techniques, poor soils, and lower quality nursery stock all play a role in the health of yard trees. Young trees may have trouble getting established in new yards with poor soils. If they survive, lawn mowers and weed whips often take their toll. Once trees have been established for a few years, their odds for survival improve.

Greenways and natural areas are one of the positive quality indicators of the health of the urban forest, but estimates for the number of trees in greenways do not exist. Because linear parks are considered greenways, some of the trees they support are counted in that grouping. However, our data-gathering techniques have not separated natural or informal greenways from parks and other more linear corridors. As one green area connects to another, like the parts of a quilt being sewed, the area we designate as greenways increases, a phenomenon easily noticed from airplanes. But as each patch is connected, it is also more difficult to separate parks, stream corridors, vacant lots, and tree-lined median strips for the purpose of calculating the numbers.

In 1987 the American Forestry Association surveyed the condition of the street trees in twenty cities and found them to be in a state of decline. The cities included New York, Boston, Baltimore, Detroit, Cleveland, Chicago, Denver, Atlanta, Salt Lake City, Philadelphia, St. Louis, Newark, N.J., Birmingham, Ala., Hartford, Conn., Richmond, Va., Dover, Del., Flint and Lansing in Michigan, and Dayton and Toledo in Ohio.

This survey suggested that the health of the urban forest is declining at an alarming rate. Only one city—Lansing, Michigan—planted as many trees as it removed, and even that city has a five-year backlog. A third of the cities plant one tree for every eight trees removed, and about half the cities surveyed replant one-quarter of their losses. New York, for example, has lost approximately 175,000 street trees, or 25 percent of its total tree stand, during the last ten years.

Throughout these city areas, plant communities struggle through stages of succession and are mostly confined to early stages. Trees planted along streets usually reach maturity, die, and are replanted to complete the cycle. Rarely does the environment created under the urban forest canopy spawn a new forest as it does in the rural forest.

There are some exceptions. Trees like the ailanthus, silver maple, paulownia, and mulberry may find vacant yards, gardens, and various other patches of dirt where they can make a home for a few years. I see a couple such trees going home from work, growing almost in midair, atop a wire mesh that protects somebody's garbage cans. When left unchecked, abandoned buildings and parking lots can easily fall into this pattern. It is a natural form of forest succession, but not one to be proud of.

Today, a central challenge for cities is to create some plant diversity, which is a more subtle but important measure of ecological health. We have great opportunities to improve ecological conditions, especially in new developments, in greenways, and where city streets and walks are being reconstructed. Building cities and suburbs with little or no space for trees is a mistake that lowers the quality of life and is costly to the pocketbook, the mind, and the heart.

Out where greenways merge into the countryside, our knowledge of the urban forest gets very sketchy. Expanding cities and suburbs are annexing the existing trees from once-rural landscapes. The amount of such area being converted is not known, but estimates range from 300,000 to 1 million acres a year. No other segment of the urban forest offers more potential to future communities or suffers more abuse. Our technical skills are limited in this area, but several sterling examples do exist that demonstrate the possibilities.

A few county governments responsible for the urban fringe where new development is sprawling have hired or are consulting with urban foresters. Trees from the existing landscape are being incorporated into new developments over extensive areas. More intensive methods are being demonstrated on corporate sites where buildings, roads, and parking are carefully placed into the natural landscape. A few planning agencies are including foresters and soil conservation experts on their design review teams.

These are important success stories that show us how cities can change, although they have not yet made a major impact on the overall state of our community forests. We might see them as seeds for more pleasant communities.

A DESERT CITY SHAPES ITS FOREST

Innovative urban land planners and designers such as Ian McCarg, Mike Hough, and J. T. Lyle have seen a challenge in integrating the natural landscape as part of the design process, using existing natural conditions in a positive way. They suggest that urban designs that short-circuit a natural cycle or reduce diversity are negative elements. Working with the natural systems creates a solid foundation for building an ecological landscape, a landscape that fits the physical environment and is able not only to survive but to thrive. Tucson, Arizona, is a case in point.

Tucson is a city in the desert. Its population has grown rapidly for the last twenty years, putting stress on one vital resource: water. For the last decade a strong water conservation ethic has developed, and city leaders took some extraordinary steps to encourage conservation when they created landscaping policies. A quick review of water use indicated the landscape was too thirsty, accounting for over half the total water used by the city. The new policies encouraged residents to tear out trees and shrubs and replace them with rocks, sand, and other nonliving landscape. This helped reinforce the so-called xeriscape philosophy (landscaping that uses little water). The policies were expressed as landscape ordinances. Additional encouragement included recommendations in public service announcements and consumer publications.

Greg McPherson and Joanne Gallaher, both landscape architects with a background in urban forestry, were convinced that city officials had shot themselves in the foot with these landscape policies. Gallaher, who works for a private firm, and McPherson, at the University of Arizona, recognized the need to conserve water but felt planners had been lured by statistics showing only one dimension of the problem. It was true that trees used water, and too much water was used on landscaping, but it was not that the landscaping was the cause of water shortages. Not that the leap of logic was without cause; planners compared water meter readings in summer and winter and found summer use much higher. They estimated the extra summer use was mostly landscape watering—much of which was wasted—because sprinkler systems were watering roads as well as shrubs.

Gallaher and McPherson saw a different set of facts. Removing the landscaping would result in water savings, but it was also true that other landscaping used only small amounts of water and in the long run could help conserve water. Removing landscaping and replacing it with rocks were the wrong things to do. Rocks soak up heat and increase the temperature, causing water loss through evaporation. McPherson and Gallaher proposed that the city take a lesson from nature and promote an ecological landscape.

An ecological landscape is one that mimics nature and makes use of natural processes to survive. Vegetation needs to be selected that fits the climate, soils, and moisture limits of a particular site. For Tucson this included using native trees that would grow and thrive in desert conditions and thus use little water. The water used by one mulberry, for example, is equal to that used by eight palo verde trees, native to Tucson's desert environment.

Modern engineering practices compound the water problem by dumping valuable stormwater into elaborate piping systems that short-circuit the natural cycle and rapidly remove water from city streets. Much of the water needs of landscaping could be met if this water was utilized. There are opportunities to slow the water movement and make use of it. The method, called *water harvesting*, can be accomplished by making minor changes in curbs and gutters. Other water conservation methods include drip irrigation, mulch, and the reuse of gray (used but nonsewage) water. By replacing grass with mulch, water is saved, and the list of potential low-water landscape material is increased.

Tucson is now changing the way it looks at trees, thanks to the efforts of McPherson, Gallaher, and others. One private group, the Southern Arizona Water Resources Association (SAWRA), has been instrumental in educating the public to the problems and ecological solutions. The use of native plants to create an ecological landscape in Tucson offers an invaluable lesson for all arid communities to follow.

WILL NATIVE PLANTS ALWAYS WORK BEST?

The city of Tucson has more in common with the desert than most cities have in common with their native environment, however. Ordinarily, if you compare the physical environment (temperature, soils, and air pollution) in a city with the surrounding countryside, you will discover major differences which limit the number of native trees that can survive in urban areas. If you live near a city circled by an expressway or beltway, you probably hear about temperature differences in weather reports. It's always hotter inside the beltway and in the city than in the suburbs. Climatologists refer to cities as *heat islands*, where temperatures can be nine to twelve degrees hotter than the countryside. This means some native trees will dry out and scorch when brought into the city, while some nonnative, southern, and drought-tolerant species will grow in a city's warmer environment.

Urban soils are anything but normal. In fact, most soil scientists say urban soils are a mess. When a core sample of urban soil is observed, it tells more about the building that formerly sat on a site or how hard the last set of construction workers compacted it than it does about standard soil structure. Urban soils are low in organic matter and have little air space, both standard requirements for the average tree and most native trees.

The trees that survive in most cities are tough trees that can tolerate drought, poor soils, and periodic beatings. These plants are rarely native to the site and are often the result of some evolutionary adaptation to help a species survive specific growing conditions. Swamp trees, for example, have developed unique root systems that can survive flooding. Their roots grow very near the surface and are somehow able to extract air from an almost airless medium. It is this ability that allows swamp trees to have the best survival record in the city. Cities may be hot and dry, but the most limiting growth factor throughout the East and Midwest is compact soils lacking the air needed for root growth.

In Tucson and throughout most of the Southwest, the limiting factors will be heat and water. Native and other adapted trees offer the best option because they are adjusted to both drought and heat. What makes good common sense in the Southwest—planting native trees in town—is not for other places in the United States. The buildings and rocks in Tucson act much like the surrounding desert, whereas cities in the East, Northwest, and Midwest become less like their native environment as the cities grow.

CHANGING THE ECOLOGY OF THE CITY

Cities have a unique environment that is literally molded by the human hand. From an ecological point of view, cities are spartan. So a major thrust of past research has been toward developing tree species that can withstand urban pressures, and a large amount of planning efforts have been aimed at finding trees that fit the spaces in which they have to live. A more important challenge, however, is to make the urban environment itself more suitable for things to grow.

Geneticists have probed the evolutionary development of specific trees in an effort to find tough trees to cope with the city environment. This strategy has led geneticists to search for trees that are survivors, trees that can take a beating, withstand the heat, and live with little air in the soil. It has led scientists to sift through the gene pool of species, such as the elm, which are suffering from major disease problems, in order to find potential survivors or create hybrids that can survive these devastating attacks.

Aboveground restrictions such as powerlines, signs, and buildings have also influenced the type of trees that are planted. Smaller trees are often chosen for cities because they are more suited to small places and poorer growing conditions. Smaller trees lower maintenance costs, avoid many of the aboveground obstacles, are less demanding on the site, and cost less to remove when they die. A concept called *tailored trees,* the result of cloning trees of specific size and shape to fit specific space requirements, was popularized by a forester in Cleveland in the 1960s. Although this technique has been very valuable in reducing spacial conflicts between trees and city structures, overzealous applications may severely limit the value of an urban forest.

In theory, a tailored tree has a specific useful shape that may be broad-spreading, narrow, pyramidal, short, or tall. In practice, however, tailored trees have also been smaller trees. Since many of the environmental advantages trees offer are directly related to size, smaller trees may be an indicator of declining environmental quality. This scenario can be seen in the central business districts of many cities, where the city streets are lined with potted plants that have little effect on the ecology of the city.

In short, scientists can improve tree health, but they aren't magicians. Some changes must go beyond the trees and address the ecological limitations of the city itself. Improving city ecology calls for a little more daring from planners, engineers, and foresters. Cities need larger trees, more trees, and better spaces for trees to grow in. The trend toward smaller trees may reduce the friction between city structures and the plant kingdom, but it also reduces the ability of trees to buffer the environment. If trees are going to cool the pavement and shade buildings, they will have to be tall enough to form a canopy above cars, people, and houses. If they are going to cool the heat island effect, they will have to be abundant enough to cover about half the city's surface. If they are going to reduce the impact of harsh winter winds, they have to be big enough and dense enough to affect air flow. If they are going to affect stormwater flows and improve air quality, the space they occupy will have to increase.

The average city today has a tree canopy over about one-third of its area, and the health of the trees forming this green umbrella is declining. Growing space is probably the most significant element limiting urban forest potential. Preliminary data show that the closer we get to the city's center, the shorter the life of the average tree. Longevity and size of trees is directly related to the size and quality of the space in which they have to grow. The city of the twenty-first century needs to double its tree cover from one-third to two-thirds of the total land area. It also needs to increase the life span of the average tree from thirty-two to sixty years.

CHARTING THE NEEDS

Making the changes needed to build a healthy urban forest requires political, social, and technical action. Citizens need to speak out for larger trees and for more trees. Political leaders need to develop policies that make the city more receptive to trees. This may mean changing the structure of the government agency or finding skilled urban foresters to supply more leadership during community development and redevelopment. It may mean changing the specifications for planting trees in the city and following the advice of a landscape expert who knows the construction details needed to keep trees alive. It surely means attention to the soils that are the foundation for healthy trees.

The movement to create greenways is one excellent way to bring nature to the city. Greenways bring a wealth of space and a mix of natural resources into the city all at one time. The strings that hold the web of life together in a natural area are left intact when long corridors are allowed to survive. The threads give strength and depth to the urban forest. There are opportunities for trails and waterways, room for wildlife, space for trees and shrubs to thrive.

Building greenways requires some tough political decisions because the economics of urban real estate favors large commercial use rather than open space. Cities develop because entrepreneurs invest in steel and concrete to build things they can rent, sell, or use to generate profit. Greenways and urban forests play a vital part in making those places livable, but they are not directly part of the profit-making scheme. Creating a greenway requires a patchwork of green spaces to be connected, and each connection competes with an entrepreneur's vision of commercial space. Successful connections require political insight and strength.

When existing landscapes can't be incorporated into growing communities, development and redevelopment should mimic nature. Designs of streets should change to allow more greenery. Modern engineering should use techniques like boulevards and wide tree lawns to make space for trees. Boulevards create a green path down the middle of the street and double the potential planting space for trees. Each boulevard mile can handle about 400 trees rather than the 200 average of a normal street because the linear curb area is doubled. Unlike the business side of the street—which presents restrictions for trees ranging from sidewalks to powerlines—the boulevard can concentrate on landscaping.

The toughest challenge comes in the downtown where traditional tree pits must undergo some innovative redesign. The technical designs used on traditional landscape drawings are grossly inadequate to grow healthy trees. New techniques will have to develop that create more space underground and improve the fertility of every inch of soil available. In a natural environment, tree roots may reach hundreds of feet from the trunk in search of nutrients. So it makes sense that in the confined spaces of the city, we must engineer sites that are *more fertile* pound for pound than the average rural site. What our spaces lack in size, they must pick up in quality.

Much more research is needed. We know far too little about urban environments and what can be done to make them more healthy for trees as well as for people. How do tree roots respond to various urban soils, and what practical opportunities exist for improving the underground? Are there designs for sidewalks and streets that will give trees more space underground to grow? How can we get more air and more nutrients into the street tree pits? How can we improve tree roots and improve their ability to use what is available? We have learned a little about improving tree genetics, but stronger efforts are needed.

The city forests, as they exist in most cities today, are alive but not very healthy. City forestry departments are often established after street designs are set in concrete, and, as a result, trees in small spaces are the resource most urban foresters have to manage. Urban forest managers who accept a reactionary management style, where they do their best to save trees damaged by other city agencies (rebuilding curbs and sidewalks) or where they spend most of their budget on tree removals rather than preventive maintenance or tree planting, are fighting a losing battle. Those who become decision makers, participate in design decisions, and are one or two steps ahead of major maintenance problems are saving money and improving the urban forest of tomorrow.

The state of existing urban forests is improved when tree planting is part of the capital budget, not just the tree maintenance budget. Properly placing trees in new construction is as much part of the cost of building as pouring concrete and putting in sewers. Conditions are improved when planners and designers have a direct line of communication with the city forester at the time concept plans are made, as well as when final plans are approved.

Tree care funds are far more effective when spent on young and middle-aged trees, yet removing and repairing dying or damaged trees often soaks up most of a city's budget. Helping trees to establish themselves in the early years pays off with lower trimming costs and a longer average tree life. Extending tree age five to ten years can more than double the value they bring to the community, yet very few communities follow this path. The state of our city forest will be improved more by managers who can communicate maintenance needs at budget hearings than by those who search for more efficient ways to care for already unhealthy trees.

Where we find healthy city forests, we usually find strong citizen support. In the end, the support of city managers and government agencies comes back to citizens. They are the conscience of the community and the clients all political leaders work for. No other group feels the sense of place trees offer or organizes a force to change conditions more effectively than citizens. City forests decline when city foresters consider citizens a group to avoid, and the forests improve when lines of communication are opened. Informed citizens can organize and make policy changes that would be inconceivable to the average agency technician.

Stephen Jay Gould dedicated his first book, *Ever Since Darwin*, "To my father; who took me to see the Tyrannosaurus when I was five." That visit led him to become a paleontologist. I wonder how ecologic wisdom would develop in our children if we took them to visit the giant sequoia or groves of liriodendron on our city streets. They could learn about ecology right in their own neighborhood if we cultivated a better environment.

3

Tough Trees for America's City Forests

Clyde M. Hunt

WHAT DO RASPBERRIES in November, Douglas fir east of the Mississippi, and chestnut blight have in common? All are the result of our desire to improve our surroundings. Consider the raspberries. We like variety in our life and in our diets. One crop a year was not good enough, so we selected berries that would yield a fall crop too! In the Pacific Northwest and in the eastern coastal areas, the climate is warm enough and the growing season long enough to harvest a second crop. Douglas fir seedlings, native to the Northwest, grow so well in some parts of the Northeast that more are now grown and sold in Pennsylvania for Christmas trees than any other conifer—native or introduced. Sometimes our search for variety also leads to unexpected consequences. We were so eager to improve on our native chestnut that we introduced bigger, exotic chestnuts—and also imported the deadly chestnut blight. All this in the name of diversity.

Biodiversity may be defined as the variety of species in the ecosystem and as the genetic variability within each species. Despite our appreciation for diversity, manifest in our development of new raspberries and other plants, globally we are losing species diversity at an increasing rate as we seek to develop more uniform plant and animal crops. That is true on farms as well as in cities.

Most people have heard how uniform many farm crops have become, all ripening at the same time, growing at rapid rates, and using large amounts of fertilizer. The situation is unnatural and monotonously lacking in variety. In city design, we've done much the same thing. Cities too are often artificial, less inviting, and less interesting landscapes than they could be. Part of the reason has to do with the state of the city's basic environment for plants: its soils and air.

DISTURBED SOILS, HOTTER AIR

In the past century, humans have altered climates, soils, and plant communities on this continent at a rapid pace, causing added stress for plants and animals. Today, superimposed over more natural soil regions and climatic zones, as indicated by distribution of native plant species, we can now draw *human influence zones.* These zones follow the travel corridors and spread out to surround our communities along the way. Center city influences are the most extreme and radiate outward toward the suburbs.

Consider the effect of buildings, for example. On its northern side, a building's shade can create conditions matching the moist and cool of north-facing slopes. However, on a southern exposure, the glare from glass areas and reflected heat exaggerates climate stresses. Tall buildings are like high rocky ridges. The heat stored in the mass of rock, concrete, and steel gives these growing sites the temperature characteristics found a hundred miles closer to the equator.

Add in the mix of exhaust gases from vehicles, buildings, subways, sewers, and pollutants and dusts from manufacturing processes, and we have another example of the influence zone spreading outward from populated areas. In brief, urban air is warmer, drier, and more polluted than air flowing through and over nearby forests or pastures. Conditions so different from native surroundings can make an inhospitable place to grow native vegetation.

Urban soils are regularly disturbed and compacted and often devoid of organic matter. This accentuates the extremes. City soils are drier during droughts than normal soils and often waterlogged following even moderate rains. If a soil is deep and homogeneous before a city's construction, it won't remain so for long after the heavy equipment, concrete, and steel move in. While top soil is moved and removed, low spots are filled in. Slopes are reduced, streams are covered over, and storm waters are diverted. The addition of cement and plaster alter the pH and nutrient availability. Little oxygen and water passes through the compacted or paved urban surfaces. Road salts, oils, fertilizers, and pesticides rarely make up for the nutrients removed in the humus and leaf layers. These, in sum, are the "desert soils" now beneath the city's blacktop and concrete.

As a result of great differences in the condition of soil and air, when we try to transplant natives from the surrounding countryside back into our cities, we often are surprised at our lack of success. Every spring, birches, dogwoods, redbuds, and maples are grubbed out of the woods and introduced back into urban areas with disappointing results. By contrast, vegetation we didn't plant invades our yards and fencerows. These "weeds," while not native, certainly seem at home. By watching, we learn that trees from the bottomlands—the sycamores and pin oaks, silver maples, willows, and gums—do well in cities. Privets, wild cherries, hollies, and poison ivy seed into fencerows and wherever they strike root. We rarely welcome the weed species, yet they are tough enough to survive. They have become our "new American city forest."

FORESTS ON THE MOVE

In their eons-long history, American forests have seen much change. If we think backward to "the forest primeval," looking to the ages following glacial advances and retreats on the North American continent, we can only surmise how plant species adapted to climatic change, seeding into areas previously too warm or too cool for normal growth. Some species failed to keep pace with these changes and became extinct. The most adaptable are still with us today. Some have genes for hidden traits that enabled their ancestors to survive the heat, drought, cold, or other threatened changes.

In more recent history, but before the European settlement of North America, new tree species were being brought to new places by humans. Early American natives near the Mississippi, Ohio, and Missouri rivers are believed to have established pecans several hundred miles north of their otherwise "natural" range. Grapes, berries, and other nut plantings have been spread farther and wider because of such prehistoric planting.

Early European settlers brought both tree and plant species with them. Evergreen seed and seedlings were introduced to change an otherwise drab native winter landscape in parts of Pennsylvania, New York, Ohio, and Illinois. Cemeteries were often the first beneficiaries of early introductions. Who wanted a final resting place without benefit of a Norway spruce or a Scotch pine? All the American trees that were leafless in winter seemed "foreign" to the immigrants.

The imports from overseas are so pervasive that in 1961 Dr. E. L. Little wrote the U.S. Department of Agriculture booklet entitled "Sixty Trees from Foreign Lands" to assist Americans in recognizing many of the diverse species that now grow in city neighborhoods. Some are so successfully naturalized that we think of them as always having grown here.

Over the years, Americans have continued to carry tree species from one part of the country to another. Blue spruce trees were brought East by family members returning from visits to the Rockies—and they thrived in their new territory. Douglas fir is now popular as a fast-growing Christmas tree species; easterners like their looks, and want them in landscaping around homes and in parks.

In the last twenty years, northern paper-shell pecans have been tested as far north as Ontario and some bordering states. These tests for hardier species have potential for city forests because pecans and hickories are bottomland species that can tolerate flooded, oxygen-poor soils. On another front, in far southern areas, Brazilian pepper, Australian pine, and melaleuca have invaded coastal areas, often outgrowing the native species. While this adds diversity, a shift in plant species results in visual changes to the native landscape and losses of dependent animal species.

Along with new imports and expanding ranges for our native trees, we are reintroducing some long extinct trees. In 1985, the Morris Arboretum of the University of Pennsylvania developed an exhibit called "The Return of the Natives." The exhibit featured ginkgo, metasequoia or dawn redwood, and katsura tree or Cercidiphyllum. All these species were grown as seedlings, photographed as established arboretum species—and also exhibited as fossils embedded in North American rocks, mute testimony to their earlier native status. In the case of these three species, it is no surprise that they grow so well here after being reintroduced. They also fit into the ecosystem as a whole. Gray squirrels harvest metasequoia bark shreds for their nests as if they were never without them. Rabbits prefer metasequoia twigs to other native species.

For the future, we may expect to see continued changes. For example, a recent report from the Environmental Protection Agency to Congress entitled "The Potential Effects of Global Climate Changes on the United States" (1988) predicts that climate changes will occur at a much faster pace than any previously experienced. While the speed and amount of climate change aren't clear, since the emissions causing them are likely to continue, we might expect changes in climate during the next century that will affect forest species. If these changes are rapid, they may not allow for the orderly migration of species. Some such as balsam fir, hemlock, and birch may either die out of their present habitat or shift to cooler, moister climates. Tree species on dry sites may be replaced by prairie grass species. Southern species may continue to advance with the warmer and drier weather, filling in for species unable to tolerate these stresses.

Should these climatic changes occur so rapidly that our native species can't fill the vacancies in our forests or cities (because of lack of seed or through lack of concern), we may in years to come find ourselves in serious trouble.

PROMOTING DIVERSITY

What can we do to promote and utilize an optimum and strong diversity of tree species for our cities? If these climate changes occur, we will need to conserve and promote the best of our "tough" city trees, even those we now regard as "weed" species. Overall, we will need to carefully weave the best of the native species in and among the toughest of our now-naturalized species. For example, baldcypress tolerates the extreme heat and water-logged soils typical of cities. They thrive in paved urban areas far from their mucky native southern swamplands. Metasequoia may also grow well in similar urban climates. We see fine urban specimens, such as kousa dog-woods, that tolerate some of the stresses that plague our native flowering species.

We will need to be aware of planting and maintenance patterns that favor, rather than further stress, our best trees. For example, when we attempt to grow drought-hardy trees and lush grass in the same soils, we may drown one to save the other. As John Kuser pointed out at the Third National Urban Forestry Conference in 1986, maintaining old but healthy valley oaks with established root systems while keeping grass green during dry summers is a nearly impossible combination.

We must avoid planting only one species or genus as we did when elms covered many of our communities. Not that elms are less desirable, because they still exhibit outstanding shape and vigor in cities. But they have not fared well where elm bark beetles spread the Dutch elm disease, and cities that once had streets lined with elms were devastated. Wherever elms were scattered through a town, their loss seemed less catastrophic.

Numerous communities today still have remnant elm populations, and we think that most of these survivors may have escaped attack rather than exhibited any measurable resistance. The fewer remaining elms, the less likely they may be fed upon by infected beetles. The fewer dead and dying trees, the less likely are continued attacks. While destruction of all breeding sites may not always be practical, the principles of isolation and dilution can work remarkably well in preventing a local infestation from becoming an epidemic. Would we worry so much about gypsy moth or oak wilt if a smaller percentage of our species was threatened?

Today several new elm hybrids are less susceptible to these pests. More resistant cultivars are now being tested so that elms need not disappear from our cities before they stage a comeback.

The early trend toward planting single species throughout an area is still having effects in some regions of the country, however. Reports from California today prompt concern for another vulnerable species: the millions of eucalypts now threatened by the introduction and outbreak of the Australian eucalyptus borer. These borers are not very picky about the

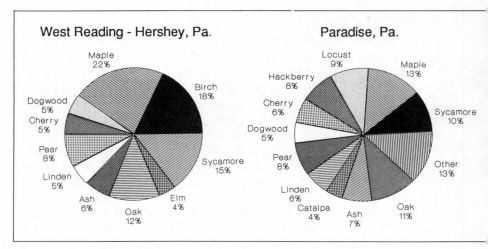

trees they attack. Most eucalyptus species, any age classes, healthy or stressed, appear to be targets. There seems to be little natural resistance to these pests. Except for periods of cool temperatures, the borers quickly complete their life cycle and are ready to move on to the next eucalypt. Transporting infested firewood spreads this pest to areas not yet under attack. Distance and cold apparently offer the only restrictions to the borers' advance. Naturally occurring predators have been left behind. Quarantines have been deemed difficult to establish and have not been imposed.

The linear patterns for planting eucalypts along highways, railroads, and boundary rows or windbreaks—even in parks and cemeteries—may hasten the spread of the disease. The adult borers are strong enough fliers to reach the next eucalypt; thus, infestations may spread quickly.

Rather than depend on chemical poisons that carry their own dangers or quarantines as a means to slow the spread of pests, we could place increased emphasis on the use of diversity among our planted species. This spreads the risks and offers a measure of protection from catastrophic loss. Whenever a major portion of our urban trees is a single species—whether an elm, an oak, or a maple—we face a greater risk of heavy loss than if we have twenty different species planted throughout our communities. In addition, if a species is represented by several cultivars, we'd expect the pests to be less successful. Tree wardens or city foresters may limit their losses to 5 percent rather than face the loss of one widely planted species.

The fewer the species and the greater the environmental stresses, the greater the risk of severe loss. For example, planting many birches in areas too warm and dry for their survival may lead to a complete loss over a rather short time, usually about twenty years. By substituting other species

Clyde M. Hunt

Paxtang, Pa.

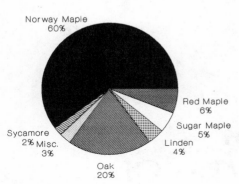

Norway Maple
60%

Red Maple
6%

Sugar Maple
5%

Sycamore
2% Misc.
3%

Linden
4%

Oak
20%

FIGURE 3.1. *Pie graphs show species diversity in West Reading–Hershey, Paradise, and Paxtang, Pennsylvania.*

rather than replanting those overly represented or at risk, we can increase diversity.

Overall, we know that the net effect of propagating single cultivars is to narrow the genetic base so that the general adaptation and resistance to pests may be reduced. Yet, for the purpose of nursery sales to the public, species for propagation are often chosen for ease of cultivation, uniform appearance, or brilliance of fall colors rather than for a species' pest resistance or longevity.

While uniformity may win favor from some aesthetic viewpoints, as rows of even teeth may help a candidate in a beauty contest, this quality has not proven very helpful for survival value. For resilience in the face of the pressures of city living, we must select our street trees based on more meaningful criteria than leaf color or shape. We must take this opportunity to retain greater resistance to pests, pollution, and climatic extremes.

By opting for diversity in our urban plantings, we can be sure all our streets won't be identical. Our elms and eucalypts, where they are planted, should prove less vulnerable. We can reweave the fabric of our mistreated urban areas by including the variety and diversity still present in our native forests together with the improved and overlooked species that survive along our streets, highways, and greenways.

Our cities don't have to be islands of overheated concrete with a scattering of small, isolated trees. They must be woven into a network of cooling greens much like the one that landscaped the country before we pushed the forests back. We need boldly to plant large numbers of trees and reestablish vegetation groups to bring the forests back to our cities. Only then will city people have an umbrella of foliage to shade and cool the urban environment.

4

The History of Trees in the City

Robert W. Miller

TREES HAVE PROBABLY been a part of cities since their first establishment. Early settlements contained domesticated plants, and among these were trees and shrubs cultivated for a number of uses, including food. Many early cities contained some residual vegetation and volunteer trees that were tolerated as long as they did not interfere with other activities. However, trees and associated vegetation were not a part of the urban design, except in private gardens of the ruling classes and on the grounds of temples.

According to Zube (1971), the first intentional use of public trees in cities was inspired by the baroque gardens of France. These gardens were developed in hunting preserves and consisted of wide pathways radiating from clearings in the forest for the purpose of shooting game during the hunt. These radiating pathways lined with trees came to influence the design of eighteenth-century villages and towns and ultimately produced the radial street pattern of Washington, D.C. In the mid-1850s Napoleon III superimposed a radial street pattern on Paris and lined the new boulevards with trees. Two objectives were realized with the new street plan: easy access to the city in time of celebration and easy troop movement in time of riot.

THE ROMANTIC LANDSCAPE

Industrialism in Great Britain produced deplorable urban conditions. The resulting decline in the quality of life yielded efforts to improve urban conditions, one of which was the introduction of public green spaces. Around 1800, trees were introduced into London in a series of squares placed in residential neighborhoods and planted with trees and lawns. Industrialization also spawned the romantic landscape movement, resulting in other attempts to introduce nature into cities and the development of the first suburbs to escape urban conditions (Zube, 1971). While the baroque garden was the epitomy of the formal landscape, the romantic landscape was informal in nature and consisted of the "natural" arrangement of plants and structures in the landscape. In its most idealistic sense, the romantic landscape embodied a mix of what was considered the best from the city and nature.

AMERICAN CITIES

Early colonial villages in New England were built around a village green. The function of the green had nothing to do with aesthetics but rather served as a place to muster militia and keep livestock during times of attack. It was not until late in the eighteenth century that trees and lawns were intentionally established in village greens. Philadelphia, on the other hand, was designed in 1682 by William Penn and contained five open spaces of five to ten acres each, filled with trees. Trees on streets and in yards were uncommon, and it was not until after 1784 that insurance companies began to insure homes with trees near them (Zube, 1971).

Following the Revolution, Americans sought to create a new identity for themselves. Thomas Jefferson believed in a country governed by "sturdy yeoman farmers" and regarded the city dweller with a certain amount of suspicion. This attitude was embraced by the populace and influenced early attempts to incorporate nature in the urban design as well as identifying nature as a source of moral virtue (Schmitt, 1973).

Examples of early legislation concerning urban vegetation were found in Michigan and Mississippi. A Territory of Michigan law in 1807 specified that trees be planted on boulevards in the city of Detroit and that squares be established and planted with trees. The commission charged with selecting a capital for the state of Mississippi in 1821 recommended that the new capital have every other block filled with native vegetation or be planted with groves of trees. The commission felt that this would provide a more healthy environment and provide easier fire control in a city constructed of wood (Zube, 1971).

The introduction of industrialism into the United States in the mid-nineteenth century was followed by the importation of the romantic land-scape movement from England. This manifested itself in city beautification efforts, including the introduction of trees on streets and construction of city parks and civic centers. The city park movement, led in America by Frederick Law Olmsted, had as its goal the introduction of naturally landscaped parks into rapidly growing industrial cities. Olmsted, de-signer of New York's Central Park, stated: "The park should, as far as possible, complement the town . . . what we want is a simple, broad, open space with sufficient play of surface and a sufficient number of trees about it to supply a variety of light and shade" (Gardescu, 1976).

Suburbs for the emerging middle and upper classes sprang up on the outskirts of cities following the spirit of the romantic landscape. Streets were laid out in curvilinear patterns and homes built on rolling wooded parcels. Communities such as Llewellyn Park in New Jersey, Roland Park in Baltimore, Ridley Park in Pennsylvania, and Lake Forest and Riverside in Illinois were designed in the latter half of the nineteenth century and served as models for twentieth-century suburbs. However, as mass housing be-came the rule from the 1930s on, smaller lots were subdivided, and, to accommodate construction, existing trees were removed and not replaced (Zube, 1971). This trend did not begin to reverse itself until the late 1960s, when home buyers started placing higher premiums on wooded parcels.

Tree planting became of national interest by the end of the nineteenth century. Arbor Day was first observed in Nebraska in 1872, following its inception by J. Sterling Morton of the Nebraska Board of Agriculture. The first Arbor Day in Nebraska witnessed the planting of over a million trees. The observance of Arbor Day spread to the rest of the country, and each April tree-planting celebrations are held, with millions of trees being planted in cities, suburbs, farms, and forests.

During the early twentieth century most large cities and many medium-sized communities initiated city forestry programs to plant and care for street and park trees. Milwaukee's forestry program, started in 1926, had as its goal the planting and maintenance of trees on city streets. Smaller cities, towns, and villages engaged in tree-planting projects, but many did not establish community forestry programs until Dutch elm disease rav-aged their tree populations.

GARDESCU, P. 1976. "A Landscape Architect's View of Better Trees for Urban Spaces." *Better Trees for Metropolitan Landscapes*, U.S.D.A. For. Serv., Gen. Tech. Rep. NE–22, pp. 135–42.

SCHMITT, PETER J. 1973. "Back to Nature." *American Urban History*, edited by A. B. Callow, Jr. New York: Oxford University Press, Inc., pp. 454–68.

ZUBE, E. H. 1971. "Trees and Woodlands in the Design of the Urban Environment." *Trees and Forest in an Urbanizing Environment*. Plann. Res. Dev. Serv. No. 17. Amherst: University of Massachusetts Press, pp. 145–50.

5

City Tree Care Programs: A Status Report

J. James Kielbaso

IMAGINE, FOR A moment, the condition of trees in an ideal city. All available planting sites are occupied by healthy, well-chosen trees which line streets and grace public properties. These trees live longer than trees in other cities in the region, and every tree removed is replaced within a year. The exact location and condition of each tree are known and monitored regularly. No decayed or weakened trees which could be safety hazards are on the public ways, and no trees obstruct vehicular or pedestrian traffic. By plan and not simply by accident, trees and utilities do not compete for space.

There is no summer heat island in the city; as a matter of fact, the city seems quite comfortable compared with several years ago. Maintenance is regular and careful. Each tree in the city is pruned every four years to remove any weak, obstructing, or otherwise undesirable branches. Trees are carefully selected for the characteristics of the soil at the planting site, following recommendations of experts for selection and planting; no trees suffer from nutrient deficiencies caused by extreme soil reaction. Few pest problems occur, and they are quickly controlled because integrated pest management utilizes effective scouting to identify any problem before it becomes serious.

In this ideal city, an information center is available for all citizens to use to assist themselves in caring for their private trees. Newspapers, radio, and television regularly carry public information about tree care and benefits. Public employees who work with trees have regular training sessions to increase and maintain their capabilities. A written management plan to care for all the city's trees is available, and a written plan for coping with any emergency, such as high wind damage, is in place.

Does this sound familiar? Can you look out of your window or look overhead as you walk and identify with these ideal conditions? If you can, you are living in one of very few cities in the United States with such an intensive management program. Count yourself very lucky. More likely, you don't see all—or even many—of these signs, but, hopefully, this description leads you to ask how your city could achieve such a goal.

COMPONENTS OF A GOOD PROGRAM

A 1986 survey of urban forestry programs, conducted by this author and graduate students at Michigan State University, allows us to draw some conclusions about what is central to those cities that do have urban forestry programs that come somewhat close to the ideal model. First is a city's commitment to making trees a high priority, usually made in view of their total environmental, economic, and aesthetic assets. Second, this commitment is legal: the city has a precise ordinance that assigns responsibility for the planting and care of all the city's trees.

As a preamble, the ordinance states that since trees contribute immeasurably to the public welfare, they will be provided adequate space for growth, both above and below ground. It also states that trees will not be removed by anyone except for strong, justifiable reasons and only after a permit has been obtained. The ordinance specifies who will be responsible for the care of the city's trees and other vegetation. It also specifies the acceptable training of this person and assures that tree care is a designated, significant, and important part of that person's job description.

In almost all cases of good, effective tree management, the 1986 survey found a tree manager with the title of forester or arborist, who served in a subunit of government with the words *forestry* or *tree* as part of the department title. Consider some examples—all of them cities with outstanding urban tree programs by today's standards—although by no means the only cities with strong programs.

- Austin, Texas, has an urban forester in the Forestry Unit, Operations Division of the Parks and Recreation Department. This professional knows the number of trees in the city, conducts cooperative research on live oak decline, offers extensive public education programs, and runs an innovative Christmas tree recycling program.
- Cincinnati, Ohio, has an urban forester in the Forestry Section of the Engineering Division of the Public Works Department. That city has a

management plan and also has an unusual ordinance requiring that all wood products of their urban forest be utilized, with revenue going back to the forestry program.

- Lansing, Michigan, has a forestry manager within the Department of Parks and Recreation. Among other things, Lansing has a formal management plan and a written emergency plan; the city has removed all high-risk trees and is in the process of replacing removals; it regularly participates in research projects.
- Highland Park, Illinois, has a city forester in a Division of Forestry within the Public Works Department. This city has organized a computerized inventory of its trees, has been named a Tree City USA by the National Arbor Day Foundation, uses systemic treatments for nutrient deficiencies, and has its own nursery.
- Charlotte, North Carolina, has a city arborist in its Park Operations Division of the Parks and Recreation Department who knows the number of trees by species, conducts cooperative research with the Bartlett Tree Laboratories, and also conducts an integrated pest management program.
- Minneapolis, Minnesota, has a director of forestry in the Division of Forestry, Department of Operations, Board of Park and Recreations, who knows the number of trees, conducts several cooperative research projects, has an urban forestry management plan, and conducts public education programs.
- Milwaukee, Wisconsin, has its forester in the Forestry Division of the Department of Public Works. This city has a street tree inventory which identifies how many trees it has and where they are, has done considerable research in cooperation with various universities, maintains a large street tree program and an extensive boulevard program, and has a large Arbor Day program in which the mayor actively participates.

In short, a city's trees must have an advocate. Since trees cannot talk, they need someone to speak in their defense whenever they are threatened. When a city's tree policies are sufficiently clear, a good manager can assure that tree spaces are vigorously defended, that tree removals are not permitted without strong reason, and that new tree spaces are provided when any new projects are contemplated. The task almost calls for a "tree czar"—so much responsibility rests on the tree manager that the city needs to be sure to hire the strongest candidate possible, define the position clearly, and then support the person. Every city with an outstanding tree program has a good spokesperson for trees who is capable of communicating with politicians and the public about the values and the needs of the urban forest.

With an enlightened city, a well-thought-out ordinance, and an urban forest manager in place, the elements of an ideal program are all possible. The fourth component essential to getting a sound program in place is an inventory of the city's trees. This must be organized to allow the manager to locate specific trees, and it must be regularly updated. Without that information, it is unlikely that any argument in support of the program and/or its budget can be successful. When the tree manager approaches the political decision makers and says, "It would be nice to have a 10 percent increase to do our work more effectively," the decision may be favorable, but, especially in a budget-tight era, it is more likely to be negative.

Consider, by contrast, the effect when the city forest manager can say:

> We have 153 trees in danger of falling, 720 planted in the last two years that are susceptible to drought stress, 360 susceptible to attack by the "greenhorn bee-tle" if not treated, and forty-one suffering from serious nutrient deficiency. In addition to these special needs, we are suggesting an increase in our normal planting from 100 to 140 new trees to satisfy requests, pruning 800 more trees per year to reach a recommended four-year pruning cycle, and need an increase in the allowance for emergencies by "x" dollars since we have a population of premanagement, large, aging, boxelders with which we can anticipate diffi-culties in any heavy wind or ice storm. To accomplish this program will require a 10 percent increase in the budget.

Given the facts, especially if they are clearly presented—perhaps with slides to show the targeted trees—the city's decision makers are much more likely to come to a favorable decision. Even an approximate inventory, based on the national average number of street trees per mile (134), is better than no approximation at all.

What values should be central to an urban forestry program? Aesthetic, economic, and environmental values begin the list. Trees are one of the important elements that tie a neighborhood together and form some sense of unity and character. They can convey a sense of well-being, of stateliness and charm. As well, trees add to the economic value of cities. Estimates have been made that trees add several hundred dollars to each home along a tree-lined street. Realtors know that trees usually help homes sell more quickly and at higher prices than homes without trees. They may increase the value of a home by as much as 20 percent, with an average value increase between 5 and 10 percent. Per tree value has been variously estimated between $544 and $1,714.

The environmental contributions of trees add other values that ought to be clearly drawn for politicians and citizens. Given pollution in our cities and the likely prospect of global warming, it is vital that we realize the contributions that trees make to a healthy environment. As one example, the volume of carbon dioxide removed from the air by an eighty-foot-tall beech tree each day is equivalent to that produced daily by two single-family dwellings. Tree canopies have been shown to substantially reduce the cost of air-conditioning homes, especially in warmer climates. One study found this savings to amount to $147 per year for a single mobile home. Windbreak protection through the use of trees has been found to reduce winter heating costs and save as much as 20 percent to 30 percent in energy use. More recently, H. Akbari and his colleagues have estimated that, because of these factors, a well-placed tree in an urban setting may be worth as much as fourteen times the value of a similar tree in a forest location in terms of its total environmental effect.

TRENDS IN TREE CARE

Despite these many values, the 1986 survey showed that the nation's tree care programs have not yet reached a desirable stage of maturity or quality. One outstanding conclusion was that in 1986 only 39 percent of responding cities thought they had a "systematic" urban forestry program. That compares with 50 percent in 1980. Although the definition of *systematic* was left to the discretion of the respondent, it was clear that the trend was downward, not upward. Only the category of cities with populations between 5,000 and 9,999 showed a small increase in the number which thought they had a systematic program. Table 5.1 shows the overall breakdown of cities which responded to the survey and those which said they had systematic programs, shown by size and geographic region.

The survey asked tree managers to provide budget information so that we could calculate such things as the amount expended per capita and per tree and the percentage of the total city budget devoted to tree care. Only 38 percent of the respondents were able to tell how many trees they had on streets with any degree of assurance. That percentage suggests that the status of city tree care is rather low, probably far less than 38 percent of all cities across the United States. The close agreement between the percentage of cities in Table 1 that have systematic tree care programs (39 percent) and the 38 percent that know the number of trees is also notable.

Overall budget information on tree care programs, which allows for estimating the amount expended per capita, was given by 71 percent of the responding cities. So the information in Table 5.2, which summarizes this budget picture, bases the per capita expenditures on considerably more respondents than does the per tree estimates. Both mean and median data are presented here. Generally, the mean can be seen as a goal for a good program, while the median represents a fallback position, a point at which the program is at least better than half the cities that responded to the survey with regard to its urban forestry program.

The budget data provided in the survey were analyzed according to two

TABLE 5.1
**Survey Response Rates and Cities with Systematic Tree Care by
Population and Geographical Categories, 1986**

Classification	No. of Cities Surveyed (A)	Cities Responding (% of A)	Cities with Systematic Programs (% of responding cities)	
			1986	1980
Population Group (thousands)				
Over 1,000	6	33	0	60
500–1,000	17	53	44	62
250–499	34	53	39	67
100–249	113	55	32	65
50–99	280	49	42	65
25–49	616	44	44	55
10–24	1,545	30	38	45
5–9	104	43	31	28
2.5–4.9	72	74	21	21
Geographic Region				
Northeast	822	29	29	47
North Central	812	41	41	52
South	710	35	29	40
West	443	54	54	63
Total, all cities	2,787	38	39	50

other categories: location on public property and various types of work activities. The figures in Table 5.3 show these breakdowns. They also show that over 70 percent of all city tree care budgets are devoted to the three categories of planting, trimming, and removal, including stump removal. Some differences appeared when the categories were analyzed by population and region (not shown in Table 5.3), although few were of any magnitude. Larger cities spend less for planting and removal and more for nursery care. Cities in the Northeast and North Central regions spend more for removal—a fact greatly influenced by the Dutch elm disease— and less for trimming. Cities in the West spend considerably more for trimming and watering and much less for removal and planting.

Overall, if a city is to achieve something like an ideal program, a more desirable balance would be to allocate about 40 percent of funds for trimming, 14 percent for removal, and 10 percent for planting. That would allow each of the remaining categories to increase by an average of 1 percent. This would reflect the importance of regular maintenance rather than the type of crisis response in tree removals and replacement that has

TABLE 5.2
**Average and Median Annual Expenditures for Tree Care in Cities,
by Population and Region, 1986**

Classification	Per Capita		Per Tree	
	Mean[a]	Median[b]	Mean	Median
Population Group (thousands)				
Over 1,000[c]	2.14	2.14	13.24	13.24
500–999[c]	1.31	1.38	9.11	7.14
250–499[c]	2.41	1.73	12.24	12.60
100–249	2.88	2.37	11.95	11.00
50–99	2.96	2.41	11.83	10.37
25–49	3.14	2.01	10.61	9.56
10–24	2.17	1.06	9.86	7.69
5–9[c]	3.29	1.10	11.98	6.00
2.5–4.9[c]	1.36	1.13	3.89	3.33
Geographic Region				
Northeast	1.66	0.99	6.92	4.84
North Central	3.22	2.24	10.26	9.36
South[c]	1.63	0.71	10.31	6.00
West	3.41	2.36	13.11	12.87
Total, all cities	$2.60	$1.73	$10.62	$ 8.04

[a] Mathematical average.

[b] Midvalue, the point at which half the cities ranked above and half ranked below.

[c] Small numbers of responses for category suggest caution when drawing conclusions from data: responses less than 12 in population group, 32 in geographic region.

become typical since the Dutch elm disease epidemic. Generally, more funds are budgeted for removal because these trees are large ones; therefore, several small trees can be planted for the price of one removal.

When a city can move to a strong maintenance program rather than a disease- and crisis-oriented one, it is likely that many fewer removals will be required. Trimming cycles will be also become shorter and less drastic, and other maintenance practices can be increased. The proper trimming of trees along streets can do much to extend their useful life and eliminate most potential problems long before they materialize.

A CHECKLIST FOR CITY PROGRAMS

Along with the overview of current budget priorities, the 1986 survey revealed how these American cities stand on such matters as tree ordinances, long-range plans, and record keeping. While 61 percent of re-

TABLE 5.3
Budget Allocated by Place and Work Activities
(percentages)

Location	
Streets	61
Parks	26
Public grounds	7
Nurseries	2
Cemeteries	1
Other	2

Work Activities	
Trimming	30
Removal, incl. stumps	28
Planting	14
Supervision	7
Storm work	5
Spraying	4
Watering	4
Office	2
Nursery	2
Fertilization	2
Repair	2
Miscellaneous	3

sponding cities had a tree ordinance that defined responsibility for tree care, only 13 percent had one that placed restrictions on the cutting of trees on private property, and only 17 percent had an urban forestry management plan. While 47 percent of the cities kept some tree records, only 11 percent had them computerized for easy access.

The following list presents the data from the survey in a form designed for additional practical use. During the survey, one urban forester from a southern state requested a copy of the survey form to use as a checklist for evaluating city programs. We discovered that this was one useful way to evaluate a particular city program while comparing it with others in the survey.

Yes/No Questions, with Yes Percentages Noted

1. Systematic Management: Is the tree program managed systematically rather than on a crisis basis? (39%)
2. Is the city responsible for trees on the street side of property lines, that is, in the public right of way? (72%)
3. Is the respondent aware of any state or federal cooperative urban forestry assistance programs? (27%)

4. Are tree records kept? (47%)
5. Are tree records computerized? (11%)
6. Are trees designated as "official" trees for a block or other section of a street? (23%)
7. Is there a trend toward planting small trees along city streets? (43%) (*Note:* With energy conservation concerns, the question of whether this is a positive trend should be reevaluated and larger trees used whenever possible.)
8. Does the city maintain a nursery to provide some or all planting stock? (22%)
9. Does the city have a tree ordinance that defines responsibility for tree care in the city? (61%)
10. Is there a tree preservation ordinance that places restrictions on the cutting of trees on private property? (13%)
11. Does the city have a program to monitor tree pest problems, an important first step in Integrated Pest Management? (36%)
12. Are any biological controls employed against tree pest problems? (18%)
13. Are systemic treatments used, which apply pesticides directly to a tree rather than broadcast the chemical into the environment? (17%)
14. Does the city conduct educational programs regarding trees for city residents? (30%)
15. Does the tree management unit conduct educational programs for employees? (59%)
16. Does the city conduct or participate in an Arbor Day program to bring recognition to trees? (49%)
17. Does the city participate in the Tree City USA program of the National Arbor Day Foundation? (26%)
18. Does the city participate in research relating to urban trees independently or cooperatively with a university or other agency? (13%)
19. Is there a current written or formal plan for dealing with trees in an emergency situation such as a tornado, wind storm, earthquake, etc.? (27%)
20. Does the city have an urban forestry management plan? (17%)

Numerical- or Percentage-Based Questions*

21. The number of full-time employees devoted to performing the work of maintaining urban trees. (7.0 employees, full-time equivalent)
22. The number of trees planted in 1986, as a measure of activity of the program. (338 trees)
23. The tree care budget as a percentage of the total city budget. (0.49 mean, 0.40 median)

*Absolute numbers are averages for cities responding to individual questions.

24. The tree care budget described as dollars per tree. ($10.62 mean, $8.04 median)
25. The percentage of cities knowing both the number of trees and the budget allocation for tree care. (35%)
26. The tree care budget expressed as dollars per capita. ($2.60 mean, $1.73 median)
27. How many years of tree care maintenance experience does the urban tree manager possess? (14.6 years)
28. The number of trees maintained per full-time employee. (3,798 trees)
29. The total number of trees in the city, as a positive contribution to the environment. (29,677 trees)
30. Is the number of trees in the city known, as a basic piece of management information? (38% know this)
31. What is the number of trees per capita? (0.50 trees)

These factors were chosen because urban forestry professionals believe they are indicators of a positive tree care program in a city. Most are directly related, that is, the larger the number, the more positive the relationship. Thus, the more cities that indicated their participation in the Arbor Day program, the more likely that we could say urban forestry was succeeding across the nation. Only one of the indicators—the number of trees maintained per employee—should be low to be considered more positive.

On matters such as whether official trees and small trees are valuable, disagreement exists. Some professionals see such directions as having a negative environmental value. But because they do at least imply a strong, conscious program, they are included as positive indicators in the above checklist, even though some of the strongest programs, overall, report negatively on these criteria.

BUDGET, PLANNING, AND OTHER SUPPORTS

An enlightened city committed to urban forestry, a sound ordinance covering multiple aspects of the public/private forest, a thorough inventory of city trees, and a professional advocate with the title of forester or arborist located in a forestry- or tree-oriented division of the city government— these are four characteristics of a strong urban forestry program.

A thoughtful analysis of the 1986 survey brings several other factors into focus. Once a city has taken those steps, the next most important need is financial. Lack of sufficient funding is probably the main obstacle to effective management of city trees. Table 5.2 offers some important guidelines. Depending on the situation, reaching the average of $2.60 per capita or $10.62 per tree is a desirable goal. However, realizing that these averages do represent comparatively sophisticated programs, attaining the medians of $1.73 per capita or $8.04 per tree may be more realistic initial goals. Smaller communities with small budgets may find that contracting work and sharing or renting equipment may be more sensible strategies. If this course is chosen, contracts must be carefully constructed, however, so that both sides have reasonable expectations.

Only 17 percent of cities have an urban forestry management plan, but such a long-range plan is essential for management of a resource that is by its very nature a long-term matter. Goals must be made and prioritized so that realistic objectives may be set and measured. A long-range plan should address objectives for planting, removing, and pruning of trees, along with the training of professionals, public relations, and funding.

The public has an important role in an effective program. A board representing the public should usually be legally constituted and take responsibility for policy and oversight of a comprehensive community tree program. A good board is invaluable for legitimizing the activities of the tree manager; it is essential if the program is to involve citizens whose energies can be enlisted by active education and public information programs. Keeping the urban forestry program in the public eye through public events, school programs, service clubs, and volunteer groups will result in a positive response to tree needs. Recognizing those people and groups who contribute to the program's success is also an essential strategy to enlist citizen support.

An additional factor involving private enterprise came into view as a result of the 1986 survey. Without the support of quality nurseries, a program will suffer from lack of excellent tree-planting stock. Everything possible should be done to encourage and reward good nurseries and tree care companies in the community. As they succeed, the general tree consciousness increases, and the city program does also.

How Many Trees?

The 1986 survey allows us to estimate that there are nearly 60 million street trees in the United States, based on the mean numbers of trees by population category and the numbers of cities in those size categories. If these trees are conservatively valued at only $300 to $500 each, then the value of this standing resource is $18 to $30 billion. Interestingly, based on the idea that trees can be planted at an average of about forty-five feet apart, we estimate that there are approximately another 60 million planting spaces waiting to be filled. That suggests an overall national goal of planting, on average, one more tree for each tree currently on every city street.

In setting such a goal, one must consider the species makeup. Not enough diversity is represented by the species currently existing or being planted on our city streets. A goal for planting diversity should be at least that no species make up more than 15 percent of the total tree population of a city. An even better goal is that no genus should account for more than 10 percent and no species for more than 5 percent of the total. Whether or not the same species should be planted on an entire segment of a street is subject to debate. Some experts fear the suggestion of "monoculture," whereas others place more emphasis on the aesthetics and maintenance efficiency achieved when trees are alike. Good arguments exist on both sides, but the 10 to 5 percent standard is a good one for long-range overall planning except where availability of adaptable species precludes such a mix.

In an article published by Resources for the Future in a 1969 report, *The Quality of the Urban Environment,* Wilfred Owen presents an idea that goes well with the notion that more street trees would enhance the future of our cities. He estimated that from 25 to 30 percent of all land in most cities is devoted to some form of transportation, ranging from roadways to airports and railyards. "If anything is to be done to improve the aesthetics of the city, the task begins with transport," Owen wrote. "Broad tree-lined sidewalks, adjacent lawns and flower gardens, sidewalk kiosks and eating places, all combine to make the right of way serve not only the movement of vehicles but also the social and recreational needs of people and the aesthetic enhancement of the downtown area. . . . The redevelopment of the blighted close-in areas of American cities could readily incorporate such islands of green along streets that have become drab and colorless."

Reaching the ideal city of trees may always lie a little beyond our grasp, but in 1989, we do clearly know the basic outlines of such a program. We can begin new programs or take one step further in the already existing program in each of our cities. Every step should be placed not simply on the cost line of city programs, but in the "investment in a strong future" category of those things that make our cities worth living in—for next year and the next century.

Note: For further details on these and other aspects of the 1986 urban forest survey, the reader is directed to J. James Kielbaso et al., "Trends in Urban Forestry Management," *Baseline Data Report* 20(1) (1988), available from International City Management Association, 1120 G Street, N.W., Washington, D.C. 20005.

PART TWO

URBAN FORESTS: THE VALUES

Through their simple beauty and symbolic meanings, urban trees bring richness to our cities. Their ecological contributions and health benefits add considerable economic worth to the already high real estate estimates of the value of a city's trees. And pondering the role of trees also gives us a deeper awareness of our connection to one another and to the earth. This section considers the many values of urban trees.

6

The Values of Trees

Sàra Ebenreck

TREES OUTSTRIP MOST people in the extent and depth of their work for the public good. Twenty-four hours every day, through the spinning cycle of the year, they're on the job creating an environment beneficial to our physical and mental health. They cool the air, break the wind, and intercept the rain. Pollution cleanup goes on noiselessly and without political argument. They cut our fuel bills and increase our property values. Their beauty rivals that of any art gallery. Stress reduction and energy recharge are available at a glance. The twin oaks outside the window of my office, for example, daily affect my perspective on life. The movement of branches in the wind relaxes my eyes while the sheltering strength of these century-old giants restores my soul.

What's the value of all that sylvan activity? As forest scientists and citizen activists are showing, the city forest has values so multiple and rich that urban forest management ought to climb right up to the top grouping of any community's funding priorities.

DOLLAR FIGURES FOR INDIVIDUAL HOMES

First, consider the hard economic values for homeowners. The U.S. Forest Service estimates that market values for homes are pushed upward by the presence of trees, at rates ranging from 7 to 20 percent.

Want to figure those values out more exactly? The Council of Tree and Landscape Appraisers has created a formula for estimating tree worth based on the portion of the market value of a property related to trees. This

49

approach starts by assigning a "basic value" for the tree's functions based on the diameter of the tree trunk. By that standard, a prime condition sweet gum twelve inches in diameter would have a value of about $1,700. The actual value is affected by its health, location, and exact species type. A free-standing tree is worth more than one growing under utility wires, and a top specimen of the species more than one that has lost limbs after being struck by lightning. (See Appendix F.)

Energy savings produced by trees casting shade over homes or breaking the force of winter winds have also been measured by scientists, although much more work needs to be done in this area. U.S. Forest Service meteorologist Gordon Heisler estimates the annual effect of well-positioned trees on energy use in conventional houses at a savings of about 20 to 25 percent when compared with the same house in a wide-open area. The building structure, climate, tree arrangements, and type of tree maintenance will all affect the savings. Windbreak trees need to be on the side from which prevailing winter winds blow, for example. Because of the seasonal angles at which sunlight strikes, pruning lower branches from tall trees located on the south side of homes allows maximum shade in summer but less loss of solar energy beaming in from a lower arc in the sky in winter.

Energy savings and property values only begin the list. The Landscape Appraisers formula doesn't begin to calculate total environmental worth, even to an individual citizen. In its formula, for example, a dead tree is worth only 10 percent of a healthy one. Yet, as wildlife specialists will point out, some dead trees are invaluable in attracting bird and animal life. Without those wildlife hotels, we'd soon note the deadly silence of a bird-free city.

In 1985, the American Forestry Association made rough estimates of a tree's value for a few of its ecological contributions to homeowners and taxpayers. The association concluded that, yearly, an average fifty-year-old urban tree would supply air-conditioning worth $73, soil erosion and stormwater control worth $75, wildlife shelter worth another $75, and air pollution control valued at $50. Total value in 1985 dollars: $273. Total value for its lifetime, compounded at 5 percent for fifty years: $57,151. It's time, those figures say, to begin thinking of trees as major contributors to our welfare, not just as optional landscaping.

CONSIDER A CITYWIDE SCALE

Scientist Rowan Rowntree, Project Leader with the U.S.D.A. Forest Service in Syracuse, New York, is working to project some of those economic values on a citywide scale. Based on an analysis of air photos, he estimates that one-third of the area of the typical American city or town is covered by tree crowns. Another third is grass.

According to Rowntree, even those figures underestimate the working capacity of the tree/grass cover. That's because the work of vegetation proceeds in direct proportion to the area of its total leaf and stem surfaces. And over most of the two dozen cities he analyzed, Rowntree found that leaf and stem surfaces outnumber the areas of building, road, sidewalk, and other humanly constructed surfaces by about four to one. So the typical city is really a dominantly live surface in which vegetation is pumping water, exchanging gases, and modifying air flow, suspected particulates, and heat. That total living landscape is what we need to keep in mind when we calculate costs and benefits.

Rowntree's research has shown that all those vegetation surfaces intercept and transpire enough water to significantly modify the water budget of an urban region. For example, in a one-inch rainstorm over twelve hours, the interception of rain by the canopy of the urban forest in Salt Lake City reduces surface runoff by about 11.3 million gallons, or 17 percent. Most cities could count a like reduction, with the values increasing as the canopy increases. That allows surface water recharge, cuts the cost of wastewater disposal, and averts the flooding and sedimentation of city streams or rivers.

The exact science of determining how much urban forest is needed to lower overall outside summer air temperatures in an urban heat island is still in the early stages. One comparison of single streets in Syracuse, New York, with and without trees showed no difference in actual heat levels below the trees, but it may be that the differences depend on masses of trees throughout the city rather than isolated tree plantings. Based on a model for Dayton, Ohio, Rowntree has projected "significant" reductions—upward of 25 percent—possible from more widespread use of woody and herbaceous vegetation in central business districts.

Lowered energy consumption for cooling also translates into lower utility plant demands at what is often a summer peak period. In 1988, H. Akbari at the Lawrence Berkeley Laboratory of the University of California compared the cost of tree planting for energy savings to the cost of gaining the same reductions in energy use through improving the efficiency of appliances or improving electrical supply efficiency. Akbari concluded that it costs about one cent to reduce peak-load energy demands one kilowatt-hour by planting trees, whereas savings from improving the efficiency of appliances would cost about 2.5 cents, and improving electrical supply energy would cost 10 cents.

Noise reduction benefits aren't easy to quantify, but we know the city would be a lot noisier if all the vegetation were removed. Some researchers estimate, for example, that belts of trees 100 feet wide and forty-five feet high can reduce highway noise by nearly 50 percent. Other researchers are convinced that people are bothered less by noise when the source is screened from view by trees or other vegetation.

Real figures are missing for the public health benefits of trees in removing air pollutants, although scientists know that the urban forest can reduce both particulate and gaseous pollutants. Los Angeles's support for planting 100 million trees in the early 1980s was based partly on that city's need to meet air quality standards. Rowntree predicts that research under way on the benefits of trees planted near sources of automobile-generated pollution will likely show these cleanup effects to be great—figures won't be available until 1995.

Looking at ecological values from a citywide perspective had a striking impact in Dayton, Ohio. In her book, *The Granite Garden*, landscape architect Anne Whiston Spirn describes a major problem site: the entry to a high-rise apartment complex for the elderly which was so windy that venturing out on an icy winter sidewalk in high wind was an invitation to disaster. Harvard University landscape architecture students, who studied the site, tried dozens of configurations of trees, awnings, and walls to control the wind but found no way to cut wind force significantly.

But a scan of the city as a whole opened up a solution. Winter winds from the northwest blow unimpeded across parking lots and other open areas, reaching the tall apartment complex in full force. Adding trees to parking lots on the northwest edge of town reduced those winds to the point that site controls were effective. Spirn summed up the importance of that study in her book: "The solution seemed simple," she said. "But the method for identifying it was revolutionary." It was, in short, learning to see the city as an ecological whole.

CONSIDER REGIONS AND WATERSHEDS

Urban trees are related to ecological health in ways that reach far beyond city boundaries. Their contribution to regional water quality is one major, but often unquantified, asset. In the Chesapeake Bay area, for example, the Maryland state legislature has officially recognized waterside trees along its rapidly developing shoreline as "the least polluting land use" for that threatened body of water. That puts it conservatively.

The Chesapeake, with a 200-mile length, is one of the world's largest and most bountiful estuaries, and surely one of the most studied bodies of water in the world. Freighters move north and south on its waters loaded with fuel, autos, and spices. On any but the most bitter days of the year, its waters are dotted with recreational sailboats; seasonally, its oystermen and crabbers harvest the region's seafood. Yearly, its waters are home to the migrating geese and swan who wing southward from Canada.

In the days prior to the white man's discovery, scientists say, the watersheds of the upper bay were covered by old growth forest. Rainstorms, often violent and heavy, were broken in their downward force by interlocking layers of leaves and branches. The rain that did directly reach the ground pelted upon centuries-old accumulations of soft leaf mold. Tree roots held the soil in place. Because of the trees, the land around the Chesapeake soaked up the rain and filtered water slowly into the bay.

Today, the bay area is home to more than 15 million people, with their numbers climbing daily. As Tom Horton of the Chesapeake Bay Foundation points out, humans seem magnetically drawn to live on the water's edge—and in the Chesapeake Bay area, that water's edge has unusual length. Compared with a typical shoreline/length ratio of three to one, the Chesapeake's convoluted shoreline is forty times the length of the bay itself. Not all of that land is urban, but an ever-escalating amount of it has been deforested and commercially developed.

The effect of the overall changes that we humans have wrought is easy to see: dirty water. The scientific numbers are also clear: most of life in the bay itself—the populations of oysters, striped bass, American shad, white and yellow perch—is in decline.

While the primeval trees caught the rain and let it flow gently and cleanly into the bay, people more often do the opposite. The Maryland Forest, Park, and Wildlife Service in Annapolis puts it simply: almost every time humans in the bay region wash their hands, water their lawns, or clean their kitchen drains, they add pollutants to the bay. Bulldozing for roads, housing developments, and shopping centers adds more runoff. And in the late 1980s, perhaps most potent of pervasive polluters is the sediment running off cleared croplands in the 40 million-acre, five-state watershed.

One study cited by the Maryland Forest Agency shows the value of trees in this urbanizing area. In the Gunpowder Falls Basin, part of the bay watershed, forestland produced about fifty tons of sediment per square mile per year; established urban and suburban land, fifty to 100 tons; farmland, 1,000 to 5,000 tons; and land stripped for construction, 25,000 to 50,000 tons. That sediment doesn't just sink to the bottom of the bay. It inhibits the growth of sea grasses which are essential to aquatic habitat. And, especially in the case of farmland runoff, sediment carries nutrients that spur algae growth; the dying algae consume oxygen from the water, causing fish kills.

More trees in urban and developing areas could turn around some of that pollution. Along with breaking the fall of rainwater, their roots remove nutrients harmful to water ecology. They stabilize streambanks and eroding shorelines.

Recognizing those facts, Maryland's legislature has limited the amount of forest that can be removed for development and identified the central importance of tree planting in buffer zones along the water's edge. Even with these regulations in hand, the Chesapeake Bay Foundation's Horton says that restoring the bay's health is a matter of "running very, very hard just to stay in place." Trees, it is clear, can help their friends in that race—in the Chesapeake and other threatened estuaries nationwide.

HEALTH BENEFITS

Many of us know we feel somehow better when we see trees outside our window, but that "feeling better" is tough to quantify. So innovative geographer Roger Ulrich, then at the University of Delaware, tackled the issue by checking health records at a suburban Pennsylvania hospital where some patients looked out windows at clumps of trees, while others stared at a brick wall. Ulrich found that surgical patients who could look at the trees had shorter hospital stays, received fewer negative comments in nursing reports, and took fewer potent pain killers.

Those effects have profound economic implications, of course. If postoperative hospital stays could be cut by the 8 percent which Ulrich's control group showed, national health cost savings as large as several hundred million dollars a year could be the result.

Ulrich has tested other groups of people for their perception of the values of natural beauty, including trees. Shoppers in Ann Arbor, Michigan, for example, were inclined to drive home by way of a parkway in preference to an interstate because the experience of natural beauty offset the longer commuting time. A group of students feeling stressed by exams felt better after viewing fifty slides of natural scenes; another group, who viewed slides of urban areas, felt worse. Overall, Ulrich concludes, city planners and officials ought to attend to the nearly universal preference for landscapes that include plantings.

In a decade, if we examined this underresearched area, we might know even more tree values. What about the health-care savings for aging people with access to tree-shaded places that include bird- and squirrel-feeding stations? What effects for the productivity and health of office workers might follow from visual and lunchtime access to tree-green courtyards? And what about the health of the urban poor if city programs targeted slum areas for cooperative planting efforts? The summer heat of cities and its load of air pollution are usually most concentrated in the dense, cement-heavy, transportation hub of the inner city, at times making those places hazardous to health, especially for the elderly. The costs of that pollution may go uncalculated, but that does not mean they are minor.

A SENSE OF IDENTITY

What makes a city special—gives it a feel that is different from any other place? In lucky cities, the answer to that question involves trees. Like other enduring features such as rivers, hills, and massive building centers, trees are in place for the long haul. The outstanding trees of a city are also those that have found a healthy niche in the ecology of that particular landscape. Whether they're the palms of Honolulu or Portland's Douglas firs, trees speak of a place on earth that is their home as well as ours. Here again, we have a value that is not well quantified but one that inclines many people to think that the least quantified values rank among the most important.

Consider Milwaukee, Wisconsin, for example, where 118 miles of city boulevards have been crafted with median strips that hold trees, shrubs, and flowers. City forester Robert Skiera talks about "a rhythm of design that provides a visual framework for streets" and also about Milwaukeeans who love their trees and the special flavor they create for the city. Instead of having to convince city aldermen that tree planting is necessary, the city forester often finds the reverse pressure coming to bear: aldermen who go to foresters with tree-planting requests because they wish to please their constituents.

Or consider Minneapolis, Minnesota. "When people in Minneapolis get out-of-town company, they invite their visitors to take a drive on the 'grand round,'" says Minneapolis Director of Forestry David F. DeVoto. The "grand round" is a series of slow, winding, tree-sheltered drives that curve southward through the heart of Minneapolis and past a series of small lakes. "Ask anybody in Minneapolis—they'll tell you it's a taste of the north woods right here in the heart of the city," DeVoto says.

In the center of downtown Minneapolis, beneath the windows of the city's skyscrapers, lies Loring Park, a couple of acres of land that lets city folk "get to the country for lunch" on workdays. The park and its greenway are so dear to citizens that "nobody can even think about building on it," DeVoto observes. Add the 86,000 elms that citizens have protected at the cost of millions of dollars, and you get a city with trees at the heart of its identity.

Even without hard economic numbers, the value of pride in one's place is clear. Beautiful Milwaukee may attract more tourists and conventions. Pride also encourages strong citizen involvement in the city. When a sense of place is strong, people have a clear idea of why they like living in a city and what they want to support with their dollars and energy.

The ancient Greeks and Romans, who originated the concept of a spirit of place, believed in living spirits in a place that gave it a special character and protected it against enemies. Curiously enough, the naming of a city's special identity can function rather like that living spirit in budget and policy-making meetings: protecting special places against any destruction. Because trees are essential to any city that has a deep sense of its ecological identity, the state of a city's trees are a clear sign of whether its special spirit is alive and working.

EDUCATION AND IMAGINATION

A value of city trees often left unspoken is their educational potential. Aldo Leopold, Wisconsin forester and author of the now-classic essay, "The Land Ethic," put the need for such education simply: even more than abstract scientific facts ordinarily taught in schools, the average citizen needs "some understanding of the living world." Why teach children to sing about "my country" while seeing "little or nothing of its inner workings?" he asked.

Pure wilderness is often far away from most cities, but almost no school lacks access to an urban tree or an even larger part of the urban forest. Here students and adults can learn, not just that trees are wonderful to look at, their leaves fun to kick in the fall, but how they interact with the entire natural world of soil, water, air, plants, animals, and humans. They may also learn how a tree's health is a signal of the health of the whole ecosystem. With many such student exercises, over a period of time, we might hope for a new era of harmony with our environment, built slowly from the understanding that begins with urban trees.

And it needn't all be terribly serious. Herbert Schroeder, of the U.S. Forest Service in Chicago, reports that one of most popular nature education experiences at a Chicago nature center is the yearly Halloween Haunted Trail. As October draws to its close, volunteers dressed as ghosts, ghouls, witches, and monsters stake out sites along the arboretum's nature trail. Parents with kids pay solid dollars for the experience of stepping, ever so briefly, into a world of terrifying mythic spirits and demons.

What's going on? Schroeder says these adventurous participants are regaining a sense of the mystery and enchantment that has so largely been lost in our scientific and technological world. The ancients, Schroeder points out, saw the natural world alive with nymphs and deities. In such a world, human imagination was at home. Halloween night allows people to open up to that part of their inner lives.

And why is that important? Perhaps because we sense with our imaginations what our science is also clearly telling us: that we are part of this natural world, our fates intertwined. In our efforts at measuring forest benefits and developing sound and scientific management methods, we "should not lose sight of the imaginative aspect of nature," Schroeder concludes. "We need to let people tell us in their own words about the significance of vegetation for their experience of the city."

SEEING WHOLE

What are the values of urban trees? The total answer, it appears, only begins in the practical estimates of additions to real estate values and energy savings. It continues through citywide and regionwide assets, moving toward unquantifiable values such as the creation of a sense of place and the stimulation of our imaginative sense of unity with all creation. Once we understand the global linkage of energy consumption, air pollution, and global warming, we can see that each step to plant shading trees also ripples outward as a practical contribution to global ecological stability.

Envisioning these multiple values is a worthwhile exercise. Once done, it has in itself a practical effect: it helps us to begin thinking in a more holistic way. When planting trees is seen not only as a beautification measure, but as an investment in tourist attraction, an energy-saving action, part of the city's stormwater management and air-cleansing systems, part of its recreational assets, a health-promoting measure, provision of multiple outdoor educational sites, creation of a sense of civic pride, and builder of a sense of community—then we have not only planted a tree but learned a new way to think, one that can shape not only our environment but our own character.

From that new pattern can come a future undreamed of today. Far from simply solving current problems with our tree planting, we can be taking important steps toward a twenty-first century in which people and planet have learned a new way to live in energetic harmony. Instead of being the antithesis of the natural world, cities can become exciting manifestations of nature's capacity to support and delight human life.

7

The
Imperative Forest

Donald C. Willeke

WHEN I BEGAN to work on the problems of our urban forest sixteen years ago, the urgency of the crisis we then faced in Minnesota forced me to speak out loudly and often of the *practicality* of our urban forests, which were being gravely threatened by Dutch elm disease and oak wilt. I had to impress upon citizens that a very valuable resource would be ruined if they did not quickly spend large sums of public and private money.

After we convinced the people and the politicians to devote dollars to the problems, I was often asked to speak about the *politics* of the urban forest and to share some of the techniques we had learned.

Now, with the luxury of time and the perspective of distance, I have begun to think of the *philosophy* of the urban forest. As I view our cities and towns, I ask myself what promotes in the minds of our urban citizens the idea that they must strive to plant a forest in the interstices of their urban environments, at great cost and at odds with a multitude of biological considerations?

Having proceeded from the practicalities and politics of the urban forest to a consideration of its philosophy, I did what philosophers usually do. One evening I retreated into my library and built a fire—using logs from trees which had lost their battles with the hostile urban environment. I climbed my library ladder and, like Carl Spitzweig's famous painting, *The Bookworm*, loaded myself down with treatises. Then I climbed down, sat before my fireplace, lit my pipe, scratched the head of the large bulldog at my side, and began to read and think.

As a result of my pondering, I have developed certain beliefs.

I believe that the planters of our urban forests are in large measure driven by considerations far beyond utilitarian motives and are impelled by larger philosophical considerations, with roots far back in mankind's history and perhaps even further.

I believe that the multitude of individual acts that are being made to plan, plant, and renew our urban forests arises because we are all acting upon a classic moral categorical imperative falling squarely within the definition given by Immanuel Kant in 1797 when he said, "There is . . . only a single categorical imperative and it is this: You should act only on that maxim through which you can at the same time *will* that it should become a universal law."

Together, those who have been united in this effort—from the tree planters in the original planned community of Williamsburg, Virginia, through people like John Adams, who planted an American elm on the White House lawn, and J. Sterling Morton who helped raise urban tree planting to a national obsession, through efforts of individual leadership such as Kirk Brown with the Tree Trust in Minneapolis, Andy Lipkis of TreePeople in Los Angeles, through the united activities of American Forestry Association members, and finally through the efforts of multitudes of citizens who pressure their governments to plant and maintain their urban forests—together, all of us are acting on a categorical imperative, one which we can rightly *will* should become a universal law.

Thus, the urban forest is truly the imperative forest—a forest mandated and impelled primarily by philosophical considerations.

ELEMENTS OF THE PHILOSOPHY

If *philosophy* may properly be defined as the study of the processes governing thought and conduct, here is my tentative attempt to categorize the processes governing our thoughts about and our conduct toward our urban forests into four different but interrelated longings or quests.

The Longing for Security Home, in our society, once was where the hearth was. Eons before that, in the plains of Africa where man is said to have originated, home was where the tree was; now, again, for most Americans, home is where the trees are.

The most inviting pictures of homes usually include what a perceptive nursery worker calls "the umbrella of trees." He rightly discerned that most Americans prefer homes that are or may become surrounded by these living umbrellas, and they usually act quickly to plant and maintain them. The resemblance between that modern-day activity and the activities of the early humanoids in those velds where grew what one perceptive anthropologist called "the trees where man was born" is almost too obvious for comment.

This should hardly be surprising. The recent University of Minnesota studies on identical twins separated soon after birth showed that even after many years, their behavior patterns—down to the smallest personal quirks—are remarkably similar. These new studies confirm in carefully controlled ways what was shown in previous studies with less exact methodology. If personalities and attitudes are "hard-wired" into our skulls far more than had been believed (or admitted) in the past, is it crazy to assume that the preferences developed by early humanoids have wholly disappeared from our own mental circuitry? I think not, and that concept goes a long way toward explaining the philosophy of the urban forest.

The longing for security contains more: humans are very territorial animals. My two careers as a lawyer and army officer are ample witness to that fact! And the elements of our urban forests are often used to mark our territories. The use of boles of trees to define streets—the most public of spaces—and separate them from homes and businesses is obvious everywhere. Urban trees are gentle boundary markers. They say, "This land is tended by and is the property of another person," and they say it beautifully. This phenomenon is perhaps best seen in newer areas where the trees are smaller and act more like conventional markers than the architecturally significant structures they will become.

The Longing for Dignity But security is not enough. When humans become reasonably secure, they become concerned with their dignity. And here, too, the urban forest plays a vast, if not fully understood, role. Every text on urban forestry has pictures showing rows of trees lining streets and approaches. Would not other structures work as well, last longer, and take far less maintenance? They would, but the people would not stand for it. The Romans tried it, and the prototypical monument-lined Appian Way was never duplicated. But the linden *allées* of Europe and the American elm-lined streets have become veritable arboreal clichés.

It is no accident that until recently the American elm, which the early botanical explorer André Michaux called "nature's noblest vegetable," lined most streets of the northern United States and that the palm took the place of the elm in the semitropical parts of our land. These most dignified and stately of trees are now sorely missed as the excess of our monoculture plantings are claiming their inevitable price. But where elm and palm remain and where replacement trees are achieving significant size, the dignity which people seek in their urban forests is eminently apparent.

Unfortunately, human dignity is often at great odds with two increasingly prominent features of our society: mobility and transience. Trees, as tangible expressions of stability, offer "an antidote to transience." As a lawyer assisting clients, I have frequently observed young couples roaming around their first home after a closing. Often I have heard one remark, "Gee, dear, we should buy a new tree to plant right over there." As their personal estate becomes increasingly dignified with the purchase of a home, they seek a tangible expression of the end of a more transient phase in their lives and thus contribute to our urban forest.

The third element of the longing for dignity is something my observant nursery friend calls "the effort to give 'depth of field' to our habitations and our lives." A few trees around a residence give that depth of field which is so necessary if a home is to be more than just a pile of lumber and rock exposed on a flattened plot.

A landscape architect recently compared a new, treeless suburb of tract homes with a well-planted older neighborhood. She said to me that trees "humanize" our urban environment. I replied that she had the right idea but entirely the wrong expression. What our urban forests do is precisely to "dehumanize" (in the best and most favorable sense) our structures and blot or blend out the starkness, irregularities, the trashiness, jarring contrasts, and all the other things which painfully assert that humans have been doing their often undignified things.

The Need for Symbolic Dedication and Rededication When the quantum leap in mammal intelligence took place—either when the serpent climbed the apple tree in the Garden of Eden or when some mutation occurred among the humanoids under the trees in the African veld (take your choice)—humans became the only creatures with any significant ability to foresee and plan their futures because they had developed the knowledge of the concepts we now call good and evil.

A number of things arose from that horrible and wonderful knowledge. One of the most remarkable is the human need for periodic symbolic dedication and rededication, for acts of faith, acts of renewal, and ritual confirmations of continuity. Given the conclusions already drawn, it is easy to infer that a large part of the philosophic base for the urban forest is found in this need.

Perhaps I am treading too close to established religions to suit some people, but continue to think about this concept for a moment. Why is the *tree* the standard synonym for the cross of Christianity? Just because it was made out of wood? If so, we could have called it *timber* or perhaps *board*. But we do not. And every December, trees (albeit sacrificial ones) decorate most of our homes. Furthermore, for centuries the standard way to recognize that a structure of any importance has reached its topping-off point has been to hoist a tree up with the final beam.

But I think we should look at how trees are used as elements of dedication, not in a sacrificial sense but in a living sense. It is not surprising that

Grant Wood's delightful painting of an Iowa Arbor Day ceremony at a country school sold for nearly $1.5 million, for who among us has not been thrilled at Arbor Day ceremonies? Similarly, the springtime scene of parents and children digging holes and planting trees has, like many other things I have mentioned, become a visual cliché. So have plantings as memorials to the departed.

Why has this arboreal liturgy developed? Why have kings and commoners, presidents and preschoolers, leaders and little people all found it both convenient and pleasing to incorporate the trees of our urban forests in their symbolic acts of dedication and rededication? Is it because trees are cheap and the process easy? Perhaps. Or is there a deeper urge? Perhaps there is something biological telling these weird animals who have learned about good and evil that our forests—especially the forests each of us see every day of our lives—are not inherited from our ancestors but instead are borrowed for a short while from our children. And as we dedicate ourselves to our children, we must also rededicate ourselves to those grand living things that will stand with them on their journey.

A Longing for Peace The last element in the philosophical structure is at once the easiest and the hardest to understand: it is the longing for peace. The trees around our homes are elements of great peacefulness and assurance to countless people, whether they be poets who have written on the subject for ages or just common folk sitting on their front steps contemplating the views from their own front doors. This is the one consideration which shows up in every survey on the metaphysical aspects of urban forests. Perhaps this is because of the size of trees, perhaps because of their strength even in the face of nature's fiercest blasts, perhaps because trees change so slowly that most people do not even notice until suddenly the tree, like a loved relative who is taken for granted, is gone forever.

Whatever the reason, trees have become an analogue for peace. Yet there are among us those who think nothing of bulldozing whole ancient forests both urban and rural, of butchering giant redwoods that have stood on this earth since Christ stood in the temple of Jerusalem and even perhaps since Moses stood in the palace of the pharaoh.

How can a few humans be so callous about trees while the vast majority revere them to the point of often refusing to prune for fear of "hurting" the tree? To this question I have no answer, any more than I know why God first commanded His chosen people "Thou shalt not kill," then straightway told them to slaughter all the inhabitants of the Promised Land of Canaan, or why a nation that could produce a Haydn could also produce a Hitler.

Although a tiny but highly destructive minority seems to be programmed in just the opposite way, for most humans the planting of a tree is one of the most hopeful things we can do. Each of us has seen it unite people of all ages, creeds, political views, races, and dispositions. It instills pride, breeds harmony, and speaks of faith in a time of peace to come. Thus, it combines all the philosophical elements of which I spoke while also tangibly expressing the characteristic of foresight which separates humans from other life forms. Squirrels bury acorns; men plant oaks.

Perhaps I am wrong in all this. Perhaps we have urban trees only because a cold utilitarianism is at work that would excite only Jeremy Bentham.

But if I am wrong, at least I am grandly wrong. Let me conclude with two thoughts.

First, these lessons are not really new. The oldest of all is that planting and tending our urban forests is a high act of peace. I learned it from the prophet Isaiah, who must have been an arborophile because he referred to trees so often in his beautiful book. I am most fond of his prophecy in Chapter 55, which is yet to come true, of a time of great peace when we shall:

> go out with joy, and be led forth with peace; the mountains and the hills shall break forth before you into singing, and all the trees of the fields shall clap their hands. Instead of the thorn shall come up the fir tree, and instead of the briar shall come up the myrtle tree; and it shall be to the Lord for a name, for an everlasting sign that shall not be cut off.

The last thought is that although the peaceful day of fulfillment for our urban forests is, like Isaiah's prophecy, yet to come to pass, the will to create our urban forest is both ancient and strongly present now. It is deeply rooted in our collective subconscious; and that will is a phenomenon so widespread that it may properly be called universal. It is our categorical imperative.

And thus it should be our maxim that we shall build a forest—not a forest away and apart from the bulk of humankind, but a great forest encompassing nearly the whole of our human habitation. Let us, then, in the words of Immanuel Kant, act on that maxim which we can at the same time properly and rightly *will* to be a universal law.

8

Who Owns
the Trees?

R. Bruce Allison

It is a feeling I get when I hear that honking cacophony of Canada geese and look up to see a distant *V* pointing north or south, moving across a lead-gray sky like a lecturer's pointer across a blackboard. I think of Leonardo da Vinci's painting—a portrait of St. John the Baptist with a knowing smile on his lips and his finger pointed skyward. The art critics would fry me alive in a pot of boiling maple syrup if I were to suggest that Leonardo's St. John was pointing to a formation of Canada geese, but I would be so bold as to suggest that both the geese and St. John are pointing in the same direction and drawing our attention to a similar truth.

I was walking across the University of Wisconsin campus past the soil science building one summer day. A storm front was pushing heavy gray clouds across the sky. Cars and students were scurrying about, radios blaring, horns honking. The chatter of humanity pervaded the scene. My thoughts were deep on the problems of a project on which I was working, the editing of an applicators manual on forest pesticides. I was wondering and worrying about the complexities of our impact on nature, feeling responsible and concerned that nature's fate was in unsteady human hands.

My heavy-browed concentration was interrupted by a tan-brown blur moving across my peripheral vision. When I looked up and focused, I saw a formation of a thousand tiny whirlybirds sweeping down across my path. They were maple keys caught in the summer breeze, each spinning like a whirling dervish. They rode the currents of the wind, maneuvering past the red brick university buildings. My concentration was pulled from the between-bells business of the campus to that little drama of procreation. What struck me most was the independence of that act from human influence. No hand cast those seeds from the tree, no electric fan was blowing them about, no spade was required to plant them. Their timing was not dictated by bells and computer schedules. Their motivation was not money, grades, or social approval. And, on further thought, I gained the insight that on the stage of life those maple keys were front and center and all the campus bustle was mere backstage distraction. I suddenly was feeling less responsible for nature and was hoping that she was feeling more responsible for me. Like Leonardo and the Canada geese, those maple keys put things in perspective and reminded me of the need to establish a healthy working relationship with nature.

A CALL TO STEWARDSHIP

Henry George, an economist and philosopher whose *Progress and Poverty* is now a classic—and like most classics seldom read—suggested a different kind of relationship with nature. In his economics, he differentiated between natural wealth and man-made wealth. He defined natural wealth, such as land, as existing independently of human labor. Not only is it not a product of human endeavor, but access to it is necessary for human survival and progress. To allow a few to possess, restrict, and perhaps deplete these natural resources deprives others of their fair share and future use. Natural objects should be used beneficially, George reasoned, but not owned. Ownership implies the absolute right to dissipate and destroy. Natural objects are not created by human labor and, therefore, belong to everyone; consequently, the user has only a limited possession. Plus, natural wealth must be preserved for the survival of future generations. Natural objects are held in stewardship, not ownership. The critical difference between owning something and holding it in stewardship or in trust is clearly understood by the ecologists and environmentalists who have documented the abuse and avaricious depletion of some natural resources by the banditry of a few who happened to be the first there or be strong enough to push all others aside. Scott Nearing, author of *Living the Good Life*, calls it the grab-and-keep society—those who depend on natural resources for survival are excluded from them, ownership rights are exalted to higher-law status, and the educational system indoctrinates the next generation with the myth that certain natural objects are the private domain of an individual, a corporation, or a state.

So what does all this have to do with trees, which after all, is my only field of expertise and the real topic of this chapter? I could make the connection with coal, which in fact is a forest of a million years ago. The unbridled exploitation of this natural resource would be alarming. Or I could make the connection with the trees of 200 years ago, the majestic white pines which swept the boundless wilderness of North Wisconsin. They were ripped down in a decade by an exclusive few, money-hungry lumber barons. That Wisconsin natural resource is lost forever. All that remains is a few patches of virgin white pine—just enough to remind us how majestic they were and to leave us a little bitter at being denied our inheritance.

But as for coal, the connection to trees is a little too strained. And as for our forests, the passing of laws and creation of agencies, such as the Forest Service, regulating their care have largely solved the problem. Such environmental laws and forest-use agencies were a way for the community at large to declare that certain forests are natural resources belonging to all citizens and that the benefits from their use will be shared by all, with the investment protected for future generations by careful management practices—in other words, a stewardship. Coal and forests are being used ethically, but what about the urban tree?

If a negligently driven automobile damages a city tree, the driver can expect a bill for damages from the city. The tree is community property and has real monetary value. When it is damaged, the community's assets have been diminished, and the city has the right to demand compensation from the responsible party. Now consider that tree in your neighbor's yard—a large white oak over 200 years old. If you mischievously sawed it down, you could be taken to court and forced to pay the owner whatever value the tree had. But what if the owner cut it down?

WHEN IS CUTTING RIGHT?

If I had a beautiful, beneficial tree in my yard, which was providing shade, soil protection, air pollution control, community beauty, and increased house property value, and a neighbor reached over the fence and cut it down, I would be irate, indeed! If the same tree was in the median strip and the neighbor cut it down, I would object vehemently. But if that wonderful tree were ten feet the other way within his property line and he buzzed it down one fine afternoon, chopped it up, and tossed it in his fireplace, what could I do then? Silently turn from my window mourning the tragic end of a life that had spanned ten generations? Would I shrug my shoulders regretting that the air would be a little more polluted, the winter would be a little colder, the summer a little hotter, fewer birds would be returning, and the neighborhood slightly diminished? But it was, after all, his tree and its death not my concern. Or would I run out and scream over the whine of the chain saw and demand, "Just what the heck is going on here?

R. Bruce Allison

Why do you think you have the right to destroy this tree which is a pleasure and benefit to many people, a tree which occupied this site long before any property lines were made up?"

My neighbor may turn to me and explain that the tree was diseased or perhaps, due to decay, a hazard to passersby, and that logic demanded it be removed. Then I could walk away saddened but satisfied and perhaps resolved to help plant another in its place. Not even trees live forever. But if my neighbor had no such excuse for his behavior other than it is his tree and he'll do what he damned well pleases, that's when I really start screaming.

He may scream back, "Property rights!" "Freedom of action!" "Man's home is his castle!" and so on. I'm not suggesting that a person shouldn't have the right to rip down his own house if that's what he wants to do. That house is a product of human ingenuity, labor, and materials. Its creation, existence, and benefits are of a personal nature. The point I wish to make is that a tree is different from a house. That 200-year-old oak is a product of the ingenuity of nature whereas that house is the product of human labor. They are two separate categories. The tree owes nothing to any person for its creation. It exists independently of any property owner. It offers benefits to an entire community of people and has been doing so for generations. The tree ethic of which I speak is not and should not be enforceable by laws and regulatory agencies. It is a state of mind, a consciousness, an aware-ness, a feeling. It is shared with others through education and persuasion.

Bill Anacker, the arborist who taught me how to climb trees, was a man imbued with the tree ethic. As an apprentice-employee of Anacker's Tree

Service in Maryland, I sometimes accompanied him in making job estimates. In one case, a customer pointed out a large, very old copper beech,
which was growing alongside the house. The owner grumbled about how
the leaves cluttered up his lawn, stopped up his eave troughs, and probably interfered with his television reception. "How much to cut it off at the
base and get rid of it?" he snarled.

While I was obligingly considering drop-rope angles, felling procedure,
man-hours, and equipment costs, hoping to impress Bill with a well-
reasoned bid, Bill, himself, was stepping back from the tree, looking up
into the rich green crown, and gathering a larger perspective. Bill, though
certainly independent in his thinking, was usually a cool-headed business-
man always courteous to his customers. That's why I was shocked when
after sizing up the situation, he turned to the customer and said, "This
magnificent tree has been here a hundred years longer than you and your
television and God willing it'll be here a hundred years from now. I'll be
damned if I'd ever take it down for any price. I suggest that you move
yourself and leave the tree where it belongs." Needless to say, negotiations
ended at this point, and I never did get a chance to impress Bill with my
carefully planned bid. The experience did leave a lasting impression with
me, however, one which I have carried forward into my years of doctoring
trees.

And it is not just arborists who understand the tree ethic. On occasion, I
meet others who feel it strongly too, though it doesn't happen often
enough. Last autumn my Madison, Wisconsin, tree care company had
contracted with the university to prune some dying limbs from an oak on
the Memorial Union terrace. This forty-foot white oak, just outside the
cafeteria, was truly an historic tree in whose shade hundreds of thousands
of students had no doubt gathered over the years to listen to music, hear
political speeches, or sip their morning coffee while reading the paper. I
manned the ropes on the ground while Ravi, my climber, scampered in the
crown dropping cords of deadwood. As the limbs dropped, an entire
cafeteria of breakfasting people studiously ignored us or on occasion
glanced out the window in disinterest. Others passed by on the way to
class stepping over the mounds of fallen wood holding their ears against
the buzz of the chain saw. It surely looked like we were dismantling this
tree, yet not a soul came up to ask if we were taking it down and why. That
tree had sheltered so many. Where were its friends now?

Then suddenly a woman in her early twenties emerged from the cafeteria line and did a double take when she spotted us. She quickly paid for her
breakfast, then deserted the tray to rush out the door, practically leaping
over the brush piles to confront me. "What are you doing to that beautiful
oak tree? Don't tell me you plan on taking it down. It may be a little yellow,
but it's still alive." Her voice was full of feeling. It was obvious she cared for

the tree as one would care for a friend. She, no doubt, would also understand about the geese and the maple keys and maybe even what Leonardo
meant in his painting.

I assured her that I was here to help the tree, not remove it, and that
chances were this tree would outlive us all.

PART THREE

WHAT
MAKES
A TREE?

In order to understand the needs of our community trees, let us take an imaginary journey within a tree's trunk, as well as down under to the world of a tree's roots.

9

Journey to the Center of a Tree

Alex A. Shigo

WHAT ORGANISMS EXISTED more than 200 million years ago and are the largest life forms ever to inhabit the earth? Dinosaurs are the largest land animals known to have existed. They approached the limit of what the earth's gravity would allow without crushing vital organs or collapsing under their own weight. Blue whales are even more immense but are saved by the buoyancy of the environment in which they live, as is evident when beached whales are crushed by their own 150-ton bodies. But you don't have to go to a museum or on an ocean voyage to see the earth's most massive living things. Most people can see these organisms, though perhaps not the largest specimens, by simply gazing out their windows.

Trees are so common that we often forget how extraordinary they really are. They live on all the continents except Antarctica and in an astonishing variety of environments, from tropical to subarctic, rainforest to desert fringe. The General Sherman tree, the world's largest giant sequoia, weighs approximately 1,450 tons—as much as nine blue whales. If blue whales can't get away with their weight on land, how do trees do it? And with dinosaurs extinct and many species of whales endangered, how have trees been able to survive and thrive?

The answers lie within that tree out your window. As we journey to the center of that tree—or any tree—we'll find that the answers lie more specifically in the structural properties and growth processes of a tree. A better understanding of these can also have practical applications, such as helping you prune your trees to their advantage and prevent unnecessary wounds.

LAYER WITHIN LAYER

A journey to the center of a tree will require you to visualize and think about trees in a way that you probably never have before. For example, do you see any similarities between a tree and an onion or a stack of upside-down sno-cone cups? How about a submarine? Well, by the time you finish reading this chapter, you will. Such analogies will be useful in helping you understand how trees stay healthy.

Let us begin by looking at the structure of a tree. These earth giants are not just wood. Within a tree's woody trunk is a variety of structures, each performing a number of functions. Trees are like onions in that they have many layers. The outside layer of a tree, its bark, surrounds the entire organism except for roots, leaves or needles, and reproductive organs. At the risk of giving trees human characteristics, we might say that the bark is similar to our skin, which covers everything except our hair and nails.

Beneath the bark is the cambium, which is a cell factory that generates a new growth ring every year (or every growth period). As we pass the cambium on our way to the center of the tree, we find those growth rings of wood. The growth rings are divided into two kinds of wood—sapwood and heartwood. Sapwood has living cells and performs many vital functions for the tree. The cells of heartwood are dead, but in healthy trees the heartwood is sound and contributes support and protection to the tree. The ratio of these two kinds of wood varies from species to species. Osage orange and locust have only a few rings of sapwood. American elms hav͟ between twelve and eighteen rings no matter how old they are, signifying the twelve to eighteen most recent years of tree growth. Birch and maple may have forty to 100 rings of sapwood and very little heartwood. At the very center of a tree is a pencil-thin rod of pith, which represents the stem that was the tree in its first year of life.

Structurally, trees can be compared to a stack of conical paper cups. Each growing season, a new cone is added to the stack. If it were possible to remove all the inner layers and leave only the most recent growth ring, the tree would continue to stand and function normally with no noticeable difference to the observer. This is possible because growth in trees occurs close to the outside. The cambium, just under the bark, is the only area of the trunk where new cells are generated. Cells formed outward from the cambium develop into phloem (the food-conducting tissue of a plant) and bark. Bark is divided into two layers—the inner bark is comprised mostly of active living cells, the outer bark of a corky protective shield. Cells

Forest Service, U.S.D.A.

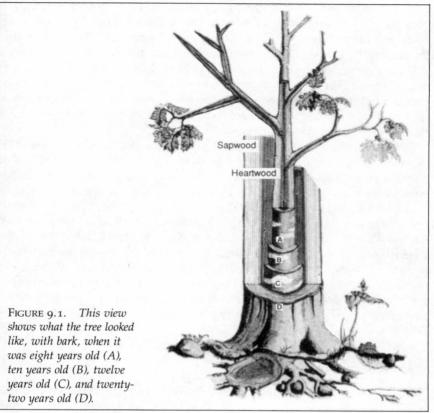

FIGURE 9.1. *This view shows what the tree looked like, with bark, when it was eight years old (A), ten years old (B), twelve years old (C), and twenty-two years old (D).*

formed inward from the cambium develop into xylem (water-conducting tissue) and comprise the bulk of a tree's wood.

By a process called cell differentiation, living cells (called parenchyma cells) develop into various tissue. Transport vessels in hardwoods (called tracheids in conifers) form within days or weeks when certain cells grow large so quickly that their contents break away from the walls, making the cells hollow. The end walls between these cells break down, creating small openings that form a conduit between cells. Food from the leaves moves down the tree in the phloem's transport tubes while water and dissolved minerals move up from the roots in the xylem's tubes.

Respiration in the roots, an energy-burning process, requires food from leaves to be pushed downward with a pumplike action. Finally, water is drawn upward, as in a straw, when transpiration and evaporation in the leaves pull fluids up like a siphon.

Fibers, on the other hand, develop when adjacent cells do *not* lose their contents for months or even years. But as with the transport vessels, the cells themselves are dead. Fibers are primarily for mechanical support. They provide tensile strength in an up-and-down (axial) direction, while the rest of the trunk provides compression (side-to-side) strength.

Functioning vessels occur only in sapwood. Most of the axial transport occurs in the current growth ring. Only a fraction of the previous year's transport system is used once new ones are formed. In some trees such as American elm, spring vessels form when the leaves emerge. As trees age, vessels clog and no longer transport fluids.

Seventy to 90 percent of the bulk of sapwood is dead, although about 80 percent of the cells in the wood are alive. This is because the cells that become wood, vessels, and fibers are very large compared with the living parenchyma cells. The woody cells have thick walls containing lots of cellulose and lignin—rigid materials that give trees their strength. These cells are bound into a grid pattern, like bricks in a wall, that makes the tree strong. The living parenchyma cells, on the other hand, have thin walls. Parenchyma cells cluster into the rays, which are visible in the cross-section of many kinds of wood. Check the oak in your woodpile for these rays, and you'll see that they divide a cross-section of wood into very thin pie-shaped wedges. Liquids move radially (in and out) through rays via parenchyma cells and a chemical process not observed in any other living organism.

SELF-PROTECTION SYSTEMS

Now that we know something about the anatomy of a tree, we can examine how it allows the tree to live and function. From their basic structures, trees have evolved protection and defense mechanisms. The difference between protection and defense is like the difference between a fortress and a battle. One is passive, the other active. For example, the outer bark not only provides physical protection, but it also contains a waxy material that waterproofs the bark and gives it an antimicrobial power.

Trees have also adapted their layered structure for protection. Trees can't heal after injury as animals do because they don't have the ability to generate new cells to replace damaged and infected cells. Neither do trees have the immunological chemistry to fight disease and infection. Once a tree is injured, it invariably becomes infected with microbes or fungi and carries the injury or infection for life. But unlike animals, trees compartmentalize, or wall off and isolate, infected areas to prevent disease from spreading to healthy areas.

Isolating disease by compartmentalization is an adaptation of growth processes. Each year trees grow new leaves or needles, nonwoody absorbing roots, flowers, and seeds. These organs are also shed annually. The

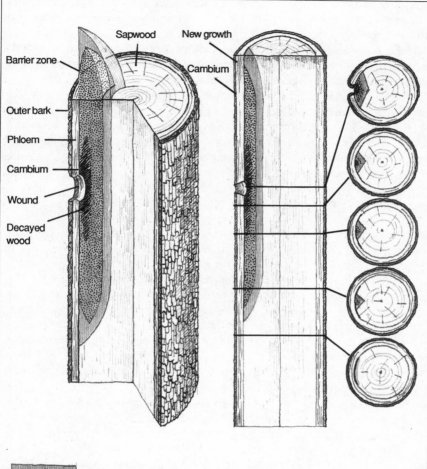

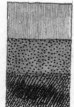

Antimicrobial substances

Microorganisms

Decay

FIGURE 9.2. *How a tree responds to a wound. At left, microorganisms in sapwood cause decay. At edges of infection, parenchymal cells make antimicrobial substances to fight infection. View at right shows the tree in a later season. Internal defenses are winning.*

cambium grows a thin corky layer of boundary cells that isolate these parts before they die. When any part of the tree is under attack from microbes or fungi, a similar process occurs.

The cell-generating cambium layer can modify cell production much the way a queen bee does. When all is fine in the hive, the eggs become soldiers, workers, or drones. But when the hive is under attack, more eggs develop into soldiers. In a healthy tree, the bulk of cells in the cambium layer differentiates into xylem and phloem tissue—the tree's pipelines between the leaves and roots. But when a tree is under attack, cell differentiation changes its priority to the production of parenchyma cells, and it varies the chemical makeup of these cells as well. They produce a class of chemicals known as phenols, which discourage infection. With this change in growth pattern, the tree produces a strong barrier zone that can encircle the tree and prevent the spread of disease.

This new type of wood is only part of the tree's reaction to trouble. Damaged areas are also sealed off inside the barrier zone. The living parenchyma tissue that is woven between the xylem and phloem during periods of normal growth can deliver needed chemicals to the dead transport cells. Radial transport of these protective liquids clogs vessels, preventing the spread of pathogens upward and downward. The infected area is walled off the way damage can be sealed off in a leaky submarine—by simply closing one door to prevent the leak from spreading to other areas.

Evidence of struggle can be seen in wood. When a tree generates a lot of parenchyma cells to isolate infection, it uses energy that would otherwise be available for growth. The result that you see is a thinner growth ring. In addition, compartmentalization discolors the wood.

The more injuries a tree has sustained, the more its activities and internal structures are diverted to seal off infected areas. This leaves fewer cells and organs to maintain life and growth. Mature trees contain hundreds, perhaps even thousands, of these compartments. It is the compartmenting process that saves trees, but like all good things, it is possible to have too much. Compartments can stop the movement of disease, but when they become too numerous, they can also stop the movement of the tree's vital fluids. That's how the natural death of a tree occurs.

Wind, lightning, and fire commonly injure trees. To these can be added other natural agents such as birds, insects, and animals. And, finally, there are people. You may have heard that trees "like to be pruned." Pruning can improve the quantity and quality of fruit and nuts as well as board footage. And like a haircut, pruning can improve the appearance of a tree. But it is important to distinguish between what is in the interest of the tree and what pleases humans.

Pruning is a trauma to a tree, and a tree will treat a pruning wound as it does any other injury. Trees actually "prune" themselves in some circumstances. When lower branches become shaded and cannot produce the energy needed to survive, they are sealed off and discarded. Trees have adapted an elaborate internal system of connecting branches to the wood of the trunk that supports the branch but can seal it off when its time has come. Within this junction, called the branch collar, there is an interlocking switching system of vessels that supplies these functions.

Visually recognizing the branch collar is of critical importance to the tree pruner. If pruned at the right spot, the collar will be able to seal off the wound quickly. But if the collar itself is damaged, the process of compartmentalization will be impaired; then the collar will become infected and add to the stress that the tree is trying to overcome. Because the vessels split in two at the collar, cutting too close to the trunk cuts into the mainline vessel as well as the branched portion.

Trees can adapt to changes in the environment, but when change occurs too quickly, they may not be able to respond fast enough. Two species, American chestnut and American elm, were driven to near extinction when people imported other species of chestnut and elm infected with diseases that indigenous trees were not adapted to resist. A journey to the center of these trees would have revealed that they were not able to compartmentalize quickly enough to fight off the unexpected foreign invaders.

Our journey has shown us that trees are far more complex than is apparent when we look out our window. We have also found that trees rely on structures and processes that no other organisms possess. Perhaps this is how they have survived all these eons and have watched dinosaurs come and go.

10

The Forest Underground

Thomas O. Perry and Gary Hennen

WHICH OF THE following statements about tree roots do you believe to be true?

- Roots contain chemical substances that can dissolve rock; in so doing, they create soils.
- Roots have a characteristic called *geotropism*, which means they respond to the earth's gravity and always grow downward.
- There are approximately as many branches in the root system as in the crown of a tree.
- A tree resembles a weight lifter's dumbbell in profile with both bulbs of equal size but one bulb under the soil.
- Taproots ordinarily extend twelve to fifteen feet into the soil; these deep root systems make trees safe during droughts.

These statements are part of the folklore of tree roots, but none is correct. These misconceptions resulted from the imagination and artistic misrepresentation of those who have not examined tree roots carefully. This chapter summarizes observations of soil scientists, foresters, and other specialists whose obscure publications are not normally examined but whose practical information is invaluable for architects, engineers, and even the average home gardener.

THE FUNCTIONS OF ROOTS

Surprisingly, the functions of roots are better known than their structures. To some extent, this is because basic functions can be derived logically with the help of a few simple observations. The two most basic functions of roots include holding the tree erect and transporting and collecting water, mineral nutrients, and oxygen from the pores in the soil. All these materials are essential for photosynthesis, which takes place in the leaves, so roots are involved in conducting fluids great distances against the force of gravity. Conversely, carbohydrates synthesized in the leaves flow back down the conduits of the branches, trunk, and roots to supply energy for life, growth, and functions to the cells of the roots.

The connection between roots and the crowns of trees is intricate, complex, and not entirely understood. The pattern of fluid conduction varies between and within species. Injecting dyes and observing their movement indicates that, in oaks and other ring-porous species, a given root is connected directly to a particular set of branches, usually on the same side of the tree. In these cases, death or damage to the roots usually results in death of the specific branches, and vice versa. In species possessing different anatomies, the dyes ascend in zigzag or spiral patterns, indicating that the roots serve all the branches and leaves. Death or injury of roots will not result in the death of specific branches. Instead, twigs and branches throughout the crown will die back.

ROOT STRUCTURE

Early observations of tree roots were limited to examining the short taproot and larger roots close to the trunk or to examining the vertical distribution of roots exposed by excavation, but this approach has proven inadequate. The complex variety of roots—big to small, tough to delicate—makes them much harder to study than other parts of a tree. The primary roots near the trunk start large and branch and taper to become the thickness of a thumb; they grow horizontally, four to eleven inches below the soil surface. From the transport roots, feeder roots grow upward to the surface, tapering to 0.008 inches in diameter, the size of coarse hair.

The heavy work necessary to excavate large roots is usually done with bulldozers, backhoes, and fire hoses, which inevitably destroys the fine roots. The delicate work necessary to study the root tips must be done with tweezers, fine brushes, dental picks, and ear syringes. In addition to being botanists, researchers must direct heavy equipment operators and possess the skills of an archaeologist.

By any method, it is virtually impossible to collect even a small portion of a tree's root system entirely. The extreme ends of root systems are about the size of the lead in a pencil. Symbiotic fungi, known as mycorrhizae, are attached along approximately the last one-third inch of the smaller roots. Fine strands of the mycorrhizae extend out from the roots into the soil. Sometimes the strands are black, sometimes white. They are about the size of a strand of a spider's web. The mycorrhizae amplify the area of the feeder roots 100 times or more as well as enhance the tree's water and mineral absorption capacities.

Despite the difficulties, usable information about roots can be derived by sampling—a method scientists have developed to study small portions of a system carefully and thoroughly, then applying the findings to the entire root system. The statistics are intriguing. A mature tree possesses thousands of leaves and *hundreds of miles of roots.* Hundreds of thousands of these are the very fine feeder roots. Yet these constitute only 5 percent of the total weight of a tree. On the average, another 15 percent of a tree's weight is made up of transport roots; 60 percent is trunk, 15 percent branches and twigs, and, finally, 5 percent leaves. Thus, the distribution by weight is approximately symmetrical.

Precise measurement of the surface area of leaves and roots is not possible, but estimates show that the surface of the root system is even greater than the surface of the leaves! This is best understood by the concepts of *leaf area index* and *root area index.* There is a limit to the leaf surface (both sides are counted) and the root surface that any particular plot of land can sustain. During the height of the growing season in a typical forest or cropland, the maximum leaf surface area is twelve times greater than the soil surface, while the root surface area is typically between fifteen to twenty-eight times greater than the soil surface area. Thus, in general, the root surface area of a tree or a pansy plant is likely to be at least twice as large as the leaf area.

The roots of a tree radiate out from the trunk to form a mat of cables, which act in combination with the adhering soil to hold the tree upright. When the wind blows from one side, the roots of that side are placed under tension (the other side is placed under compression). In the words of an engineer, the tree is an inverted cantilever. When the wind of tornadoes strikes the tree tops and the soils are dry, the trunks and limbs snap off. When the rains of hurricanes or long-soaking storms have saturated the soil and turned it to soup, the roots can no longer hold the tree upright; then even a moderate, forty-mile-per-hour wind will blow the tree over— roots and all will be heaved out of the ground to produce wind-thrown mounds.

Ninety-nine percent of a tree's roots are found in the top three feet of soil. Root-spread area is often four to seven times the cross-sectional area of the crown or one, two, or more times the height of the tree in diameter. Rather than the weight lifter's dumbbell, a more accurate image of a tree's shape is a wine glass sitting on a dinner plate. The root systems of many trees are matted together under the soil, making it impossible to determine which roots belong to what trees. Under these conditions, natural root grafts commonly occur when trees of the same species grow in the same stand. This great clutching tangle and joining of roots also inevitably contributes to the stability of trees against gravity and wind.

ROOT GROWTH

The first root to emerge from the seed of some species (e.g., pines and oaks) sometimes persists and grows straight down into the soil to depths of four to seven feet or even more, until the supply of oxygen becomes limiting. If this taproot persists, it is usually largest just beneath the tree trunk and decreases rapidly in diameter as secondary roots branch from it and radiate out horizontally through the soil. The primary root of other species, such as spruces, willows, and poplars, does not usually persist. Instead of a taproot, the first formed roots of these species are characterized by multiple branching to form a system of fibrous roots that dominate early growth. (See Figure 10.1.)

Whether they have taproots or fibrous roots during their early stages, most mature trees have a root collar, which can be recognized as a bulge on the trunk at the ground line. From this root collar, four to eleven woody roots originate and grow horizontally through the soil. These major roots branch and decrease in diameter as they spread away from the trunk. In so doing, they form an extensive network. These major roots and their primary branches are woody and perennial, that is, they persist from year to year and usually show annual growth rings just like trunks and branches. These woody roots, often called transport roots, constitute the framework and support system for the tree. They generally extend to occupy a horizontal area several times larger than the projection of the crown of the tree.

A complex system of smaller roots continues ever outward and predominantly upward from the support/transport root framework. These smaller roots branch four or more times to form fans or mats, terminating in thousands of fine, short, nonwoody tips. The tips vary in size from less than an eighth of an inch to about one-half inch long and are about the diameter of a grain of rice (or, as mentioned previously, the lead of a pencil). These are the roots that account for the majority of a tree's surface area. Since they are primarily the site of water and mineral absorption, they are called feeder roots. It is here that the symbiotic mycorrhizae fungi, which enhance absorption, are located.

Because these root tips are so delicate and occur primarily in the topsoil and litter layers, they are susceptible to hazards such as drought, extremes

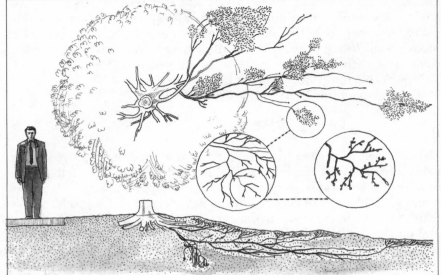

FIGURE 10.1.   *Idealized view of a major root and its branches. Roots are thick near the trunk and decrease in diameter with branching and distance from the tree. The transport roots grow horizontally and parallel to the surface while the feeder roots grow predominantly upward. The feeder roots are concentrated in the surface layers of the soil. During warm, moist periods, the feeder roots can be found in the decomposing layers of the litter. During cold or dry weather, they die back. Several "suits" of feeder roots can form and die during a single growing season. Insets show progressive magnification of roots with far right inset a representation of root tips.*

in temperature, and frost heaving, not to mention human activities. They also provide food for nematodes, springtails, rodents, and soil microfauna. Injury and death of these fine roots are frequent. New roots form rapidly, however. Altogether, there is more shedding and new growth in this part of a tree than in any other, including the leaves. This ephemeral aspect of roots has only recently been recognized.

WHERE ROOTS GROW

The distinction between shallow-rooted or deep-rooted species of trees is not a real one. Roots grow where the mineral nutrients, water, and organic matter necessary for life are available. Trees grow best in light clay-loam soils about three feet deep. Root growth, and hence tree growth, is restricted in shallow or wet soils or in excessively drained soils. Roots do not grow toward anything. They cannot grow where there is no oxygen or where the soil is compacted and hard to penetrate. The number of soil pores and the availability of oxygen decreases exponentially with soil depth. The amount of clay, silt, and other fine textured material also increases with depth. Dense, fine-textured soils resist penetration by both roots and mechanical devices. However, most species of trees will grow roots deeply into the soil, down cracks, and even down sewer lines if oxygen and water supplies are adequate.

Frost action and alternate swelling and shrinking of soils between wet and dry periods heave, break, and loosen surface layers of soil. Decomposing organic matter provides food for millions of insects, worms, and nematodes, which burrow and tunnel through the surface layer, fluffing the soil even more, until approximately 50 percent of its volume is air. Air, water, minerals, and roots penetrate this layer with ease. The surface layer contains the highest concentration of available water, oxygen, and minerals and thus the majority of roots.

ADAPTIVE VARIATIONS ON GROWTH PATTERNS

Other patterns of root growth may develop under certain conditions. Roots can grow thirty feet or more downward if oxygen, water, and nutrients are available. In drier soils, pines and some other species often form striker roots, which are somewhat like taproots in that they grow downward until they encounter obstacles, such as insufficient oxygen or too much water. But unlike taproots, they do not grow down from the trunk. Instead, they grow from the horizontal woody support roots. Some black gum trees are known to send out extensive striker roots.

Both taproots and striker roots may branch out horizontally to form a second tier of roots. (See Figure 10.2) The lower tier tends to occur just above the soil layers where oxygen supplies are insufficient to support growth. Water holds less than 0.0001 as much oxygen as air; thus, oxygen scarcity is associated with wet soils. Spruces, willows, and other trees that grow in wet sites ordinarily have root systems that are shallow and multi-branched. Drainage ditches and swamps illustrate this adaptation by revealing an impressive concentration of matted roots just above the permanent water table. Tupelo, cypress, black gum, sycamore, and other species common to swamps and flood plains, on the other hand, have evolved special anatomies that permit conduction of oxygen a foot or more below the water table.

Pines and other trees tend to develop a two-layered root system in the deep sands of the American Southeast as an adaptation to drought. The surface layer of roots absorbs water and nutrients available from intermittent summer rains. The roots of the lower tier allow survival during droughts. Some trees, like longleaf pine, have yet other special adaptations for survival in sands and other deep soils. For the first four or five years of life, these trees remain very grasslike. They squat close to the ground and show little sign of growth. This condition is known as the grass stage. Once an extensive root system is established and has penetrated through to the layers of soil where there is a reliable supply of water, longleaf pine seedlings break out of the grass stage and grow rapidly.

APPLICATIONS FOR TREE HEALTH

Understanding where roots grow and what they do provides many opportunities for improving tree health. This is particularly important in cities where stresses are many. Growing space is limited; there is often too much

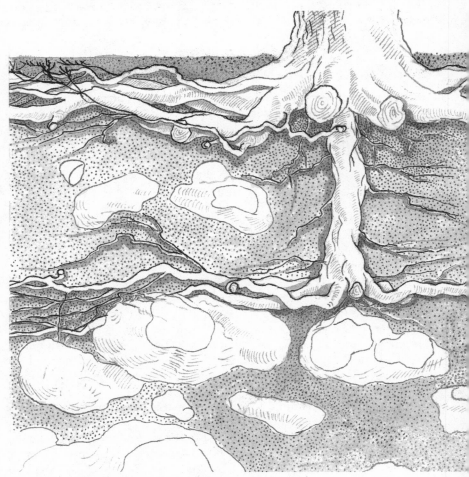

FIGURE 10.2. *Idealized view of a tree with two tiers of roots.*

water and not enough oxygen. Since so many roots occur just under the surface of the soil and root systems spread so far, herbicides used for other weed control purposes can also cause major problems when used near trees and shrubs.

Most tree deaths are accidental and most often involve misconceptions about roots. The largest single killer of trees is soil compaction—a condition most frequently encountered in urban areas. Compaction results from excessive use by people, livestock such as penned animals, heavy machinery, construction, the installation of powerlines, sewers, streets, and sidewalks. Even pigeons have been known to damage trees. Though small and lightweight, pigeons have small feet which causes them to exert as much pressure (weight per area) as larger, heavier animals. Compaction col-

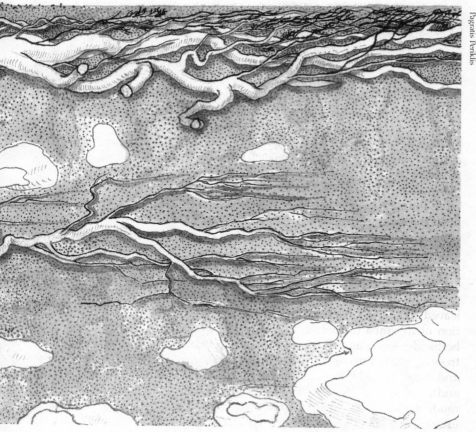

Pagratis Periklis

lapses the pores of the soil, thus affecting oxygen and even water supply. Surprisingly, these adverse conditions are best tolerated by trees adapted to swamps and flood plains such as pin oak, willow, willow oak, sycamore, and honey locust because these species are adapted to conditions of low oxygen.

Any grading or other activity that buries or cuts off tree roots will result in death to a corresponding portion of the crown. During house construction and utility line installation, over 90 percent of the roots in yards may be destroyed. The soil structure in the entire yard is usually completely destroyed by compaction and the spreading of heavy excavated soil over the top of undisturbed soil. Even as little as a few inches of clay soil can seal out the oxygen supply and prevent the penetration of water sufficiently to kill a tree. Careful watering and thinning tree crowns to compensate for root losses allow the residual roots to supply extra water and nutrients while new roots grow and become established.

The greatest threat to urban trees is the condition and amount of soil space available for root growth. An oak or maple, which typically lives well over 100 years (some times several hundred years) in a forest environment, may live only twenty-five to thirty years in a heavily used city park (e.g., Central Park, Boston Common, or the Mall in Washington, D.C.), and only five to twelve years in sidewalk pit locations.

Urban tree-planting and landscaping success can be improved by a variety of strategies related to good root growth. These include choosing a species appropriate to existing conditions; grading, aeration, landforming, and preparing the soils; planning (and limiting) access by people and animals; avoiding problematic locations; and limiting vegetation so as not to exceed the carrying capacity of the site. Since all of these factors must be planned in a new park or street in any event, planning them right costs no more than planning them wrong. Doing them right will result in longer-lived trees and more attractive landscapes.

Since roots generally spread far beyond the crowns, the use of chemicals anywhere in the vicinity is likely to affect a tree. Soil is a matrix of chemical reactions that produce the richness of minerals, air, and so on. Various chemicals affect soil properties; the rock salt that melts ice can kill trees as can hydrated lime used to make concrete. Trees are affected like broad-leaved weeds when lawn weed killers are used. For example, the application of dicamba (also called Banvel) alone or in combination with other herbicides such as Trimek or in combination with fertilizers can injure trees. Improper use of dicamba will distort the leaves of oaks and sycamore and defoliate and kill sensitive trees like yellow poplar. Roundup herbicide and its formulations are supposedly inactivated when they contact soil or muddy water, but these chemicals do not have to penetrate the soil to interact with roots growing in a litter layer, lawn, or mulch. Dogwoods and other trees, for instance, may show extreme leaf distortion and crown dieback even when herbicides do not strike the green portion of their trunks or foliage. Other common chemicals such as rock salt, used to melt ice, the lime from concrete, and the solvents used in cleaning fluids can all do damage to tree roots.

Since roots grow in cracks and crevices of pavement, application of Valpar, Bromacil, and other sterilants and herbicides can kill trees sixty feet or more away. Even large residential lots which average 105 by 150 feet are not big enough to contain the root systems of large trees. To save trees from damage, neighbors must cooperate when planning to apply chemicals. Besides, the roots of as many as nine different trees are frequently intertwined. Roots of the same species such as oaks, poplars, and sweet gum often graft to each other so that fluids, chemicals, and microbes can and do travel from one tree to others.

CONCLUSION

Contrary to popular belief, the following facts about roots are true:

- Most roots grow horizontally and upward through the soil.
- Most roots are in the top foot of soil, few are deeper than three feet.
- Many roots extend radially, far beyond the tips of tree branches—thirty feet is not uncommon.
- Roots grow best in the upper layers of soil because the available oxygen, water, and nutrients are concentrated in these layers.
- Roots will not grow where moisture and oxygen are unavailable.
- The surface area of the root system is larger than that of the leaves and branches.
- The small root hairs that make up the majority of the root surface die and regenerate periodically.

PART FOUR

PLANNING
FOR TREES

Getting trees integrated into the basic design of our cities requires the involvement of many different kinds of urban forest professionals. Working side by side with city planners, we need horticulturists, landscape architects, arborists, and many more. Together, they create a sense of place, provide for wildlife within the urban area, and improve the overall health of the trees already in place. And with strong city ordinances and the latest computer technology, we can strengthen and simplify all our efforts. This section gives practical information on planning, planting, and maintaining an ecologically sound city forest.

11

A Blueprint for Tomorrow: Getting Trees into Urban Design

*James Urban, with
Ralph C. Sievert, Jr., and
James Patterson*

IN THE LATE twentieth century, urban trees are being forced to survive in city systems that are increasingly hostile to tree growth. Take, for example, what has happened to one downtown street in the nation's capital. Imagine yourself walking down Washington's K Street—a major east/west roadway—on a hot summer's day fifty years ago. Overhead, the branches of trees planted in the 1880s reach outward, almost touching branches from trees on the opposite side of the street. Beside you, landscaped garden space between sidewalks and buildings gives tree roots room to grow. Just ahead, a construction worker loads bricks from a horse-drawn wagon into a wheelbarrow and then pushes the load across the walk into a construction site.

Now let us visit K Street in 1989. The sun beats down, unmercifully hot. Shimmering heat waves are reflected back through the air by concrete that stretches, almost unbroken, from the street to the edge of continuous, interlocked high-rise buildings. A few small trees have been planted, but their branches do not yet provide much shade. Added lanes of traffic speed by, releasing fumes to the air.

You stop abruptly as the boom of a crane lifts a load of bricks high into the air above your head and lowers them into a forty-foot-deep hole that is soon to become a new building. The flat-bottom truck carrying the bricks is parked on the sidewalk, and a construction worker motions you out into the street. Beyond the truck, another worker is operating a large vibrating compactor that tamps the soil for a new sidewalk. Glancing ahead, you decide to risk jaywalking to the other side of the street in hopes of catching a little shade in the shadow of the buildings.

Fifty years have not improved the urban forest. As the scene on K Street demonstrates, the pressures of the city environment affect almost every facet of tree health. City streets have less soil with the proper drainage and structure to support tree roots. Wide roadways, bigger building sites, street signs, light poles, and fire hydrants are all necessary additions to the cityscape, but they compete with trees for valuable space. More urban trees are dying, and fewer replacement trees are being planted. Tight city budgets have reduced the planning and maintenance force required to help overcome the problems created by these obstacles. In short, within a fifty-year span, our urban forests have gone from good health to a status in which we almost expect these trees to decline and die at a young age.

It is time to make some changes in the design and construction of our cities. Trees are a major element in the city structure, with their own economic, ecological, and aesthetic values. Because they are living components, we need to pay attention to the air, water, and space they need in order to grow—both above and below the ground. Just planting more trees is not the answer. Trees have long been fit into spaces left over after everything else is written into the design. This approach will not work if we want our trees to be a major element in a city's structure.

Today, urban forest professionals are recognizing the declining state of our urban forests and are working to change those conditions for tomorrow. But the problems they face are not simple. Ultimately, the situation demands changes in the entire long-range approach we take to planning for trees in urban America.

THE CLEVELAND MODEL

Trees are constantly competing for space in the city. In areas that are already developed, these conflicts can be reduced by carefully identifying the spaces available for trees and choosing the best trees to fit the site.

Cleveland, Ohio, is known in the arboreal world for its active pursuit of this technique. Its urban foresters have developed a process for selecting and planting trees with aboveground shapes that match available air space. For example, if the site has only a narrow space between the street and a row of buildings, a tall columnar tree is selected. On a wide street lawn with a powerline overhead, a short spreading tree is chosen.

Thanks to continuing research by horticulturists and nurserypeople and to testing in urban environments, a wider range of tree types, sizes, and shapes are now available to cities across the country. Choices from this expanded list of trees can be made based on size, tolerance to moisture extremes, shape, and color.

Cleveland has developed checklists to help determine where a tree will fit. These standards help prevent conflicts with existing buildings, utilities, driveways, and traffic signals, and they allow the city forester to restrict planting to areas where the trees are likely to survive, thus conserving limited maintenance and tree-planting budgets.

In brief, one Cleveland checklist requires that no tree is planted:

- beneath overhead wires lower than twenty-five feet above the ground or centered beneath wires;
- within ten feet of a fire hydrant or driveway apron;
- within twenty feet of a stop sign or other traffic marker or within thirty-five feet of street intersections;
- within fifteen feet of a utility pole or twenty-five feet of a street light;
- within five feet of any underground utility; or
- within twenty feet of a building or structure.

In addition, the size that a tree will attain is noted when it is planted. Large trees are planted fifty feet apart, medium trees thirty-five feet apart, and small trees twenty feet apart. Tree lawns for the three categories of size are required to measure greater than eight feet, five to eight feet, and three to five feet, respectively.

Once the Cleveland planting professionals have worked out compatible sites for new trees, a second checklist helps in selecting the right species. Desirable trees are categorized by the size and shape they will have at maturity. Three size groupings are used: fifty feet or taller, thirty to fifty feet, and less than thirty feet. The trees may be listed by shapes under the headings of oval, spreading, columnar, pyramidal, weeping, etc.

Finally, trees are selected according to:

- shape and size to fit the site;
- the best chance of surviving transplanting and the greatest longevity based on resistance to drought, insects, disease, or poor soils; and
- aesthetically best suited to the neighborhood.

A computerized street-tree inventory makes it possible to examine past species selections and make choices that reflect compatibility with existing trees.

The Cleveland checklists aren't perfect, however. They are still based on the idea of fitting trees into available spaces rather than giving trees priority in the planning process from the start. In fact, Cleveland's spacing standards are so restrictive that they would preclude planting trees in downtown areas of most cities. And the Cleveland approach does not provide a comparable checklist to determine where new buildings, utilities, driveways, and traffic signals should be prohibited to avoid interference with the growth of existing trees.

Clearly, if urban trees have value, a more radical approach to planning is essential. We can no longer ignore the fact that even an advanced approach, such as the Cleveland model, may still be leading us down the street toward treeless—therefore, lifeless—cities. A stronger approach is especially important on urban sites where new construction or reconstruction means that forest planning could still be built into the process.

THE PORTLAND MODEL

Portland, Oregon, provides one example where trees have priority, or at least equal footing, in a city's development. With a cooperative effort between the city's park bureau and its planners, tree-planting requirements have been built into zoning and building regulations. All new development must include tree planting, with the amounts specified in the zoning codes for diverse types of sites. Building codes specify that the city forester must sign off on plans, ensuring that a development has met its tree-planting requirement.

What's the effect of this approach? Steve Goetz, grounds manager for the Portland Park Bureau, points to the fact that private sector investment in tree planting can become the norm rather than a pleasant exception. He tells of a $50 million downtown commercial building complex with belowground parking. In other cities, the project might have proceeded without tree planting. But as a result of Portland's code requirements, the developer put in large suspended pits to the tune of $20,000 to provide planting space for trees.

Portland has other success stories—one of them the winner of a Federal Highway Administration award. That prize went for planning of a tree-friendly ten-foot median and wide buffer strips in redesigning a roadway through a rundown industrial/residential riverside neighborhood. In downtown Portland, trees were also included in laws that set aside some downtown streets for pedestrian- and bus-only use.

The Portland model is successful because it not only conserves public funding by getting the developers to finance tree care, but it also gets the developers to think about trees early in the design process. To make this approach work, the urban forest planner must shift roles from supervising the planting of city trees to facilitating for private sector action. Such planning also demands that foresters get in on the development process very early and stick with it to the end. What Goetz calls the "window of opportunity for trees" exists at the first meeting with the architects. Because changes in staff can affect whether trees are kept in the planning and construction process, some mechanism for carryover is also needed among the ranks of urban foresters.

How did Portland get its regulations into place? That was another window of opportunity, according to Goetz. This window opened when the city decided to revise its zoning and building code language, and park and city planners got together to figure out how to build trees into the process. Portland isn't the only place working to get trees built into the basic planning process. In Milwaukee, roadways are now regularly designed with medians that provide both above- and underground space for trees. In Maryland, all new development is now required to put utilities underground, thus avoiding aboveground conflict with growing trees. Each of these achievements provides components of a strong future model for healthy urban forests.

ENGINEERING THE UNDERGROUND SPACE

Sound urban forest planning like that in Portland or Milwaukee requires not only aboveground locations for trees but serious consideration of underground matters. Competition for underground space is one concern, especially in dense urban centers where underground utilities are taking increasingly large amounts of room. But another major issue has to do with soil.

Most urban soils are no longer suitable for adequate root growth. As larger buildings, wider roads, and larger and more powerful construction equipment press down on soil surfaces, the overall result is massive soil compaction. Soil scientist James Patterson cites some startling facts. In Washington, D.C., he found that the soils on the Mall stretching between the Capitol building and the Washington Monument are so compacted that the average soil density is about the same as a cinder block or brick. In some urban areas, soil density is comparable to concrete!

We can think about soil density in terms of pore space, that is, the ratio of soil particles to voids where air and water can be found. While the ideal pore space for growing trees is about 50 percent, the average pore space on the Washington Mall is often less than 35 percent and sometimes drops as low as 13 percent. The effect, Patterson says, is extreme stress on tree roots when soil is either completely wet or dry. Soil oxygen decreases and plant roots congregate in cracks or grow right at the surface rather than penetrating the rock-hard soils.

POOR DIRT: WHY URBAN SOILS NEED LEAVES

In the forest ecosystems, where there is constant replenishment of organic matter through the accumulation and decay of leaves, organic matter favorably influences the soils. A similar influence is lacking in urban soils. In the urban ecosystem, leaves and organic matter are usually removed as soon as they begin to accumulate. As a result, urban soils tend to deteriorate, and therefore need consistent replenishment of organic matter, as the following comparison clearly shows:

Natural Soils	*Urban Soils*
Leaf litter accumulates and decays atop the soil surface to favorably influence the soil.	Organic materials removed
Easily worked	Difficult to work
Well structured	Poorly structured
Familiar dark brown color	Varied colors, including gray or gley (a claylike soil that indicates poor aeration within the soil layers)
High level of microorganism activity. Speeds breakdown of leaf litter and enriches the soil.	Reduced microorganism activity. Results in limited breakdown of existing organic matter, with subsequent reduced availability of nutrients to plants.
Favorable conditions for storing, transporting, and releasing water	Minimal water movement through the soil limits moisture available for plant

Recent research in root development has shown that, even in relatively good situations, only the top six to twelve inches of urban soil have characteristics that allow root growth—not enough for the growth of healthy trees—and in downtown areas, often no soil is suitable for root development.

Clearly, we can no longer dig a hole in the pavement and expect trees to grow. Without attention to rooting needs, the average tree, after planting, begins to decline as soon as it outgrows the soil with which it was planted. Street trees studied in suburban Washington, D.C., for example, showed substantial dieback in less than five years. When the rootball of one tree was excavated, the entire four-by-four-foot planting pit was a solid root mass with hardly any soil. No rooting activity was found beyond the edge of the original tree pit. Rather than expect tree roots to thrive anywhere

Natural Soils	Urban Soils
make increased amounts of moisture available for plant growth and facilitate handling of heavy rainfalls with minimal adverse effects.	growth. Rain can easily dislodge and displace soil particles.
Increased drainage in the soil mass and between soil particles	Reduced percolation makes soils difficult to wet and, once wet, difficult to dry.
Low densities. Soils are more resilient to compaction.	High densities. Soils can become hard as concrete.
Favorable insulation from temperature extremes	Extreme temperature variations
Root channels provide few physical barriers to both root growth and water movement.	Increased physical barriers (concrete, asphalt, oil). With particles packed more tightly, roots have more difficulty penetrating soil.
	Increased metal content from car exhaust and industrial emissions. Effects of heavy metals are aggravated.
	Frequent exposure to salt from melting snow and ice on streets and sidewalks. Destroys soil structure and impedes gas exchange.
	Higher alkalinity from lime applications and breakdown of man-made materials. Imbalance of nutrients results, with calcium tending to predominate

American Forestry Association

they are placed, we must design and build the space for roots to grow. Poor soils may actually need to be dug out and replaced.

The volume of roots required to support a tree is roughly equal to the volume of tree branching above. Although much research is needed on potential ways to solve some of the space problems, we do have some answers. The tree lawn—the space between the curb and sidewalk—needs to be wider. The soil used to fill these spaces after construction must have better air and water movement. It should be topsoil rather than gravel, bricks, clay, and building debris. This soil should be more than one foot deep and should not be heavily compacted.

Sidewalk construction should change to allow sidewalks and trees to coexist. Although the techniques need to be refined, we know that the use of geotextile cloth can limit the need to compact soil under the walks.

Grouping urban trees into blocks rather than rows provides room for root growth, as well as beauty and focus in a courtyard.

Gravel layers permit air to reach the soil beneath the sidewalk, allowing roots to grow deeper. Styrofoam "popcorn board" can also be used as an underlayer for concrete sidewalks. The foam allows roots to grow under the walk without causing damage to the walk.

Grouping trees in urban tree islands is a method that tackles the underground space problem. It is working well in New York and other cities. Areas along the street are identified where a sizable planting pit—ten by twenty-five feet or larger—can be created. Several trees are then planted there and share a large volume of good soil.

One or two islands on every block can produce larger trees, thereby providing the city with more shade and green area per tree. This solution is clearly more successful than lining the streets with small trees that have a significantly lower chance to reach maturity—or even survive. Clustering trees also reduces maintenance costs.

Another idea for improving upon rooting space is to create interconnected tree pits. Here, a continuous street tree pit three feet deep and four feet wide is excavated for an entire block prior to placing the sidewalk. Drainage lines and loosely compacted planting soil are placed in the trench, followed by a four-inch gravel cushion that allows air and water to flow between sidewalk and soil. Finally, a new concrete sidewalk is poured over this zone, with adequate spaces left open to plant the trees.

This system, with variations, is currently being tested in Washington, D.C., New York, and other cities with positive results. When such large areas of suitable soil are designed as part of the urban environment, it is possible to control soil compaction, pH problems, and nutrient, water, and oxygen levels.

DESIGNING TOGETHER

The urban forest is only one part, although a vital part, of the larger urban development scene. To grow successfully, the urban forest must be designed as an integral part of the urban whole and considered by all members of the design team over the long period of planning and construction.

Today, urban foresters and landscape architects are working for a better understanding of the urban forest. Although the technology to keep trees healthy and living longer is a major challenge, many successful techniques have been tested. But we need more than technology.

Major changes need to be made in the philosophy of designing and building our cities. Engineers, architects, developers, construction companies, politicians, and citizens need to join the effort to make space for trees. Too often, such professionals know a great deal about blueprints, concrete, or political constituencies, but very little about the ecological values or biological needs of trees. Even landscape architects, who generally consider trees as architectural elements in their planning, may not know the biological requirements of trees chosen for their attractive appearance.

The overall economic, ecological, and human values of urban forests need to be more clearly presented to and understood by these individuals and groups. Citizens and professionals must also have the information that allows them to grasp at least the basics of the relationship between tree growth, open spaces, root growth, soil quality, and maintenance.

With that information in hand, action must be taken to include tree planting and maintenance needs in all city plans for new development or reconstruction. Only then will our cities see real movement toward healthy, mature urban forests for the next generation.

12

The Green Team: Who's Working on Trees?

Jan Goldstein and Steven Teske

IT'S 8:45 A.M. and Steve Sandfort's Cincinnati team already is in high gear. The task: reforestation. Fifty trees are on the truck, fifty of the 100,000 in Sandfort's long-range plan. Sandfort is a forester, and these ten-foot tall maples are en route to Interstate 75 in downtown Cincinnati, where they may live—with help and a certain amount of luck—for generations to come.

It's 9:15 A.M. and Jim Urban, landscape architect, is about to set pencil to paper. He has been selected by a Washington, D.C., real estate firm to landscape a commercial property slated for total redevelopment. The price tag for the project is $25 million. Urban has just lobbied for and won a bigger-than-average slice of the pie: an extra $20,000 to plant trees in a manner that will reduce maintenance costs and increase longevity. He has spent much time studying the site, given some thought to a new twist on his recently revised planting detail, and is now ready to roll.

Bailey Hudson has already been out with the utility company line trimmers for two hours, and it is barely 9:30 in the morning. Each of the dozen or so specimen sweetgum lining East Cypress Street are prized by residents of suburban Santa Maria, California, and no cut will go un-noticed. Hudson's eyes are riveted to the spinning blade of the saw in the

Gary Moll

Tree trimmers perform 80 percent of the maintenance work in urban forests.

trimmer's hands. Though his title is park superintendent, his training is in arboriculture, and as an arborist he is the voice for the town's trees.

It's 10:00 A.M. in Seattle when Jim Clark's lecture to his environmental horticulture class begins. "Before the year is over," he says, "you will be able to recognize 300 trees and shrubs suited to this climate and describe their flowers, their fall colors, and the problems that plague them. But, most importantly, you will possess a basic understanding of the conditions under which each will thrive. And you will be expected to share what you learn. Over and over and over again."

The urban forest that most of us call home is the domain of no one particular profession or discipline. Its relative health and well-being is shaped by people from many walks of life. Foresters, landscape architects, arborists, and horticulturists are four professionals with the technical know-how needed to improve the health and value of our urban forest. All of the skills needed to meet the challenges of building, developing, and maintaining a healthy urban forest will not be mastered by any one of these groups. Each must contribute its best attributes to form the alloy needed to forge tomorrow's urban forest.

Foresters, for example, tend to be farsighted. They understand the natural systems of the forest and are trained in managing systems to benefit tree communities. Whether the goal is profit, as in woodlot management, or the protection of a valuable and protected area, such as a

CAN YOUR CITY USE A SWAT TEAM?

Donald C. Willeke, urban forestry activist from Minneapolis, Minnesota, has come up with an idea to help urban foresters strengthen their programs. He calls it a SWAT team. That means forming a group of highly skilled professionals who can be called on fast when danger threatens or a specific objective must be achieved.

Who should be on a SWAT team? Start with one or two *lawyers*. A good lawyer, says Willeke (who is one) is trained to be a good generalist. If you pick two who are also interested in urban trees, they'll give you sound pro bono advice that ranges from how to handle the politics of a situation to fund-raising contacts. A *corporate leader* should be on the team to provide insight into working with the business community. A *plant pathologist* and a *horticulturist* can give expert advice on technical matters. A *public relations expert* can advise on meaningful public service messages and media contacts. A *reporter* and an *editor* add by representing the actual working press. A *city engineer* can provide invaluable advice on actual working plans in city construction. *Someone wealthy* and *someone powerful* add to the SWAT team—perhaps a category that overlaps with a corporate leader, but perhaps not. Certainly, the advisers should include at least one reputable *politician*.

Find folks who show some interest in urban forestry, and then cultivate them just as you would a tree seedling, Willeke recommends. Have lunch together. Offer to visit their office or to give them a tour of a special tree site. Ask them to come along on an overview look at the city's forest to give you their advice about the program. Listen to their comments about trees, but also about politics and lines of approach to program development.

A SWAT team can help in budget battles as well as providing valuable insight into gaining citizen and business support or resolving technical issues. If you're not an urban forester, but can see that your forester needs such a SWAT team, well, offer to help him or her build one!

Sara Ebenreck

wilderness, a forester is a manager. Project scales tend to be large and perspectives broad. "We back off from a city to see where the trouble spots are," says Sandfort.

Landscape architects are trained to approach problems of a different scale—ranging from a few hundred square feet to the division of large parcels of land into individual lots. Traditional landscape design that addresses the structural/human/plant interface is their main focus. Through the design process, landscape architects seek to accommodate the needs of their client within the unique context of the site. Once a design is finished, landscape architects are often hired to bid and supervise the construction of their designs. In this role they assume responsibility for the quality of plants and method of installation used. According to Urban, the landscape architect's influence is also strongly felt in the planner's arena. "We make basic decisions on how much land is allocated to open space and how much is left for existing trees or new ones," he says.

Looking at trees on an individual basis is the business of arborists. They are the people who know trees inside and out. An intimacy with tree structure, function, and characteristics is at the very core of an arborist's training. To people who are not so trained, the arborist's ability to assess a tree's vitality seems almost magical. The arborist supplies the facts needed about the condition of individual trees so that action can be taken to keep them healthy. Arborists have recently become central players in the game of hazard management—anticipating hazardous tree situations before they become problems.

The focus of the horticulturist is the cultivation of plants, including shrubs, trees, and ground covers. His or her goal is the production and maintenance of the plants we crave to fill our stomachs and beautify our surroundings. Research and technical training in the function of plants of all sizes and shapes is part of the horticulturist's special skills. To the urban forest, horticulturists bring a knowledge of numerous plants and cultivated trees that will do well as companions.

But even these four kinds of professionals must seek out help from still others to cope with the full complement of problems posed by the urban forest. Plant pathologists, entomologists, agronomists, hydrologists, silviculturists, geologists, and geneticists also supply much needed skills and information.

While there may sometimes be turf battles between these disciplines, lines of communications and cooperation are clearly opening up. Teams of urban foresters from different disciplines are forming in both the public and private sectors. The International Society of Arboriculture and the American Forestry Association have created forums and networks that promote information exchange between urban foresters.

Still more communication is needed, however. Urban foresters need to learn the language of other professionals so they can effectively lobby for the cause of their trees. As Charles C. Weber, arborist for the city of Huntsville, Alabama, puts it, "We must listen to what others—civil engineers, planners, elected officials—are concerned about, learn to talk their language, and then be ready to show them what our skills and training have to offer, when the right time comes to speak."

The alloy formed from the professional melting pot that has the ability to interact with those trained in engineering and developing the city will produce the formula to turn our cities a deeper shade of green.

13

Building a Sense of Place

Steven J. Anlian

"THERE'S NO THERE, there." With these words, the early twentieth-century author Gertrude Stein aptly described an American location which totally lacked any memorable identity. By contrast, urban planners and landscape architects aspire to create a sense of place—different from any others—in the spaces they design.

In the built environment, this sense of place may exist on the scale of a small urban courtyard, a park, a neighborhood, or an entire city. Designers of particular areas are deliberate in selecting the materials that are required to make a physical statement. Architects may define the space with walls that enclose or by installing an arrangement of windows responsive to the exterior environment. Even if a building is inwardly focused, it still contributes to the exterior landscape in the facade that exposes itself to the public eye.

The art of the landscape architect frequently lies in public view, in created places within towns and cities, along transportation systems, and in natural conservatories. While employing synthetic materials and man-made forms, the landscape architect strives to incorporate design elements derived from natural features such as rock, earth, water, and vegetation. The most dominant element, and often the most memorable, is the tree.

As a college student in New York, I recall my daily stroll across the campus quad, which was artistically lined with hackberry trees. Today, my most vivid images of that quad include these specimens and their dynamic, ever-changing features: the umbrella of shade in the summer, autumn's yellow foliage, winter's calligraphy of cherrylike fruit hanging from sloping stalks, attracting birds when everything else seemed lifeless. This mental picture goes beyond the quad, conceptually encompassing an entire campus and implanting in my psyche positive thoughts of this place, of my college experience, and beyond to the phenomenon of higher education in general.

Most of us can readily recall other memorable places where trees play a dominant role: the tidal basin of Washington, D.C., where the Japanese cherry trees embellish the Jefferson Memorial; the elm-lined streets of Milwaukee or Minneapolis; the gracious live oaks surrounding Louisiana's old plantation houses.

Landscape architects employ trees to create such recognizable imagery, to embellish architecture, and to enrich the urban environment. Trees give a scale to architecture through their size and familiarity. They provide shade, enclosure of spaces, screening, framing, and other important assets. As a result, they are vital tools in responding to difficult contemporary design challenges.

DESIGN FOR CORPORATE AMERICA

Consider, for example, the way trees help fashion a response to design demands made by the accelerated growth in major commercial centers and office parks in the United States. The proliferation of new service industries means that entire town centers are growing, encompassing hundreds of acres and millions of square feet of building floor area. Such commercial hubs always involve multiple players, each with corporate mandates about architectural imagery, signs, and logo-type vocabulary. Major department stores are the proverbial "thousand-pound gorillas," who assume a dictatorial role in the evolution of urban central business districts and suburban shopping centers. Development lying outside the commercial core consists of national chains—from service stations to fast-food restaurants, all of which insist on their own identity.

Creative planning can accommodate the individuality required in established corporate architectural forms by using unifying tangential elements. These design elements include paving, walls and fences, groundcovers and shrubs, and, most significantly, trees. A defined palette of canopy, coniferous, and ornamental trees can project cohesiveness and integrity for the master landscape plan.

At the St. Charles Towne Center in Charles County, Maryland, a 500-acre mixed-use commercial and office project, which includes a super-regional shopping center, trees are the common denominator. Dozens of national retailers are represented in varying but compatible architectural solutions. A comprehensive master landscape plan and tree species list

Rows of trees form an arch over a Charlestown, West Virginia, plantation walkway, creating a sense of enclosure.

have been established, and each owner or tenant must comply with contractual design guidelines and architectural convenants. As each parcel develops, the individual user must incorporate the predetermined infrastructural landscape plans, which include the planting of specified trees. The result is a cohesive design, subtly unifying multiple elements while accommodating corporate autonomy.

DESIGN FOR STREETS AND NEIGHBORHOODS

On a different scale, such a sense of place can be created for streets, blocks, and entire neighborhoods by the repetition of selected species of trees. Separation of "places" occurs where a distinctive change occurs in tree size, spread, texture, and overall character.

Kingstowne, Virginia, is a thousand-acre planned community near Washington, D.C. It is evolving at an intensely accelerated pace because of its location close to the expanding nation's capital. A hierarchy of streets has been structured to respond to anticipated traffic capacities. The corresponding streetscape plans enumerate types, sizes, and locations of trees, reflecting specific design objectives. The communitywide collector roads include sufficient publicly controlled land on either side for the creation of landscape zones. These employ mixed hardwoods planted in a manner that imitates the existing indigenous woods, reinforcing the feeling of a forest. Internally, residential pods of fairly intensive housing densities utilize trees to project a more urban feeling through even spacing and repetition of trees of identical size and type. Adjacent land bays, although similar in residential character, employ distinctively different street trees, which lend different feelings and a separate perception of place.

In many other locations, trees that follow lines of transportation networks such as roadways, paths, and canals create a more pleasant environment than utilitarian connections would do. Trees clinging to a parkway create a clear sense of lineal place absent in a treeless highway. Anyone who has driven along America's scenic routes, such as the George Washington Memorial Parkway in Washington, D.C., has experienced this concept. When we consider how much of America is seen through a windshield at forty-two inches above the ground, it seems that more attention should be directed to enhancement of these "linear melting pots."

Trees are playing a major role in the downtown revitalization phenomenon that is sweeping across America's older towns and cities. Main Street USA is getting a facelift, and in doing so, it is attracting merchants, office workers, and shoppers back to central business districts formerly plagued by a deteriorating image and a perception of being somewhat less than user friendly. Fundamental to most of these streetscape projects is the use of extensive tree planting, a dominant design tool to help capture the community's heritage, whether it be a 1950s suburban or eighteenth-century colonial sense of place.

Many other ways exist to utilize trees to achieve design objectives in the built landscape. Containment of a space certainly defines the limitations of that place, its borders, and its area. Tree rows in regimented configurations may create outdoor rooms by their sense of enclosure. The definition of the space with living walls terminates views and prevents "spacial leakage." When off-site spaces are screened, the internal area is minimally influenced by external forces, thereby maintaining a designer's control of that particular place's ambience. French garden design frequently employed tree rows to define spaces, such as the axes of horse chestnut trees enframing the views of the Luxembourg Palace in Paris.

Trees which form a distinctive continuous overhead plane through their branching patterns and canopy define spaces in a subtle architectural way. A single tree with a significant spreading crown can define a particular space simply by the impact of the perimeter of its umbrellalike canopy. Remember the legendary spreading chestnut tree under which the blacksmith stood? Careful crown pruning of multiple trees planted in close proximity to one another so as to form a continuous intertwining of canopies and a solid overhead plane is called *pleaching*. Used in formal garden design, it is a strong technique in spacial definition. Colonial Williamsburg, Virginia, demonstrates how effectively London planetree arbors may define spaces in this manner.

INFLUENCING PUBLIC PERCEPTION

The condition, posture, and form of trees in a design will influence the mood of observers, who may speculate about what stimuli have contributed to those factors. For example, the sinewy, contorted, grotesque form assumed by a lonely Jeffrey pine atop a Yosemite peak is suggestive of a harsh environmental condition. In a more controlled setting, a pruned bonsai, an espaliered pear tree, a topiaried holly, or a sheared pine all project an image of human intervention; each may even bear a distinctive cultural overtone which affects the perception of a place.

Landscape planners are continually faced with the challenge of integrating new places into established communities, in-filling older neighborhoods, and trail-blazing "undeveloped areas," such as converting farmland or forestlands to accommodate population expansion. Here again, trees are flexible devices for facilitating transitions between old and new.

In a changing Virginia countryside where orchards had been the major visible imagery within the declining agricultural economy, a mixed-use community has been planned to include an "orchardscape." By continuing the recognizable scheme of regimented plantings of fruit trees into the new development, we project an established sense of place into the new land use. Such design elements can also help gain public acceptance of the new place.

A similar approach has been taken at Trinova's corporate headquarters in Lucas County, Ohio, where building clusters designed by architect Charles Moore assume a "farm vernacular" style to blend with the agricultural landscape. The expansive parking fields that surround the structures have been systematically penetrated with planters containing rows of trees, resulting in "parking groves" that soften the pavement and reinforce the farm theme.

Conversely, trees in environmental design should respond to the dominant sense of place, if one is evident. A "lakescape," for instance, can be strengthened by use of the kinds of trees which people expect to find along the lake, either by previous interaction with this ecosystem or by established perceptions of the forms and textures one longs to see around a natural water edge. The element of water, with all its calming qualities, can be amplified in its effect by similarly relaxing tree forms. Weeping willow trees, for example, strategically placed around a lake in informal patterns, will echo the lake and solidify the "sense of lake" beyond the water's edge.

THE SENSE OF TREES

Joyce Kilmer's renowned phrase reminding us that "only God can make a tree" subliminally suggests that trees are a blessing and that, therefore, a place with trees is indeed blessed, even though their presence and location may well have been contrived by "fools like me."

The sense of community celebrated by the very presence of trees is perhaps the most inspiring of all effects. Our care for the trees in our communities is a reflection of our care for the environment at large. A well-groomed urban forest reflects the community's insight, self-esteem, and graciousness. "Green cities" are unselfish places, "value-added" zones, and superior places to live and work. Trees make sense—a sense of pride, a sense of community, and a very memorable sense of the unique places we've visited.

14

Critters in the City

David Tylka

A CANADA GOOSE patiently incubates five eggs in a flower box on the tenth-floor balcony of the Community Federal Savings and Loan Building in St. Louis. A red fox begins its nightly mouse hunt along Rock Creek Park in downtown Washington, D.C. And each fall, cedar waxwings devour ripe crabapples and viburnum berries in backyards across America. Happily, for people and animals alike, wildlife has adapted to the urban landscape.

The main ingredients of wildlife habitat—food, water, and cover—are plentiful in many parts of the urban environment. The vegetative diversity found around homes, schools, and businesses furnishes food and cover to a wide array of wild animals. Lawn sprinklers, swimming pools, and fountains supplement urban creeks and ponds and are available to thirsty critters even under drought conditions. Although there is a noticeable absence of large predators such as bobcats, wolves, and mountain lions, wildlife thrives in the green spaces of our urban environment.

For the most part, people enjoy sharing their urban environment with wild animals. In backyards throughout the nation, people go to great lengths to invite songbirds and butterflies to visit. Each year Americans spend over half a billion dollars on birdseed and millions more on nature field guides, camera equipment for nature photography, feeders, and birdbaths. Thousands of urban residents have paid to enroll in the Backyard Wildlife Program of the National Wildlife Federation.

PARKS, CEMETERIES, AND ROOFTOPS

Although backyards may offer the most diverse habitat to city wildlife, other urban landscapes are also important. To the benefit of wildlife, the management of public parks is evolving to meet America's growing interest in natural experiences. Urbanites still go to parks to play softball, but more and more Americans are frequenting neighborhood parks to observe wildlife, hike on trails in the woods and meadows, and take wildflower photographs—all popular recreations involving nature.

As a result, expanses of mowed grass, so expensive to maintain within our park systems, are being broken by areas of natural vegetation. The increase in diversity of plants will, in turn, furnish more habitat for wild animals. Monarch butterflies utilize the milkweeds and black-eyed Susans. Wrens feed on insects. Cottontail rabbits eat the succulent green vegetation. Owls and foxes prey on the rabbits. And people—the ultimate benefactors in this scenario—smell the wildflowers, photograph the natural landscape, watch the animals, and listen to the song of the wren or the trill of the screech owl.

The residents of Boston have extended the idea of wildlife observation in parks to their cemeteries. About one-third of the remaining open space in Boston exists in cemeteries. Several cemeteries across the country, such as Forest Lawn in Buffalo, New York, publish brochures about the plants and animals found on the grounds. Golf courses and corporate and institutional grounds are generally similar to cemeteries in vegetative composition. The diverse ornamental plantings, as well as the natural vegetation on undeveloped portions of these properties, offer habitat for chipmunks and many songbird species.

Other urban spaces that wildlife have taken advantage of are steep slopes and flood-prone areas where development has been limited. Rock Creek Park in Washington, D.C., and the Wheat Ridge Greenbelt in Denver are good examples of vegetated creek corridors that are veritable havens for many wildlife species. These forested corridors provide homes for foxes, frogs, and salamanders, but box turtles and raccoons also use the corridors to reach other suitable urban habitats. The linear configuration of these corridors lends itself to nature hikes, jogging, horseback riding, and bicycling. Local nature organizations conduct regular bird surveys along the trails. The four-mile-long Rock Creek Park contains roads that allow motorists to enjoy the mature second-growth deciduous forest from their cars.

Not all urban wildlife corridors follow creeks, however. Highways, railroads, and utility rights-of-way furnish nesting and feeding sites as well as dispersion routes for wild animals. Municipalities and highway departments are doing wildlife a favor by mowing less frequently and planting wildflowers along road embankments. These wildflowers provide habitat

A raccoon perches on a ledge high above downtown Clayton, Missouri.

for insects such as butterflies and also for many small mammals. Kestrels, or sparrow hawks, commonly patrol highway medians preying on grasshoppers, small snakes, and mice. Kestrels have adapted well to nest boxes attached to the backsides of highway signs.

Because of the high cost of keeping the common grounds of subdivisions manicured, some trustees have taken a more natural approach to managing these parcels. Great-spangled fritillary butterflies have been attracted to grounds that have been allowed to grow up as meadows, while indigo buntings prefer forested grounds. Mallards and Canada geese will utilize stormwater-retention basins constructed to catch rainfall from the street and rooftops in subdivisions. Children use these basins to get a firsthand look at dragonflies or bluegills.

Buildings in subdivisions and citywide furnish some of the most unusual kinds of cover for wildlife. Large school and industrial chimneys are home for hundreds of chimney swifts. Bats seek roosts within building cracks and behind loose siding. Pigeons and peregrine falcons fancy ledges. Graveled, flat rooftops furnish nest sites for killdeer and nighthawks. But perhaps the most unusual nest site for birds is the tenth-floor balcony flower box occupied by a pair of Canada geese. The geese likely chose this site to reduce the chance of nest predation. Their efforts have

apparently paid off—the pair have successfully raised goslings each year
for the past six years.

Canada geese—like squirrels, raccoons, and woodpeckers—can aggra-
vate as well as delight. Geese defecating on a golf green, squirrels eating
birdseed from a feeder or gnawing into an attic, raccoons raiding garbage
cans, and woodpeckers splintering the wood siding on houses easily
irritate urban residents. Public and private agencies and organizations
commonly offer alternatives to remedy such situations, however. And, in
spite of these conflicts, the overwhelming majority of urbanites still consider wildlife around the home an asset.

According to initial findings of the 1985 National Survey of Fishing,
Hunting, and Wildlife-Associated Recreation, conducted by the U.S. Fish
and Wildlife Service, 109.7 million people (over half of all adult Americans)
participate in nonconsumptive wildlife-related activities such as feeding,
observing, or photographing wild animals. Of these, 96 percent enjoy
these activities around their homes. As our population continues to move
to the city, attracting wildlife to the neighborhood is a way to bring some
"country" into the city. Urban wildlife may very well represent a link with
our past—a way of coping with the more crowded conditions of city life.

Residents of the upper penthouse suite have a bird's-eye view of St. Louis, Missouri.

David Tylka

PLANNING FOR WILDLIFE

All animals need food, water, cover, and space. You can help by considering the following:

- Plan proactively for wildlife from the very start. Don't treat wildlife as "add-ons."
- On construction sites, save all possible trees, shrubs, and ground cover. For wildlife, trees need not be perfect specimens.
- Remember that a whole series of reptiles, amphibians, mammals, birds, and invertebrates are associated with trees as they decline and die—including bluebirds, flying squirrels, woodpeckers, and hundreds of others. All dead trees are not hazards, nor are they intrinsically ugly. Like snakes, dead trees have a serious public relations problem. We recommend retaining at least one dead or dying tree per one-quarter acre lot.
- Multilayered vegetation with a diversity of plant species is more stable and attracts more wildlife species than monocultures or tall tree and grass combinations. Lawns are a stubborn holdover from a European heritage. They connote wealth and property—and they are necessary for play and recreation. But they are labor- and energy-intensive and sterile in terms of wildlife—what you are doing with a lawn is freezing a very early, unstable successional type. Give some thought to how much area you really need for lawns and convert the rest to beds of trees, shrubs, or native grasses.

- Mulch tree and shrub beds with leaf litter, tree trimming chips, or melaleuca mulch. Mulches are a rich food source for ground foragers like towhees and thrushes, provide cover for small mammals, reptiles, and amphibians, and also enrich the soil.
- Select plant species tolerant of urban conditions, preferably native species that provide food and shelter for native wildlife.
- Use native plants to dramatically reduce disease and insect pest populations, thereby eliminating the need for pesticides, which are lethal to wildlife.

Susan Cerulean

Clearly, urban wildlife enriches our lives. The look of excitement in children's faces when they have a close encounter with a lizard or when a fat, green caterpillar drops onto a picnic table tells it all. Children who are not exposed to these natural experiences are woefully deprived.

PLANNING SPACE FOR WILDLIFE

So how do urban residents make their cities and towns more attractive to wildlife? The same conservation practices employed in the country will essentially work in the city. The approach is basically to provide wildlife habitat (food, water, and cover), and the animals will find it and use it. The more abundant and diverse the habitats, the greater the numbers and kinds of wildlife that will be attracted to urban areas.

State conservation agencies and the University of Arizona, responsive to a changing public clientele, are beginning to assist municipal planners and administrators by conducting inventories of urban wildlife habitat. These inventories have been conducted in seven urban centers in New York, in St. Louis and Kansas City, Missouri, and in Tucson, Arizona. Three counties near Denver, Colorado, with a rich wildlife fauna have also been surveyed for critical wildlife habitats. Identifying critical habitats and then conserving them by limiting development or certain land uses around them will benefit not only the animals but also the animal watchers.

The Missouri Department of Conservation has been a pioneer in the area of urban wildlife habitat conservation through its land-acquisition activities. In a program called Urban Wild Acres, the agency purchases small wilderness tracts in and around the urban environment and then leases these lands to local governments to manage for the enjoyment of nature.

Some cities have made an effort to conserve patches of wildlife habitat, but if these efforts are to be truly fulfilled, we need to provide avenues such as wooded creeks for animals to reach these patches. Corridors allow many types of animals to move from areas of higher to lower population densities. Young animals, after leaving their nests or den sites, use these corridors to find new territories of their own. Corridors are also utilized if habitat conditions change, such as food supplies running short or water sources drying up. And some mammals, like foxes and raccoons, hunt or forage for food along creek banks.

It is commonly perceived that only animals from dense populations outside the city use the corridors to enter urban areas. However, given the lack of large predators, the high diversity of plant life, and the local abundance of some foods, the opposite may also be true because urban squirrel, rabbit, and raccoon densities are typically much higher than those in the surrounding rural lands. In Tucson, sensitive wildlife corridors have been identified and protected to ensure the passage of roadrunners and javelina in and out of the city limits.

Butterflies, songbirds, and other winged species are wonderfully adapted for city life. They obviously do not require corridors to move about in the urban landscape. Unless the surrounding land is a biological desert of pure concrete and asphalt, these mobile creatures have little difficulty finding necessary food, water, and cover. This mobility is one of the reasons many people manage their own yards to provide habitat for butterflies and birds. The aesthetic appeal of these two groups is also unsurpassed in the wildlife kingdom.

Who can the general public contact for information about urban wildlife, such as how to attract birds and butterflies to the backyard? Cooperators in the Backyard Wildlife Program of the National Wildlife Federation are given technical assistance, and if their yards furnish the basic needs of wildlife, the yard is certified by the federation. Also, several fine publications are available from the National Institute for Urban Wildlife in Columbia, Maryland. (See Appendix D for addresses.) Many books and articles about urban wildlife have recently been published and are available at libraries and bookstores across the country. However, the best person to contact is your local or state conservation department representative. The more progressive wildlife or conservation agencies will have many urban wildlife publications available free to the public.

The mutually beneficial coexistence between people and wildlife in the urban environment can be enhanced. Architects are beginning to design buildings to accommodate the needs of both, and some land developers are harvesting the economic benefits of integrating wildlife needs into housing projects, realizing that people will pay more to live in homes surrounded by wildlife amenities. Urban foresters and landscape architects are tailoring the vegetation in residential areas to attract songbirds and butterflies. Planners are recognizing that municipalities and counties that have incorporated green space into their policies and ordinances will appeal to business and residential developers.

The urban wildlife biologist is a bridge spanner who takes the principles of the wildlife profession and helps to integrate them into all these other disciplines for the benefit of all. Much like the urban forester, however, the urban wildlife biologist operates on the outer fringes of tradition. Wildlife programs at universities and state conservation agencies are reluctant to break with tradition and conduct research involving this urban coexistence. Wildlife research is much simpler if studies are confined to the world of animals. To bring in other disciplines and involve the toughest variable of all—people—offers a new challenge for schools and conservation agencies. Many of the studies concerning the urban interrelationships between wildlife and people have come from a handful of investigators at the State University of New York at Syracuse, the University of Arizona, Yale University, and the National Institute for Urban Wildlife.

As we near the twenty-first century, we are pioneering ways to make the urban environment a better place to live, for both humans and wildlife critters. Urban forestry initiatives can help by considering in their focus the coexistence of *all* our urban residents.

15

Improving the Health of the Urban Forest

Gary Moll

MUCH LIKE HIGH blood pressure in humans, the decline of the city forest is a creeping crisis. We don't recognize the malady for many years, and when we do, it is already a serious health issue that requires immediate and aggressive action. To reduce high blood pressure, a series of actions are prescribed including medication, changes in diet, and stress reduction. Improving the condition of city trees also requires immediate action. First, at least as many trees must be planted as die each year, and more if we are to meet the challenge of cooling cities as a whole. Second, the quality of the trees planted must meet a set of standards that include the selection of quality genetic stock and expert care of the trees in the nursery. Third, the environmental stresses must be reduced. And, finally, a periodic maintenance program must be carried out throughout the life of the tree.

THE LOSS/PLANT RATIO

In an urban forest, trees have a limited ability to regenerate themselves, so we must replant to replace trees that die. The relationship between trees coming into the forest system and trees going out of it offers a simple but valuable measure of forest health: just as your personal checking account is not healthy if you take more money out of it each month than you put in, the same is true of the urban forest. If your community can't answer yes to the question "Are you planting at least as many trees as die each year?" an urban forest is in real trouble.

Planting brings young trees into the forest and balances the urban forest account, but planting alone does not make for a healthy forest. A healthy city forest needs a mix of young, middle-aged, and old trees, and the majority of the trees in that forest should be vigorous. A quick count of trees that remain in good condition at middle-age and beyond will give the most accurate picture of the condition of a community's forest. Large, old trees supply more value to the community in every category—environmental, aesthetic, and real estate. Planting brings young trees into the urban forest, but keeping them healthy into maturity offers the real rewards.

LONG-TERM SURVIVAL

Four possibilities exist for extending tree life: choosing the right trees to plant, improving the genetic quality of the trees planted, improving the quality of the trees purchased from the nursery, and improving the cultural practices the trees receive once they are planted on the street.

Nature supplied our cities with a few jewels, in the form of native trees suited to grow under city conditions. These few species—American elm, green ash, and pin oak, for example—were planted extensively during the first sixty years of this century, and they were good for our cities. Urban forests got off to a good start, but some disastrous events were close at hand.

The American elm was considered the perfect street tree but has now been almost eliminated from the streetscape because of a disease brought into this country. Green ash suffers from borers and a compendium of diseases called dieback. The pin oak suffers from iron chlorosis on many soil types, graft incompatibility in nursery propagation, and a disease related to chestnut blight that can be transmitted on pruning tools.

We have learned a great deal from the dramatic decline of these great urban trees. Decisions about which trees to plant and how many of one species to plant should not be taken lightly. We need to seek out trees that do well in urban areas and to search scientifically for improved varieties of the species we plant. We need to see that these trees are available in the nurseries and are promoted for gracing our city streets. The list of trees we plant needs to be large enough to supply diversity. The rule of thumb is to let no species occupy more than 5 to 10 percent of the community or city.

Scientists and nurserymen have identified and reproduced improved varieties of trees that can be added to the planting arsenal. In the Northeast alone, there are some 280 cultivars in use. Nurserymen were the first to

Environmental stresses—limited growing space, pollution, mechanical abuse—are taking their toll on city trees.

recognize the need to grow better trees. They selected trees mostly because of their outward appearance and neglected other important traits.
Although their breeding work was not scientific, they did hit on some
cultivars that are performing better than average on the streets. Scientists
have entered the tree-improvement scene during the last ten years and
have also provided a number of improved species. Their work has been
slow but accurate, while the efforts of nurserymen have been prolific but
random. They have patented approximately 1,000 cultivars while research
scientists have bred less than 100.

Perhaps the most important trait passed on by nursery work was accidental. The cultivars, as they are called, are usually reproduced by grafting
a bud from the desired tree onto the rootstock of a tree of the same species.
Since grafting involves wounding the tree, the trees that survived the
grafting process had at least that survival trait. Wounding is one of the
most common and severe stresses a tree must endure, and a tree that can
survive wounding by automobiles and lawnmowers has a good chance of
survival in urban America.

Along with picking good species, there are tremendous opportunities to
improve the ability of trees to survive tough urban conditions. It would be
a mistake to write off trees like the American elm entirely. Our ignorance
almost eliminated it from the continent, but now we look to science,
technology, and skilled management to bring it back to the city. Research
scientists are testing many potentially superior elms that may prove resistant to the Dutch elm disease, and a couple of cities—Minneapolis,
Minnesota, and Evanston, Illinois—have kept their American elms
through well-organized and well-financed maintenance programs. Our
urban forest can be as impressive as the elms once were if we supply an
adequate level of financial support and commitment to such research and
management.

GENETIC PROGRESS

During the late 1960s and early 1970s, when tree geneticists took up the
cause of urban tree improvement, research took on a much-needed scientific approach. The more random approach to tree improvement in nurseries had created a nightmare of confusion about which tree possessed
which traits. Consider the case of the sycamore, for example.

The sycamore, or planetree, is liberally planted along city streets
throughout the country. The American sycamore (*Plantanus occidentalis*)
has its problems as a street tree, first because it grows very large and also
because anthracnose disease can cause the tree to lose most of its leaves.
But, not to worry—a planetree of superior genetic stock has existed for
quite some time. Called the London planetree, it is the result of an acciden-

tal cross that occurred in Oxford, England, about 1670 between the American sycamore and the Oriental planetree (*P. orientalis*) to produce the London planetree (*P. x acerifolia*). The tree was noted for its ability to survive the sooty city air and was propagated extensively in England.

Americans recognized the ability of this tree to survive city conditions and introduced it to our urban forest. The London planetree has proven resistant to anthracnose disease as well as air pollution. However, much of the value of this tree has been lost because of lax propagation practices in the United States. Any planetree exhibiting visual traits similar to the London planetree was given that name. Of course, the visual similarity offers no guarantee of resistance to anthracnose or air pollution. But this story may have a happy ending yet. Dr. Frank Santamour at the National Arboretum has made the first intentional cross of the American sycamore and the Oriental plane. We now have a true London planetree, and two improved cultivars—Columbia and Liberty—have already been introduced into the nursery trade.

Overall, breeding work has shifted from selection for aesthetics to selection for survival. The number one survival problem is stress, which can take many forms. City soil, which may be more accurately described as the substance under the sidewalk, lacks the characteristics used in soil classification everywhere else. It may be too wet or too dry to accommodate optimum root growth, and it is almost always too compact. To add insult to injury, people add excess amounts of toxic substances like road salt, dog urine, and automobile oil. Closely following underground stress is physical abuse to trees that causes wounding. Insect and disease problems can be disastrous, causing major destruction to some species while not damaging others. Air pollution, too much sun, or too much shade also become some of the fine details considered in breeding for survival.

In the last few years, scientists have focused considerable energy on the rootstocks of trees because underground stress is so significant. Very little was known about root growth and health just a few years ago. Even though nurserymen spent a lot of time looking for good stock for scion material (the aboveground part of the tree), little concern was given to rootstock. We now realize that roots are responsible for the winter dieback of some of our city trees. Southern rootstock is indeed more susceptible to freezing in winter. Incompatibility between the rootstock and the scion causes many trees to fail. Improving our understanding of roots and their connection with the rest of the tree offers many possibilities for tree improvement.

Red maple is a case in point. It will survive and grow nicely on both wet and dry sites and has a wide range of variability in growth habit when reproduced by seed. Some good-looking red maples have been selected for city planting, but grafting the desirable cultivars onto rootstocks has caused many problems. The wide genetic diversity has created practical problems in matching root and scion material, and a large number of grafts have failed. Scientists at the National Arboretum have now identified the cause of the graft failures and can identify compatible pairs of trees for grafting by mapping the trees' enzyme makeups.

Tree improvement research is under way at the U.S. Department of Agriculture, some arboretums, and at state universities. The amount of activity is still modest, but the potential of these efforts is significant. For example, tissue culture, the process of producing clones of a particular species from cells or small pieces of tissue, has already produced some trees. The technique prevents incompatibility problems between roots and scion because no graft is needed.

Breaking incompatibility between genes would open an entirely new frontier for plant scientists. A new process called symotic hybridization (the fusion of vegetative cells of two dissimilar plants in the laboratory) would allow scientists to mix a wide variety of genetic material for evaluation and testing. The reproductive processes would prevent many of these combinations from occurring while others would take thousands of years to occur. Genetic material from entirely different species—for example, oaks and maples—could be mixed and potentially valuable combinations screened and selected for use. Statistical models produced on computer software could help geneticists evaluate some of the biological phenomena before extensive field or laboratory testing is undertaken.

The Department of Agriculture has just created a program for preserving germ plasm, which will also help the diversity of the urban forest. Many trees do not grow naturally on this continent and are threatened in their native habitat. Without the U.S.D.A. germ plasm bank, many species may be lost forever. Once the program is developed, samples from all the genetic stock being brought into this country can be added to this bank, giving many more scientists opportunities to find the genetic combinations they need.

Improving the genetic condition of a tree requires the utmost patience. A geneticist studies how to improve a tree, makes the appropriate crosses, and then waits for the trees to grow. Sometimes success can be determined by evaluating pieces or parts of a young tree. For other information, however, the geneticist must wait for the trees to reach maturity. So while genetic improvements offer much hope for the future, they are on the whole a very long-range effort. Closer at hand is a hard look at how we choose what stock to plant.

FINDING QUALITY AT THE NURSERY

Quality is the single most important factor affecting the value of a tree at the time of purchase. Simply stated, a community that selects quality trees makes a wise investment. Quality trees have a better chance of surviving the transition between the nursery and the street; they establish themselves quicker and require less care. Science and technology are improving our opportunities to obtain healthier and tougher trees, but the marketplace sells both good and bad trees. It is up to the buyer to make the final call on quality.

A big mistake is often made in a community's bidding process—trees are selected on low bid without consideration of quality. The low bidder offers the best deal only when he supplies a product of the same quality as that of the higher bidder. Yet trees of the same species and size, bought from two different nurseries, are often very different. The bidding prospectus should address this issue. The community buyer needs to know how the nursery plants, cultivates, and maintains its trees. A street tree will be a resident of the nursery for many years and requires a lot of specialized treatment to prepare it for the street. Trimming gives the crown a strong structure and raises the branching to a proper height up the trunk. Branches help the tree put on caliper growth, but if the tree is not trimmed when young, the later pruning cut can cause considerable damage. Roots require pruning so that a fibrous and compact system is produced. If a tree isn't properly root-pruned, most of the roots needed for survival will be lost when it is transplanted. The tree may survive but will grow slowly and require a great deal of care.

The best way to recognize quality in the bidding process is to develop a set of specifications. The American Association of Nurserymen long ago recognized the need for standards and identified the important elements in the production of healthy plant material. Anyone buying more than a few trees should obtain a copy of the publication "American Standard for Nursery Stock," published by the association, at 1250 I Street N.W., Washington, D.C. 20005. It is an essential reference for writing specifications, and it addresses the growing requirements of many landscape plants beside street trees. The publication includes discussions of caliper and height measurements; recommended height of branches and relationship of height to caliper measurements; general, bare-root, and balling-and-burlapping specifications; and suggested root spread for nursery-grown stock. When these requirements are added to your bid prospectus, the selection of lowbidder is more likely to give you the best deal as well as the cheapest trees. It allows all potential suppliers to compete with one another fairly.

These are not the only factors that a community buyer needs to understand, however. Trees that originate in a different climate than the one in which they are ultimately planted may be damaged by planting shock. It is not unusual for local landscape contractors or nurseries to bid on a planting job for a city and then provide trees bought from a wholesale nursery in another part of the country. You need to know where the trees originate in

FROM NURSERY TO PLANTING: A CHECKLIST

The city of Minneapolis receives truckloads of trees every year. Its guidelines may help you avoid planting problems. When the trees arrive, check for physical damage.

- Look closely at the bark. Has the tree been handled carefully during the growing, digging, and shipping processes? Can you see scrapes, bruises, and old wounds that will cause later problems?
- Are there broken or damaged roots on bare-root material, and are they of sufficient size and number?
- On the balled-and-burlap-wrapped plants or those in wire baskets, is the ball in good condition? (Is it really B&B or was it dug bare-root and put in a bag filled with dirt? We have actually uncovered this in the past.) How about the moisture content? Has the tree been allowed to dry out at any time?
- What about the top of the tree? Is there evidence of broken or damaged limbs and/or twigs? If so, can the damage be corrected without causing future trouble?
- Is there indication of insects or diseases? Although all nursery stock must be inspected prior to shipment, it is not uncommon for some insect and disease problems to be missed. Therefore, stock must be carefully looked over at the receiving point. Look for the presence of egg masses, cocoons, cankers, or lesions that may be evidence of unhealthy past, present, or future conditions.

Once the trees have been accepted, particular care should be taken during the off-loading process.

- The tiny hair-roots on bare-root material should never be allowed to dry, even for a few minutes, as they will not survive any amount of drying out.
- A good mulch material should already be at the staging area before the truck arrives. There will then be no delay in covering the roots.
- If larger ball-and-burlap-wrapped material is being used, there should be machinery on hand to gently lower the trees so that the balls are not damaged. I have seen some off-loading methods that remind me of beer haulers rolling kegs off their trucks and letting them fall onto an old tire to break their fall. Tree balls are too fragile to survive that kind of treatment.
- If the trees are to be left at the staging area for any length of time, there must be a water source on site so they may be periodically watered to continue maintaining their critical moist condition.

Once the trees have been properly inspected, received, and stored, they need to be moved to the planting location. Again, *protection* cannot be over-emphasized. Too often we've seen planting crews hauling a load of trees on a flatbed or pickup truck without any protection provided for roots or tops. Be sure this is not the case with your trees; they need all the care you can give them, especially during this crucial transition period.

David F. DeVoto

order to make decisions about the quality of the stock, its chances of surviving in your climate, and the need to inspect it. If the tree is a grafted variety, you need information on the source of the rootstock as well as the scion or top of the tree. (Note: since it takes several years to grow a tree large enough to transplant in a city, many nurseries may have trouble remembering the source of rootstock and often don't have good records. We suggest that you request source information in your bid specifications anyway, so that nurserymen know that it will be required information in future years.)

Ideally, the quality of the trees is inspected at the nursery at the time the bid is awarded. If the nursery is not nearby or expertise is not on staff, a consultant can be hired to perform the inspection. The cost of the inspection should be the responsibility of the supplier. Although the buyer reserves the right to reject trees at the time of delivery, inspection at the nursery can save all parties time and money.

The delivery is the final opportunity for quality control. A clear set of requirements will make the job of accepting or rejecting stock much easier. The requirements may include specific instructions, depending on the timing of the shipment. Trees should be covered while in transport if they are not dormant and protected from extreme heat or cold. How the trees are to be unloaded needs to be specified, and anything that damages the roots, main stem, or larger branches should be disallowed.

PLANTING AND MAINTENANCE

Trees have basic requirements for survival just as people do. The planting site must supply the basic elements of air, water, soil, and sunlight. Air and sunlight are sometimes less than desirable in cities but are usually adequate for growth. If a site is particularly limiting, the species must be carefully selected and/or the site modified before planting.

Urban soils are usually very compact and lack air space and organic matter. To improve their condition, a large portion of the existing soil must be replaced. Incorporating improved soil in a planting pit slightly larger than the root ball is no longer an acceptable planting method. New construction projects should require that the entire area between curb and sidewalk be replaced with topsoil to a depth of at least two feet. Adequate drainage must also be assured.

The major problem with water is supplying enough for survival during times of drought. Some source of water should be identified during the summer months. The root system of newly planted trees is cut back during transplant and cannot maintain the tree during dry conditions. At the other extreme, if the planting site is poorly drained, the tree can get too much water. The site should be inspected during wet periods and drainage created if it becomes a problem.

No single activity can improve the immediate health of urban trees more than maintenance. Once a tree becomes part of a community, it occupies a spot for a long period of time. Keeping trees alive, healthy, and safe requires a considerable amount of maintenance. Trees in cities—including those in homeowners' yards—receive too little. About 40 percent of the urban forest budget should be earmarked for tree maintenance, but a study of tree care programs produced by Dr. James Kielbaso at Michigan State University shows cities spend only about 30 percent on this health care activity. Cities are trading off the maintenance budget for planting and removal. They are in the business of being tree morticians rather than tree health experts.

Maintenance includes pruning, fertilizing, damage repair, and control of pest problems. Trimming is the single most important item, making up about 80 percent of the maintenance budget. Trimming, or pruning, is most effective when it is started early in the life of the tree. Nipping a problem in the bud allows workers to use small tools to make cuts and haul away debris. It allows the tree to expend its energy on growth that improves its shape and health, and prevents the large wounds that are caused by the removal of bigger branches.

Maintenance should be a planned activity. A tree's basic needs can be anticipated as easily as airplane maintenance. Although very few cities have put this philosophy to work, the ones that have are showing impressive results for their efforts. In Milwaukee, planned maintenance keeps the city's trees living twice as long as those in the average city. In Minneapolis, street trees not only live longer but also have overcome a major biological threat—Dutch elm disease.

Trees should be trimmed every two years for about six years after planting and every three to four years after that. If stakes are used to stabilize the tree at the time of planting, they must be removed after one year. The activities of insects and diseases must be monitored and control measures scheduled as needed. The science of integrated pest management is giving managers new skills in controlling pests with a minimal use of chemicals, but reduced chemical use must be balanced by increased inspections and timely preventive actions.

The information that is needed for an effective management program can be obtained through surveys and inventories of the urban forest resource. Over the last few years a number of excellent systems have been designed to meet the needs of communities large and small. Inventories can range from simple (supplying only basic information about the size, condition, and type of trees) to detailed (supplying projections on growth and development of the forest).

Regular pruning helps urban foresters stay out of the business of being tree morticians.

Although cities with professional urban forest managers are still in the minority, the value of this investment has proven effective. The cost of trimming programs can be reduced considerably if managers have the tools to properly evaluate the forest and the skill to utilize local resources. Some cities have reduced their costs by tabulating areas needing trimming during the summer and bidding the work to contract crews for the winter, the slack period. By carefully evaluating new planting sites and selecting the right tree for the right spot, many trimming costs can be eliminated altogether.

We have considerable knowledge about the needs of trees and the skills to improve their health through the science and practice of urban forestry.

Technology will help us do the things we want, but our city governments will have to recognize a basic need to maintain their resource before this technology can be put into practice.

As citizens, professionals, and urban leaders, the health of our urban forest is in our hands.

16

Planting for Long-Term Tree Survival

Gary Moll and James Urban

HUNDREDS OF THOUSANDS of trees are planted in urban and suburban America each year, but only a small percentage of them will be alive at age forty. The closer a tree is planted to the center of the city, the shorter its lifespan. Those planted in sidewalk pits in center city will be lucky to live ten years, even if planted by skilled experts. What are we doing wrong? Why is it so hard to get trees to live in the city? How can plantings that start with enthusiasm, dedication, and hope come to such an untimely end? Observations by many experts identify restricted tree space and outmoded planting methods as the main causes of tree decline.

Planting seedlings on a farm is an everyday occurrence each spring. It's a relatively simple job: a spade or tractor opens a hole in the soil, the roots are positioned properly and covered with dirt, the seedling is watered as needed, and the planting is complete. But seedlings are usually too small to survive the active urban and community environment, so larger trees are recommended. The *traditional* planting specifications—well documented in landscape journals, books, and nursery catalogs and illustrated in Figure 16.1—read something like this: Dig a hole about six inches wider than the root ball and a few inches deeper; place some loose dirt and peat moss at the bottom of the tree; backfill the hole with a mix of peat moss and dirt. Build a berm of dirt around the edge of the planting hole to hold water; stake the tree, and mulch.

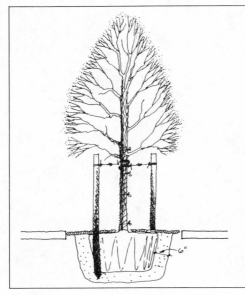

FIGURE 16.1.   *The planting procedure used in most cities today entombs tree roots and contributes to the tree's early death.*

James Urban

Although these planting specifications have evolved only over the last decade or so, today almost none of these recommendations is correct. This time-tested formula was originally designed as a standard for planting on large estate grounds where soil was good and the planting conditions favorable. Use this same method to plant in today's rock-hard urban soils, and you create a nightmare for the tree—it is doomed to a slow death by drowning or suffocation.

Nowhere are these problems more pronounced than in the city center, where trees are planted in standard pits. The pits usually measure four by four feet on the surface and three feet deep. Such a pit (or tomb, if you're up on planting humor) will hold forty-eight square feet of soil, air, and water. The poorer the surrounding soil, the more tomblike the pit becomes. The impervious walls hold moisture in and defy penetration by tree roots. The situation is much like the large houseplant kept in a too-small pot—the roots are forced to encircle and strangle the stem.

Research on root systems has begun to shed light on some of these underground problems. Tree-root systems are naturally shallow and wide-spreading, not deep, and tightly packed around the root ball used to transplant trees. As roots develop, almost none grows below three feet. They normally spread out horizontally two to four times the height of the tree. The roots of a ten-to-fifteen-inch-diameter tree would easily take up a block of soil twenty by twenty by three feet, or 1,200 cubic feet. When a two-inch-diameter tree is transplanted, it carries only fifteen cubic feet of soil with it. If all goes well, the transplant will fill the average four-by-four-foot pit (forty-eight cubic feet) in about five years and then enter a state of decline that will be unstoppable. Add a little road salt, chemical debris, mechanical abuse, and/or air pollution, and you see why the average tree in center city lives no longer than five to twelve years.

If this is a major cause of urban tree decline, what can we do? First, divide urban plantings into three categories: pit, street lawn, and residential. A starting rule of thumb is to assign the largest potential root space possible for each tree. With suburban plantings, the ideal situation is to prepare the site with a rototiller rather than a shovel. This opens up a large rooting area near the surface (most of the roots will be in the top foot of soil) and eliminates the need to dig deep into hard, airless soils where tree roots won't grow.

If the soil has a lot of clay or gravel or is easily compacted, incorporate organic matter with the rototiller before planting. It is important that the soil be consistent from the center of the planting hole to the outermost location you want the roots to reach. If the soil is good, you need not add

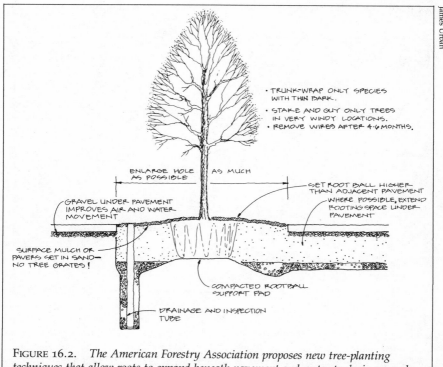

James Urban

FIGURE 16.2.   *The American Forestry Association proposes new tree-planting techniques that allow roots to expand beneath pavement and water to drain properly.*

anything, but rototilling is still recommended. The tree should be set in the hole uniformly, resting on a solid piece of ground so it doesn't sink after the first rain, with the top of the root ball at ground line and the trunk at a right angle to the earth. Only then is the soil backfilled.

In the average street lawn, space will be more limited than in suburban and rural plantings and may affect tree growth and survival. The best option on an existing site is to till up as much of the tree lawn as possible and incorporate good soil or organic matter if needed (and it almost always will be). If the sidewalk has not yet been put in place, create a space for growth underneath so that roots can reach the reservoir of soil in the lawn area without destroying the sidewalk. By digging a four-foot-wide by three-foot-deep trench just opposite the tree and backfilling with loosely compacted soil, tree roots will be encouraged to grow through the passage deep enough so that the walk won't be destroyed. Another option is to supply oxygen to the roots through the installation of a gravel bed before the sidewalk is built.

Perhaps the biggest challenge is planting in a sidewalk pit where space is at a premium. Without question, the techniques in general use today are not good enough and need to be improved dramatically. Figure 16.3 is our

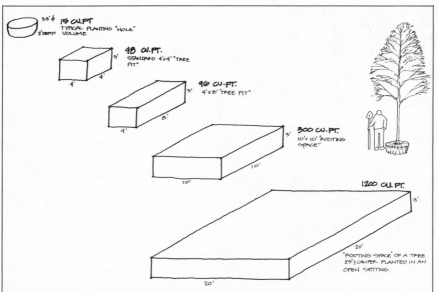

FIGURE 16.3.   *The volumes here represent the rooting space given urban trees under different conditions. To grow a tree 25 inches in diameter, more than 1,000 cubic feet of rooting space is needed. The roots of a tree 4 inches in diameter will fill a 4-foot-by-4-foot pit in less than four years.*

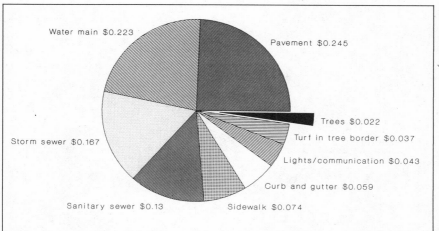

American Forestry Association

FIGURE 16.4. *Milwaukee has successfully integrated tree-planting into its road-building budget.*

best attempt at creating a better tree-planting specification. Some changes must come in the way we engineer streets and sidewalks. We will have to find innovative ways to maintain air space and organic matter in the planting pits, as well as ways to increase the total volume of growing space within. With these cautions in mind, we propose this planting model as an improvement over existing standards and suggest that future streetscape designs be adapted to consider these ideas as soon as possible.

Including trees in a cityscape plan is not expensive when considered as part of the project. Robert Skiera, city forester of Milwaukee, and his staff put together the pie chart in Figure 16.4 to show the costs of an integrated construction package. Milwaukee is one of the few cities that includes the cost of making space for trees in the capital budget for road building. Its lead is one that every city in the country should follow.

Compared with pavement, which takes twenty-five cents of every street construction dollar, and sewer and water facilities, costing fifty-two cents, the two cents spent on trees is nominal. Even the grass growing beneath the street trees can be expected to receive more monetary attention.

Integrating tree planting and maintenance with roadway construction and repair is a simple idea that can have a profound long-range effect. Two cents is not a lot to invest in the regreening of our communities and can go a long way in helping planners, architects, and engineers establish an ecological landscape in America's cities and towns of the twenty-first century.

17

Branches and Wires: The Conflict Above

Gary Moll

IT WAS A clear spring morning in 1978 when William O'Toole planted six white pines along the property line in his back yard. As his spade sliced through the turf, O'Toole's eight-year-old son anxiously waited for the moment he could help place the trees in the ground. Finally, father and son planted the trees, one by one. As O'Toole cut the burlap loose, visually squared up the stems with the powerlines of his house, and backfilled the soil, he imagined what fine trees they would be when his son graduated from high school in ten years.

In fact, by the time the tenth anniversary approached, O'Toole's dream of tall trees had not materialized. Instead, the power company crew was busy topping the trees to keep their lines clear of limbs, and they would be back in three years to trim again. "The pines are growing well, but should never have been planted under the lines," the crew leader said.

O'Toole's dilemma is not uncommon—many thousands of tall growing trees are planted under utility lines each year. They are planted with visions of leafy canopies and shade, but in reality they will become arboreal cripples, victims of saws and hydraulic pruners as an aerial path is cleared for utility wires. It is a tragic conflict that deserves serious consideration by people who plant trees and by those who plan utilities.

You don't have to go very far into the facts and figures to notice the extent of the conflict. Street trees and utility wires coexist along the majority of public roadways. Street trees, valued at $25 billion nationally, account for about half the value of the publicly owned urban forest. This value will increase substantially in coming years as communities adjust the value they put on trees to reflect research on the economic, health, and social benefits connected with trees. But trees also cost utility companies over $800 million each year in maintenance and clearing.

Although you need only look up to see the conflicts, opportunities for improvement also exist. They are as simple as supplying information to the O'Tooles of the world who mistakenly plant the wrong tree in the wrong place, and as complex as rethinking the overall planning and design of public rights-of-way.

A POLE IS A POLE, OR IS IT?

When I was growing up, all wooden poles with wires on them were called telephone poles. I don't know how that term got started, but I didn't think about the different purposes of poles until I went to work for a power company. I soon realized that the average pole is more likely to carry electric than telephone lines and that many poles carry several types of utility wires. Each wire has a different owner and a different set of restrictions for trees.

The public utilities include electric power, street lights, telephone, gas, water, sewerage, and a new utility called cable television. These services, delivered via wires and pipes, are either set on poles or buried underground. Discussion about trees and utilities tends to focus on aboveground utilities—not just because these are visible but because that's where most of the conflicts occur.

With the exception of leaky sewer lines that attract tree roots, there is little interaction between trees and underground utilities once the lines have been established. Utility lines are usually set three feet deep. Most tree roots are in the top foot of soil and almost never go below three feet. The reason more utilities aren't put underground is because it costs more initially to avoid damaging existing trees.

The most volatile aerial conflicts involve electric lines. Electricity is conducted through the wires at high voltages, and the higher the voltage, the greater clearance the lines will need. High voltage can arc out beyond the lines if grounded by something like a tree, resulting in an interruption in service. Dependable service has always been a goal of the utilities, and the demand for quality service is increasing as computers and other high-tech electronics become part of our daily lives.

Electric wires are the highest on a "telephone" pole and always have insulators between pole and wire. The more current flowing through the wire, the more insulators are needed and the more distance is required between trees and lines. Telephone service is usually a large single wire attached halfway up the pole. Cable television is the newest of the wires in the pole spaghetti, and its placement varies. Telephone and television lines carry only a few volts, so tree conflicts occur only through direct contact with branches that rub the protective layers off these wires.

Since electric lines require the most clearance, it helps to know a little more about their construction. There are two basic types—transmission and distribution. Transmission lines are the big lines on large poles and towers with many insulators hanging between pole and wire. They bring large volumes of power to a substation near your community. From there the power is stepped down to distribution lines that run down your street or alley. The utility companies have a different clearing specification for

Attempts to make large trees fit beneath utilities usually cause conflicts with the wires.

Gary Moll

each type of line and amount of voltage. Clearings range from a couple of feet on lower distribution lines to twenty feet on the large transmission lines running across country. This chapter will focus on distribution lines common in communities.

RIGHT TREE, RIGHT SPOT

If you are going to plant a tree under a utility line, stop and think first. What "envelope" of growing space is available to the tree? Imagine the tree when fully grown. Will the mature tree fit into that space? Or can you move the tree to one side of the wire and get away with a little larger variety? You can usually obtain a list of recommended trees, including information on sizes, from your state forester, local Extension Service, or arboretum.

A large tree is almost always a bad choice under powerlines. In the 1930s maples, ashes, oaks, and sycamores were commonly planted along the street. All are large trees. The sycamore is a fast-growing species that can grow to a height of 160 feet, four to six times the height of the average line. Those that still stand are veterans of a war with the overhead utilities that has lasted for decades and left many of those trees wounded beyond repair.

Finding trees that better fit growing spaces has been a challenge accepted by urban foresters, geneticists, and nurserymen. Numerous tree cultivars are now available for planting in restricted locations. Cities like Cleveland have a history of planting these smaller trees with more predictable growth patterns. The cultivated varieties are sold by brand names and are clones of the parent species. Because they are exact duplicates, their shape and size is generally known before the trees are planted.

These clones not only help solve height restrictions but also provide the best shape. The shape of each tree and the width of its crown can be used to engineer the trees into the available spaces. If the planting location can be set off to one side of the overhead lines, a narrow or conical tree might fit nicely into the spot, with minimal side trimming needed to maintain line clearance. Unfortunately, most public tree plantings must be done in the narrow tree lawn next to the road and directly beneath the lines. The success of these efforts depends on the skill of urban foresters and their ability to understand and work with the restrictions of the utilities.

One battleground in the urban forest is around these wires. It is here that branches are cut away from cables at a cost of about $3 million a day nationally. That's a lot of money, but much more is literally being trimmed off tree values as trees are turned into hazards that should be removed from the urban forest. From one point of view, the only way to handle large trees in the wrong places is to trim them somewhat severely. Some should never have been planted; others are simply victims of expanding utility needs and poor trimming practices.

What can we learn from this experience to improve the urban forest of tomorrow? Perhaps one of the biggest challenges occurs in small and middle-sized towns that have mature trees. Many of these communities need large-scale tree replacement. Removal and replacement are often traumatic and always expensive, but communities don't have to make such tough decisions alone. A survey conducted by Charles Weber in Huntsville, Alabama, showed that 40 percent of the utility companies have tried working with communities on removal and replacement programs, and that 14 percent of them do it on a routine basis. Communities should look at these programs carefully; there is no need to remove healthy trees that require average maintenance, but there is something to gain by working with the utility foresters to remove problem and high-maintenance trees.

Trimming methods can improve trees that have not lost their natural shape. Drop-crotch pruning (trimming to remove large branches back to a branch union rather than continually cutting off branches x feet from the line to maintain clearance) removes fewer branches and maintains the natural shape of the tree. The technique can also reduce the size of a tree considerably. Cutting to suit clearance creates dangerous wounds in a tree and promotes prolific sprouting. Sprouts are weakly attached to the tree and grow back into the wires quickly, thereby accentuating the problem.

In high-value areas, large valuable trees can be directionally trimmed to extend their growth on either side of the lines. In some locations, these quality trees have been allowed to grow up past the conductors, and they branch out above the wires. Trimming these takes a little extra skill by both utility engineers and foresters, but it can be done.

In rural locations, selective trimming can reduce maintenance costs. selective pruning removes some of the large and fast-growing trees to favor the smaller, stronger, slower growers. There is a catch, however—the desirable trees must already exist under the lines. Dogwood, holly, and redbud are a few good choices. Large trees with strong branches can be left next to the line. A white oak, for example, makes a better tree near (but not under) a powerline than does a yellow poplar or American linden.

Another technique for trees near powerlines is the use of growth regulators. These products slow the growth of a tree, allowing the utility more time between each trimming. The most commonly used growth regulator at this time is a product with the trade name Clipper. The utilities have been working with such chemicals for about twenty years and have made some significant advances in their use. Successful applications vary according to the species and the method used. Injection treatment has had some success, but there is concern about wounding around the injection holes.

REDESIGN WITH TREES IN MIND

Efforts to improve tree planting and maintenance on public rights-of-way need to continue, but we also need to look at the possibilities of changing the design and structure of this element of the forest that we live in.

One good move is the effort now under way to route utilities underground in new suburbs. Perhaps the ultimate solution is to go underground with all lines. The higher initial cost will be paid back in the larger, more valuable trees we are able to plant and the electricity those trees save us in air-conditioning bills. Where trees already exist, the burial of cables should prevent major damage to existing trees. High-value species in the tree lawn may need to have tunnels put under their roots, and the routing of utility services to new buildings should skirt tree groups.

As new rights-of-ways are designed into cities and communities, space should be made for trees and other plants of the urban forest. Trees need to be part of road budgets and not just an afterthought. Giving trees a home means giving them space to grow both above and below the ground.

18

Developing a Successful Urban Tree Ordinance

Charles C. Weber

AS NONPOLITICAL AS trees might seem, tree ordinances can be very divisive issues. Consider a list of the people whose jobs or property would be affected by a tree ordinance: arborists, realtors, developers, the mayor, homeowners, building contractors, nurserymen, horticulturists, utility engineers, the city attorney, city councilmembers, an urban forester, a public works manager, and many others. Each has distinct ideas about what a tree ordinance should be—and which trees should be included—but to write one acceptable to all is another matter. Usually the people in the vanguard of a tree ordinance movement are strong-willed and uncompromising. In most cities, however, compromise is the only route to an ordinance that truly addresses serious tree problems.

Faced with such diversity, how does one start? Huntsville, Alabama, began with a few Beautification Board members, appointed (after a decade or so of hesitation) to draft a tree ordinance for city council approval. This project was undertaken only two years after public objections watered down and nearly killed a parking lot landscaping ordinance and less than six months after a tree ordinance proposal was crushed in Alabama's capital city. They turned to me, as the urban forester for a seven-county district of the state forestry commission, for ideas, precedents, and technical information.

The best single recommendation I made throughout the whole process was my first: to broaden our support base so that no interest would feel left out of the decisions, whatever else happened. We invited representatives of every commercial, governmental, and educational agency that we could imagine to have a stake in the outcome, plus anyone else—Sierra Club, garden club, Rotary Club, individuals—anyone willing to talk . . . and to listen.

The committee's first question was, "What *is* a tree ordinance?" The process of answering that question set the pattern for all else that followed. Clearly, the thirty-two members of the full committee could not work efficiently, so the chairperson selected an "inner committee"—seven persons with the time, resources, and inclination to correspond, study, write, negotiate, and then report to the remaining twenty-five for reactions and eventual concurrence.

The inner committee gathered copies of other cities' tree ordinances, but the approach of comparing any one of them against the others failed. We reviewed at least thirty-seven ordinances plus several general studies *about* tree ordinances. The process of parceling them out to committee members to read, summarize, and report on for comparison turned out to be tedious and meaningless. To avoid such a dead end, I cut these ordinances apart and sorted the pieces by topic, in order to reflect the diversity of approaches on any given subject. The following areas were established:

Legalities
1. Statements of purpose
2. Tables of contents
3. Statements of the value of urban trees
4. Definitions
5. Changes to other ordinances
6. Severability clauses
7. Effective dates
8. Sanction by higher government bodies (e.g., state legislatures)

Administration
1. City forestry departments
2. City tree boards
3. City arborists
4. Funding
5. Promulgation of rules by the city tree agency
6. Interference with the city tree agency
7. Penalties for tree-related offenses
8. Appeals and administrative review

Standards
1. Permits and inspections
2. Planting and maintenance standards
3. Public and private tree maintenance responsibilities

4. Damage to trees
5. Miscellaneous technical standards

Licensing

Other Subjects

These areas were assigned to sub-subcommittee members, picked for their familiarity with the topics—not necessarily for their sympathies. They compared various approaches, noting any that related to our situation—both those that might work and those that seemed especially inappropriate. These topic headings bore a strong resemblance to the headings of our ordinance as finally adopted:

General Articles
Administration
Tree Maintenance and Protection
Work Standards for Trees on Public and Semi-Public Lands

As they worked, the members of the inner committee viewed each issue from their own perspectives; yet they soon cultivated a feeling for the limits that conflicting interests might accept. Few moments of controversy, or even bargaining, arose; while biases were in the open, an unexpected but welcome spirit of conciliation marked the discussions so that the inner committee was practically unanimous when the draft was reported for the consideration of the full committee. Few technical or philosophical objections were encountered before going to city hall.

There was one incident, however, which almost proved to be fatal for the entire effort. Among other ordinance models reviewed was one apparently composed by members of the Chattahoochee Group, Georgia Chapter, of the Society of American Foresters, in response to a request by the Atlanta Regional Commission. The urban forestry section chief in my own organization's state headquarters had borrowed this model, had written in "Alabama" in place of references to Georgia, and then had circulated it among the urban foresters in our district offices. One of the models that our thirty-two-member committee saw at the initial organizational meeting contained several serious traps:

1. It was long, detailed, and highly regulatory.
2. It set up a tree commission and a paid municipal forester, clothed with police power (and presumably with an office staff) to administer a flock of permits and regulations governing not just public and right-of-way lands, but also practically all privately owned lands as well, including those to be developed and those already developed.
3. It was undoubtedly meant to solve some very real tree problems, but it was not attuned—philosophically, psychologically, politically, fi-

nancially, or any way—to reality in a conservative southern city with strong real estate interests in its government, especially during a time of deepening economic trouble.

4. This was essentially the same model crushed the year before in Montgomery, Alabama, when it was proposed by a group of concerned citizens who failed to consult with diverse parts of the public before they approached their city council.

Little wonder, then, that our real estate and construction interests sensed a conspiracy, even though none existed! We survived—but only because we quickly acted to set the record straight as soon as we saw the trap that we had fallen into.

We see a close parallel between this process and the work to find "Areas of Agreement" that the American Forestry Association adopted in mediating natural resource disputes on a national scale. A few suggestions include:

1. Meeting times and places are important. Convenience and regularity affect the members' attitudes, and "neutral turf" helps moderate people's biases and suspicions, at least at the outset. Our work sessions were held in the Huntsville Utilities' conference room. The timing of meetings affects those who can attend. A lunch meeting at a restaurant may serve well for reports from the inner committee to the full committee, but work sessions go better late in the regular workday or just after work when members are looking forward to supper. Momentum is important, so drafting an ordinance in summer risks absences or postponed meetings because of vacations.

2. The chairperson must coordinate and constantly encourage, remain open to ideas from all sides, maintain member interests, and sense individual involvement.

3. Someone on the committee other than the chairperson—preferably some professional and unbiased individual—must work out details of the final product. It takes time, technical background, and willingness to gather, synthesize, and record the ideas of the members. I was able to visit other members individually between meetings, coordinate with the city's attorneys and engineers, and otherwise serve as the committee's legs.

The fundamental direction of the ordinance will probably determine its success or failure—in the committee, in the city council chambers, and on the streets. Practically any elected official will vote for and support a city improvement ordinance, *if* (1) it is within the city's financial means, and (2) it is in keeping with the current local philosophy of government.

In the largest sense, the "appropriate" tree ordinance is shaped by four basic forces, which interact in strange ways:

1. *Nature.* Climate, soils, native species distribution, insect and disease problems, the existing condition of the city's tree canopy (if you can count this as a part of nature), and related factors will largely determine what *ought* to be done. Nature helps decide whether the soil between street edge and right-of-way edge is a beautification zone or whether it must be carefully managed as a snow-disposal strip with its complement of salt, abandoned cars, wrecks, etc. And nature forces the people of a dust bowl city to govern themselves in ways that might seem overly protective in the coastal plain or the Appalachian Piedmont.

2. *Ethnic Traditions.* Without documentation, I sense distinct differences in the attitudes of various groups and nationalities toward regulations, requirements for permits and inspections, etc. What is it in the psyche of Pennsylvanians or Michiganders that allows regimentation on a scale that we rednecks find both surprising and threatening? If you look, you will see the trends.

3. *Political-Economic Traditions.* Environmental work is basically a political process that takes its cue from economic conditions: when we feel reasonably affluent, we protect our grandchildren's heritage; but when things get tough, we mortgage our future quality of life in favor of immediate prosperity.

4. *Legal Framework.* Adding to the complexity are some legal facts of life that can be turned to good use, such as Connecticut's state law supporting local tree management activities. Some have, unfortunately, missed opportunities, such as Alabama's law excluding pruning, right-of-way clearance, and tree removal from the list of activities requiring a state tree surgery license. Others are simply facts of life that you must adapt to, such as Alabama's legal precedents supporting landowners' claim to trees on rights-of-way adjacent to their property.

These circumstances boil down to decisions about *fundamental approach*—regulations *versus* education or permits *versus* pamphlets. A good regulation must have:

1. A reasonable purpose
2. A sound technical foundation
3. General public support
4. Money, manpower, equipment, and administrative support
5. A policy of uniform enforcement, with balance between vigor and mercy

In short, enforcement is a fairly expensive form of mandatory education, with the potential of doing good—or harm—to the cause at hand. An alternative is a purely educational approach, including:

1. Continuing, aggressive work
2. Good, readily available materials

3. High visibility
4. Dependable benefits to the public
5. A cost low enough to be affordable but high enough to command attention

There are gradations between these extremes, and different approaches may be appropriate for different parts of your tree management program.

However you solve this question of fundamental approach and carefully tailor your ordinance to the community's psyche, some individual will judge it by the first few words—the title. About halfway through our drafting process, and just about the time when we saw that we must win back the homebuilders' understanding, we recognized a glaring misnomer in our ordinance: though we had worked long hours to deregiment the ordinance—emphasizing planning, standards, and education instead of permits and inspections—we awoke to the fact that the ordinance was still titled "Tree *Protection* Ordinance." We quickly changed this to "Tree *Management* Ordinance"—a positive term that includes protection but provides a more appropriate glimpse of the contents. It is impossible to know exactly what value this had. I'm certain it was prudent, but it may have been crucial. It has also helped our Tree Commission to maintain the proper perspective toward their job.

Local limitations may suddenly change—when Dutch elm disease or gypsy moths arrive or, gradually, as the economic outlook darkens or brightens. Be sure that your tree ordinance is flexible so that in good times your tree program can grow without overstepping its authority, yet survive the hard times. Leave room for innovations.

In summary, any group setting out to write a tree ordinance for its community needs to keep in mind several fundamental principles:

1. Gain and keep a broad support base.
2. A workable compromise is better than any impasse in which each side feels justified in having nothing to do with the other.
3. An ordinance does nothing in itself; the *process* of writing an ordinance starts motion, for better or worse, and success lies in channeling that momentum properly.
4. While substance is important, don't underestimate the role of terminology—including buzzwords—that create first impressions among potential supporters or opponents.
5. Finally, the right ordinance for any community is the one that makes its people *want* to have and care for trees.

Note: See Appendix E for more on tree ordinances.

19

The Urban Forest Balance Sheet

David R. Smith

THE TERM *urban forestry* is often considered a contradictory term—rather like jumbo shrimp, freezer burn, and military intelligence. But urban forestry is not a contradiction of terms; it's an integral part of a city's infrastructure, just like the street systems, water systems, and lighting systems. If trees are a part of the infrastructure, then they must be managed like any other part in order to maximize their benefits and minimize their costs.

When compared with most parts of the city, the beautiful aspect of trees is that they appreciate in value. Most other city systems depreciate as soon as construction is complete. The city administrator is given the depressing task of slowing the rate of depreciation by designing the particular system well and then properly maintaining it. Trees, however, appreciate in value with some care, so there is a greater incentive to manage them to maximize their benefits and minimize their liabilities.

Dayton, Ohio, is among many cities that have been establishing computerized database management systems. Dayton hired ACRT, Inc., of Kent, Ohio, to conduct a street tree inventory, set up a computerized management system, and produce tree management plans for each neighborhood. The inventory, which began in 1986, is expected to take three years and will cover the entire city—an estimated 65,000 trees and 30,000 planting sites.

The cost of the inventory is $1.30 per tree or planting site. The software cost $4,700 and included a week of installation and training. The data collected included tree location, species, diameter, height, spread, maintenance requirements, condition class, location class, presence of overhead wires, and position in relation to the sidewalk. The software is driven by dBase III with a variety of custom utility programs written by ACRT. The program generates work orders that are tied to each tree. Maintenance on any tree will be automatically updated, with the time, equipment, and cost recorded. The program runs on most IBM-compatible computers.

The ACRT software is an accounting system for locating and tracking any money, labor, or equipment spent on street trees. The system operates like an accounting system where you monitor the flow of resources in and out of an operation that produces goods or services. It allows us to create an urban forest balance sheet.

Every balance sheet describes the health of a business by listing assets, liabilities, and net worth. Fixed or tangible assets of the urban forest include:

1. The cast operating budget
2. The trees themselves and their dollar value, which is automatically calculated in the ACRT software using International Society of Arboriculture formulas
3. The equipment used to plant, maintain, and remove trees
4. Sales from forest products such as firewood, mulch, etc.

Intangible assets are benefits measured from the presence of the trees rather than the trees themselves. These include:

1. Dollar savings in reduced runoff due to a reduction in the size and number of storm sewers
2. Savings in summer air-conditioning loads from lower ground level air temperatures
3. Savings in health care costs due to cleaner air
4. Increases in property values and neighborhood character.

Liabilities include current and long-term ones. These are the costs associated with:

1. Tree removal
2. Leaf removal
3. Storm damage, disease, and spraying
4. Safety prunes and trims
5. Planting sites

Long-term liabilities include maintenance and planting. These were projected over five years by ACRT as part of the neighborhood tree man-

Individual trees add up to a large total city asset.

agement plans. This projected the scope of future costs and raised discussion on ways to pay for these future expenses, such as a street tree assessment.

The ultimate purpose of any balance sheet is to determine the net worth or value of the business or, in this case, the entire street tree system. This is found by subtracting the liabilities from the assets. The goal of any business, including the business of municipal government, is to increase the value of its stock, or in this case the green system. To find the value of the trees to the "stc kholder," divide the net worth by the number of taxpayers.

Of course, the balance sheet concept should be put into the context of municipal decision making. City administrators do not make allocation decisions solely on the merits of low cost and high benefit or the return to taxpayers. There is much politics mixed in, both favorable and unfavorable, that influences allocation decisions. But the framework proposed here offers urban foresters a stronger case for both justifying an inventory system and for evaluating the management of trees once the accounting system is established.

The value of Dayton's street trees is approximately $55 million. A private company with $55 million in assets would spend at least $130,000 to establish an accounting system to manage them and to evaluate management decisions. City administrators must take the same view toward publicly owned trees. This balance sheet can be used to show how systematic management of trees can yield dollar dividends to taxpayers and political dividends to the elected officials and administrators.

Note: See Appendix C for more information on computer programs useful in urban forestry management.

PART FIVE

RURAL PLACES AND THE CITY'S OUTER EDGE

Outlying communities, whether they are small rural ones that have been in place for a century or new "megacounties" feeling the explosive force of city growth spilling out onto new lands, have different problems from urban areas. They also have different opportunities. This section looks at ways to resolve conflict between trees and development through ordinances and the use of innovative methods in construction. It also considers ways that smaller rural communities can successfully build and fund a strong tree program.

20

When the "City" Is a County

Edward A. Macie and Gary Moll

IN ANNE ARUNDEL County, Maryland, home of the state's capital and the national Naval Academy, 175,000 acres of trees that had covered the rolling landscape in 1950 had dwindled to about 110,000 acres by 1985. In the same period, Fairfax County, Virginia, lying on the outskirts of Washington, D.C., lost about 80,000 acres of trees. The likely culprit? Ex-urban sprawl—the building boom in near-metropolitan areas that has created what *Time* magazine calls "megacounties." Fulton County, just outside Atlanta, Georgia, is another one of those accelerated-growth areas. In the Atlanta area, land in transition to new, more urban uses was estimated at fifty acres per day in 1988.

In these places, and hundreds like them across the country, the central decision-making authority in control of the spreading development is not a city government, but a county commission or a board of supervisors. The most pressing issue is not planting or maintenance of street and park trees, but the protection of a preexisting forest cover from the ravages of bulldozers as new development replaces a rural economy and rural land uses.

Sometimes the loss of forest cover is gradual, a one-acre lot at a time. Sometimes—when large tracts near a highway are logged and bulldozed—the change is dramatic. Hills are flattened, soils displaced, water courses altered, and whole new communities constructed. A few decisions in the planning office, and the ecology of the surrounding countryside is in upheaval. The assets of hundreds, even thousands, of trees can be canceled as an "obstacle to building."

In each of the three counties named above, awareness of the effects of rapid development resulted in some policy changes. In Maryland, forest expertise is weaving its way into development decisions. The state forestry agency is assisting a number of county planning agencies with technical reviews of development plans. The opportunity to save trees is being considered along with the needs of roads, utilities, and other engineering concerns. Maryland lawmakers took an aggressive step by establishing a protective forest buffer around the Chesapeake Bay. Development in that strip is restricted, and forestry focuses on managing trees for clean water, not for sawlogs.

In Fairfax County, Virginia, a development ordinance that affects all new property slated for development has been in effect for about ten years. Sediment and erosion requirements are the strongest element of the law, and tree protection is part of this solution. A county arborist office has been established and staffed. The county arborist must sign off on each plan, showing that forestry requirements have been met.

In 1985, Fulton County, Georgia, developed a strong ordinance, taking a lesson in part from Fairfax. The Fulton County tree preservation ordinance and its strong enforcement are now considered models by many urban foresters. The ordinance applies to all properties subject to development within unincorporated portions of the county, although single-family home construction was excepted. The county followed the ordinance by hiring a full-time arborist to enforce it and work with developers. Every application for a land development permit in the county must be accompanied by a tree protection plan, which is reviewed with a site inspection by the arborist.

In 1988, the Fulton ordinance resulted in active protection of over 700 acres of trees and the planting of over 39,000 trees. That represented an 11 percent reforestation of land developed in the county since 1985. On the average, developers have exceeded the requirements of tree protection and planting by 50 percent.

The Chick-fil-A headquarters, which won a Fulton County award for both design and land development, is one example of how the city can grow without complete destruction of the natural environment. Chick-fil-A's executive, Truett Cathy, requested that his architects and construction team work to save every possible tree. Tree protection guidelines were established by the architectural team. In compliance, during construction, red "save tree" banners went up across the acreage. As a result, mature trees continue to shade the building, and employees walk through a stand of mixed hardwoods on their way to and from the parking lot.

In a second model development within the county, Life of Georgia's corporate headquarters, the tree protection program included a $500 contractor's fine for every tree lost from a "tree save" area. Life of Georgia proudly announces that it never had to levy even the first fine.

These two successes, and many others, didn't result simply from passing an ordinance, however. They were the result of a wise and flexible regulation combined with a strong education program and an interested and positive outreach to the business and development community.

KEYS TO SUCCESS

Land development is a complicated process, and so are the biological processes of trees. The needs of trees can restrict the options of the developer, and, obviously, the developer's intentions can kill the tree. So a key element of the Fulton County program is flexibility. The original ordinance called for "administrative guidelines," which allow adjustments to the program without going through a new legislative process.

In addition, the Fulton County program incorporates tree protection directly into the land development permit process. This involves two major steps: the petition for rezoning and the application for land disturbance permits.

Zoning ordinarily breaks land down into classifications of residential, commercial, and industrial areas. Each class of zoning carries with it a set of restrictions and guidelines. Much negotiation goes on when zoning is changed, and during that discussion, there is an opportunity to protect trees. In Fulton County, the ordinance and its guidelines outline conditions for rezoning that prohibit premature tree removal (removal prior to permitting), require a site visit by the enforcing agent to discuss tree protection, and provide additional space for trees such as buffers, landscape strips, and parking lot islands. Compliance with these conditions can also be preconditions for a development permit.

The permit process usually involves two stages—a concept stage and a final stage. In Fulton County, tree protection plans are required as part of the concept plan being submitted by developers. They are carefully reviewed along with the other construction drawings since grading, drainage, road improvements, utilities, and erosion can all affect the survival of trees. A land disturbance permit is not issued in Fulton County until a tree protection drawing has been approved along with the other development-related drawings.

On some projects, protection of existing trees is just not possible. Although it may be a hard decision, it is often more practical to remove a tree whose survival is doubtful and replace it with a new tree. A newly planted tree will remain functional for a longer period of time than will a tree declining from construction damages. A tree point system (based on the tree basal area), developed as part of the administrative guidelines, has been an effective tool in Fulton County. Developers are required to demonstrate a prescribed density of trees per acre upon project completion. This density can be satisfied with either existing trees, replacement trees, or both.

As one example of the importance and potential of flexibility in protection, consider the process of trying to save a forty-inch-diameter white oak on a one-acre parcel with a 10 percent slope, targeted for development as a convenience store. The extensive grading required to stabilize the site for building would destroy substantial portions of the tree's roots. No matter how articulate you may be in describing the environmental values of the tree, other interests will perceive a greater value in the development project and the parking spaces associated with it.

With the tree replacement formula used in the Fulton County ordinance, the developer who took down that tree would have to replace it with about thirty two-inch caliper trees, comparable in species quality to the preexisting one. Even if the site had been barren of trees, in Fulton County the developer would still have to plant the thirty trees. The conditions for zoning and permits outlined above would suggest space for tree plantings in the form of strips, buffers, and parking islands.

All developers are required to provide the same density, regardless of the predevelopment condition of the site. Keep in mind, for example, that an open pasture that is converted to another land use may need trees that didn't exist earlier. During the first year of the ordinance's implementation, Fulton County developers exceeded these tree density requirements by almost a third.

Perhaps the most important key to a successful program in Fulton County has been its education component. As soon as the tree protection ordinance was passed, an informational seminar was held for developers and engineers. Two hundred and fifty attended. In fact, tree protection can improve the marketability of projects and, in some cases, even save the developer money otherwise tied up in clearing and grading costs. Many developers are aware of the possible benefits of protection but don't understand why the trees they do leave standing end up dying. Education by site demonstration is by far the most effective means of circulating good information, but this requires an almost continuous field presence. Land development newsletters, seminars, and the use of local media are also valuable tools.

A SHARED RESPONSIBILITY

Tree protection in land development should be a shared community responsibility. Developers need to approach their projects with some environmental sensitivity. Citizens need to understand the needs of developers. And local governments must be flexible, yet recognize and support the need for tree protection and replacement. If all three sectors cooperate, our cities can grow while remaining beautiful and environmentally healthy.

The projects in Maryland, Georgia, and Virginia show that the benefits of forestland can be mixed into new development and improve the quality of the communities that result. However, we would be a little naive to think that the ordinances discussed solved all the conflicts between urban development and the local ecology. They are a good start in reducing conflicts considerably; but the ordinances and the individuals who lead the protection programs are fragile, while development companies and the hunger for urban expansion are very powerful.

The written law must generalize solutions for some very complex situations and be put into practice by individuals that are easily outgunned by the opposition. The laws require changes in standard development practices. These changes will continue to activate the confrontational juices in some seasoned developers, start many battles, and result in a lot of uncertainty in government agencies. Some of the challengers will find holes in the arguments that rationalize the ordinances and then use their community influence to weaken the law or create special exceptions when it is convenient. To meet these and other challenges, we will undoubtedly have to change, revise, and rethink many of the methods and models we are using today.

It is possible—and even desirable—to gain some tree protection through voluntary cooperative programs that complement the intentions of full-fledged ordinances. Some developers will always understand the economic as well as environmental values of protecting trees and go the extra mile to improve the quality of the communities they are building. But the need to protect the forest resource of an area as a living whole is presently much bigger than the cooperative spirit of the development community. In this climate, an ordinance appears to be the best method to assure countywide protection.

21

Construction That Fits the Forest

Gary Moll

LIKE A CHAMELEON turning from green to brown, millions of acres of forest land are subdivided for houses and business each year. The urban sprawl that was talked about often in the 1970s has quietly continued through the 1980s. Changing land uses have taxed the forest land that surrounds this urban expansion and presented a challenge to the conservation community—to secure the ecological integrity of the land by maintaining a healthy tree cover in new developments.

Until recently, the science of forestry had little to do with the development of land for urban uses, except to supply the boards and beams needed for construction. However, new information about the value of trees is helping to change our attitudes. A healthy tree in an urban area is easily worth twenty-five times its rural counterpart, and a few trees left on a lot that's being developed add thousands of dollars to the site's value. The ecological and sociological benefits supplied by trees may be more important to the community in the long run, but economic values remain a primary incentive to the developer.

Protecting the integrity of the land is usually not a question of stopping development but rather of changing the methods used to develop the land. In the last decade we have seen many examples of quality development that treads lightly on the land, carefully working its way into the natural landscape and almost becoming part of the forest.

Adverse impacts of development on the land are greatly reduced when developers and builders use natural features of the land as assets rather than obstacles to their construction plans. However, such planning can be complex. Existing conditions must be evaluated and incorporated into site design. Contractors need to adjust their equipment and construction techniques to the site, instead of adjusting the site to fit the equipment. Ripping through forests with bulldozers has a tremendous impact on the interconnected web of forest life. Large, seemingly indestructible trees are easily killed by bulldozers that may not come within five feet of their trunks.

Bioengineering can be part of a better solution. The term refers to the use of engineering principles to change, develop, or modify nature. Many of us think of genetic research when we hear the term, but that is only one example of bioengineering. Moving from the microscope to the macroscale of land development, the opportunities to improve the quality of our communities through bioengineering are significant.

A few foresters are using special engineering techniques to fit buildings, homes, streets, and sidewalks into the flora of the natural landscape. Their efforts have opened some eyes to a whole new frontier of forestry—one that challenges our understanding of ecology and our skills in creating procedures that can be implemented by the developer.

In writing this chapter, I talked with three foresters about their bioengineering techniques. Charles Stewart started working on development projects in the Chicago area over ten years ago, and Steve Clark began about the same time in Houston, Texas. Each has developed a business that immerses him in a project from start to finish, much like a landscape architect or civil engineer. The third forester, Bob Smiley, started working in traditional forestry and for almost a decade has been applying forestry techniques to development projects.

SAVING TREES WITH HYDRO AXES AND PVC PIPES

It didn't take Steve Clark long to realize that saving large trees on a Texas construction site was going to take a special effort. Difficult soil conditions, limited tree canopy, and rapid development presented major challenges. To save trees, Clark worked out a regimen to guide each step of the development process.

The type of equipment he selects to prepare a construction site is often different from that used by most developers. A hydro axe, a machine with a 600-pound blade that spins at 1,000 revolutions per minute, is often used to replace a bulldozer in clearing trees and brush. The hydro axe creates little soil disturbance while leaving mulch where trees once stood. A vibratory knife is used to surgically slice roots that cannot be incorporated into the new design.

Forester Bob Smiley grins at the job ahead of him. He innovatively uses wheel stops to stabilize slopes along a streamside trail, while permitting vegetation to take hold.

To keep trees alive near pavement, Clark often raises the height of the roads and walkways above grade. If transportation corridors come too close to tree roots, an aeration system is constructed in the root zone. Roots must have air to survive, so air is piped to the old soil line under compacted roadbeds. Clark has designed an air infiltration system using PVC pipe, a special mix of gravel with few fine particles, and a geotextile cloth as a cap. The cloth allows the soil above the aeration device to be compacted enough to meet the construction code but without damaging the air space created around the PVC pipe.

Clark uses existing trees for transplant whenever possible. If a healthy tree must be removed to accommodate construction, it will be moved to another area of the site. Transplanting very large trees requires innovative procedures. Trees may be dug in stages, giving roots time to regrow between diggings, and final movement may require very large equipment—such as cranes—usually not found in a nursery. Moving these large trees around on the site means that the developer saves costs for landscaping. The savings on the tree-moving alone often pays most of the initial consulting costs for the other planning work.

Steve Clark and Charles Stewart have learned to become part of the development team, joining engineers and architects. The work should start with planning and finish with a maintenance program specially designed for the site. Most of Stewart's projects, such as McDonald's Hamburger University and Arthur Andersen's Corporate Training Center in the Chicago area, include a plan for future maintenance. Existing trees are located by a survey team and entered into a computerized record-keeping system. The records show the exact location of the tree and describe its health when development starts. Damage that occurs during the construction process is also noted.

At the Arthur Andersen site, locating the building in an area that would save the largest number of trees was made difficult by a stream passing through the site. The development team decided to reroute part of the stream to allow room for the building and to save some valuable trees. Special operating procedures were designed for access to the site by construction equipment.

The backhoe used to dig the new stream channel was backed out to empty each shovelful of dirt, since swiveling the bucket would have damaged trees along the new channel. The trees were root-pruned to prevent damage from construction in the new channel. Temporary walkways were built for workers, preventing soil compaction around the tree roots. Finally, a large crane with a 200-foot boom was retained to lift the building construction materials over the trees as was done on earlier segments of the project.

As the project came to completion, information on critical trees was added to the original survey information and placed in the computer, and a maintenance plan started. Any insect or disease problems noticed before construction can become especially damaging to trees stressed by the construction activities. So the maintenance plan indicates exactly when to treat those trees for problems and lets the owner know what to budget for maintenance long before the work is needed.

SAVING STREAMS

Though stream corridors are one of the highest priorities in efforts to save natural areas, they can be one of the most difficult areas to stabilize. The force of water moving along a stream bank can be very powerful and is most damaging when the flow is highest. Peak flows are exaggerated in urban areas where vegetation has been removed from part of the watershed and concrete surfaces added.

Bob Smiley, a forester in northern Virginia, has demonstrated impressive results by using a bioengineering technique on a very difficult section of a stream. In addition to the stream, the site houses a large office complex developed by Hazel-Peterson and Metropolitan Life. A greenbelt was saved around the perimeter of the complex and a hiker-biker trail installed. The problem involved having the trail cross a flood plain and meandering stream.

The engineering firm's initial proposal was to straighten and widen the stream, slope the banks, and add riprap. Smiley's alternative was to retain the meandering character of the stream but stabilize the bends with special streamside structures that would be built by hand. Precast wheel stops, held together with reinforcing bars, were used to form a wall. The wheel stops were separated into a fan shape at the ends, and each one was secured to the bank to supply extra strength. The wheel stops create a honeycomb structure with holes for vegetation. As the cavity behind the wall was filled, carefully selected plant material (mountain laurel) was placed in the soil with the tops growing horizontally through the spaces between wheel stops. The structures allow the trail to brush against the stream in three different places without actually crossing it.

The concrete wall holds the stream bank while the plants become established. Later, the mountain laurel will spread throughout the remainder of the structure and provide a thick vegetative cover to protect the bank. The concrete structure will hardly be noticeable under the foliage after a few years. The structure also allowed the saving of a yellow poplar, which protects a corner of a parking lot that was slowly washing into the stream.

A WORD ABOUT PLANNING

Incorporating the resources of the land into new development is not a simple process, but it is a rewarding one. Techniques that support natural

ON-SITE PROTECTION FOR LARGE CONSTRUCTION PROJECTS

The first step in preparing any specific plan of action for protection and enhancement of a forested landscape under development is site analysis. An analysis should consist of (1) an assessment of the project area that concentrates on the qualitative aspects of the project and (2) an inventory that quantifies the vegetation on the site and its relative condition.

The assessment should describe zones or areas of the project by forest types, soils, slopes, ground and surface water, and general overall condition of material by area. It should also address the main problems that need to be corrected, the site's susceptibility to construction-related damage, and a general outline of work required to protect and enhance the site.

The inventory should include the following items for all trees reviewed: identification number, location, species, size, condition, and specific remedial work required.

The assessment and inventory should form the basis for both project design (the enhancement of the site), protection during construction, and the start of a record-keeping system to guide future maintenance.

American Forestry Association

Proper protection techniques can help save old trees for new buildings.

PRECONSTRUCTION

Prior to construction, the assessment and inventory are used to help guide the locations of new improvements. Important groupings of vegetation are avoided, and vegetation with current and future problems are given less of a priority where a tradeoff must be made. The inventory allows different alternative building and parking sitings to be examined in detail and evaluated. Roadway and utility alternatives can also be weighed to assess their relative impact on vegetation.

When a design is set, a plan can be formulated to protect vegetation not in the construction areas and to transplant vegetation out of buildings and parking areas into nondisturbed areas. At this time, provision for special treatment of trees in the project should be made (i.e., root pruning, boring under trees with utilities, retaining walls used to preserve root zones, etc.).

Concurrent with a tree protection plan should be an erosion control plan. These plans are usually done to protect off-site surface waterways from siltation. Equally important, but often overlooked by the engineers who do them, is the protection of on-site resources from siltation. Silt fence and diversion ditches should be used to prevent siltation in root zones.

Maintenance of existing vegetation is important to implement early in the process. During construction, the vegetation will be under stress from changes in water table, dust, vibration, mechanical damage, compaction, and so on. All these weaken trees and make them more vulnerable to insect and disease problems. Using the inventory as a guide, a program of pruning (root and crown), spraying, fertilizing, pH modification, and watering or dewatering can be instituted prior to construction. This early maintenance is often required to make up for years of neglect or change in land use. Such maintenance can also save much work in the future.

Prior to construction, the locations of temporary facilities (i.e., signage, staging areas, dump site and wash down areas, temporary utilities, parking areas, etc.) also should be planned and manipulated to minimize the impact on vegetation.

systems need to be promoted by planning agencies and embraced by the development community. Foresters need to stop hiding in the woods, and developers need to acknowledge the existing values of the landscape.

To make the best use of natural features, planning needs to start on the largest possible scale and carry through to the design and protection of individual sites. From the broader perspective, the planning process should be used to protect the integrity of the landscape. Before development is considered, basic landscape elements should be determined and then protected as a project proceeds. These elements should include an interlocking network of greenways—parks, buffer strips, stream corridors, slopes, and flood plains. Such natural landmarks are the fiber that holds

IN CONSTRUCTION

The key to protecting woodlands is in education of the contractors about what is permitted and what is not permitted on the site. They must be convinced that they can make a difference, that even minor injuries will affect the trees and ultimately hurt both the trees and the contractor (via fines for damage). Education must be followed with enforcement.

Even with the education of contractors, some damage is bound to occur. When it does, there must be some provision for emergency work (e.g., pruning, watering, spraying, etc.), on an as-needed basis. Concurrent with emergency work is the maintenance of protection devices (silt fence, tree protection fencing, etc.) both to keep them functioning and to keep a visible presence on the site.

Construction phasing is also important to consider. Many operations are seasonal (e.g., transplanting). Damage (e.g., compaction on frozen or dry ground) can be minimized if it occurs in some seasons. New planting should be coordinated with the preservation of the existing woodland. The new plantings should not infringe on the root zones of existing trees but should be used to supplement the existing woodland both visually and functionally via protection from excessive wind and sun damage.

POSTCONSTRUCTION

The key to maintaining and enhancing a forest environment is a maintenance plan that is integrated with the work done prior and during construction. The initial inventory should provide a list of trees with a history of insect or disease problems that should be monitored. Record keeping prior and during construction would indicate trees that were stressed during construction that should be monitored after construction for signs of stress. Lastly, the new planting that was installed to enhance the existing vegetation should also be inventoried, and the maintenance required of new planting should be integrated into a comprehensive maintenance plan for the entire site.

Thomas R. Ryan and Charles Stewart

the land together and allows us to maximize the benefits of the natural landscape.

The planning process can also set guidelines that encourage development to walk softly into existing forests. We know that a few foresters are working with a few developers to successfully engineer houses into the landscape, but the numbers of both are too small. The techniques described in this chapter, though illustrated by examples involving business sites, are just as applicable and even more practical in housing subdivisions. The planning process needs to reward builders who work with trees and penalize those who do not.

Large equipment crushes soil structure, changes water movement, and introduces chemicals that damage the vitality of the land. Trees act like ecological barometers indicating changes in the health of the land. When trees lose their vigor, so does the land. Development will always change the land, but by learning to work with the land, we can get closer to nature's grand plan.

22

Timber Cutting and the Law

Robert A. Herberger, Jr.

IT WAS A cold October morning when I answered the phone. Bill, my neighbor, was exuding enough energy to push the forsythia into chaotic bloom. "They shut me down, damn, they shut me down!"

"They" was the county, whose inspector hadn't been impressed by Bill's tale of how his family had been farming and logging their 150 acres without a permit for two centuries. Resting on precedent, Bill and his logger had not called the town clerk for the necessary cutting permits before starting his current harvest.

My neighbor's story is not unique. The town I mention is ninety miles north of New York City. Its character, like the seasons, is changing. Once rural, its primary industries were agriculture and forestry. As industry moved in and transportation improved, the woodland was transformed into forested communities. Raised ranch houses replaced holsteins, and the drone of lawnmowers replaced the whine of the chain saw. The new citizens, very protective of their new lifestyle away from the city, questioned any practice they perceived as damaging to the environment. Many became politically active and joined planning and zoning boards or formed conservation advisory councils and environmental committees.

Meanwhile, firewood and an explosive oak market brought increased harvesting and loggers from outside the area in addition to a continuation or resurgence of logging activity from longtime landowners like Bill. The newcomers did not understand the cutting and felt that cutting the virgin forests was deplorable. They failed to realize that most woods are not virgin forests—that the average U.S. woodlot has been cut at least twice

WHAT TO KNOW ABOUT ORDINANCES

- The number of communities regulating timber cutting is increasing.
- Regulations are instituted at the state, county, and town levels.
- When considering a local ordinance, all other overlapping regulations should be taken into account.
- Loggers, foresters, and the governing body should work collectively to create an ordinance.
- Forest management that includes timber cutting is an ecological land use, and the forest owner must be able to make long-term decisions about management techniques. A badly considered cutting ordinance can cause major economic problems to these owners.

A local harvest ordinance should:

1. Maintain long-term forest health as well as vitality of the local economy.
2. Establish a permit system that is easy to use by landowners and loggers and easy to administer by the government.
3. Consider the following items:
   - Visual screening of timber-cutting operations from main roads, residences, and businesses
   - Soil-erosion-control measures
   - Entrance and exit requirements for town roads
   - Weight-limit requirements
   - Special requirements for seasonal weather changes
   - Performance bonds—are they needed, and if so, what is reasonable and who should hold the bonds—the county or the landowner?
   - Map of the cutting area
   - Plan for skid trails and log landing
   - Plan for rehabilitating the site
4. Avoid complications or conflicts with state or county regulations.
5. Encourage a formal contract between logger and landowner.
6. Encourage the involvement of a forester in contract negotiations.
7. Include definitions for all the key terms—tree, forest, forester, harvest—and any technical or confusing terms.

already. The way concerned citizens used to stop or regulate the timber cutting was to put pressure on the town's environmental commission, and this is how many logging ordinances are developed.

Getting a timber ordinance established, however, does not have to—and should not—be a painful or hostile process for anyone concerned. When a municipality is thinking about putting a logging ordinance on the books, everyone who might be affected—loggers, landowners, foresters, concerned citizens, environmental leaders—should be encouraged to contribute their ideas. It might even be decided that the issue at hand cannot be solved via a new ordinance. The first time a town requested my advice, the situation focused on large virgin oaks that were being cut along someone's jogging path. The path turned out to be a woods road located in a woodlot that was next to the jogger's housing development. The oaks were not virgin but second-growth woods in the eight to ten-inch-diameter class. The farmer who owned the woodlot was completing a timber stand improvement project marked by a forester. The issue involved a conflict of perspectives, not one worthy of legislation.

A second incident in the community did precipitate an ordinance, however. An area with steep slopes was being logged, and the lack of water bars, contoured logging trails, bailed hay barriers, and common sense resulted in a muddied reservoir. A timber ordinance was enacted in the hope of preventing similar problems in the future. My neighbor, Bill, just happened to be caught up in this hope.

Before considering a timber ordinance, local government officials and others should be aware of the pros and cons of taking such an action. An ordinance may allow a community to solve a particular problem, but the problem should be real and not just a perceived one, as in the case of the jogger. And although a single incident may cause an ordinance to be adopted, the law should not be so specific that it cannot regulate activities on all environmentally sensitive areas within the jurisdiction. The ordinance can establish a legal instrument for its enforcement, but it should be remembered that there will be costs for implementation, enforcement, and training. Landowners should know that bonds, licenses, and red tape may slow harvesting activities.

The ordinance must be well written—with terms clearly defined, limitations and restraints specifically stated—to prevent it from being ineffective, but it should not be so restrictive that it needlessly infringes on what people do with their land or how people make a living. An overly restrictive ordinance, for example, can make timber harder to sell because loggers will go where it is less of a hassle to operate.

Some ordinances are very simple, providing only that information be gathered. The town may want to know only who the landowner and logger are, the time frame of the timber harvest, and that the necessary permits are obtained. The more common situation, a comprehensive ordinance, may contain specific regulations to protect bordering properties, soil, streams, and roads. It may also spell out erosion-control measures, encourage or require buffer zones along public roads, and require reporting of the size, type of cut, and quantity of trees by species.

If individual towns and counties continue to develop their own ordinances, a patchwork of timber-cutting legislation evolves. At some point, a statewide logging ordinance may serve better than this legal mosaic. California, Massachusetts, and Oregon have already gone this route, and Virginia also has a forest practice law in effect. Whatever the situation in your area, it pays to be aware of it.

23

Resolving Conflicts in the Urban/Rural Forest Interface

Gordon A. Bradley and B. Bruce Bare

As AMERICAN CITIES, new towns, and even small communities spread out over increasing tracts of rural land, conflicts over the most appropriate use of that land are almost inevitable. One central question is whether urban development can coexist with commodity uses of forest land in areas where the two interface. And if the two can coexist, how can they be made more compatible?

Because of the traditional assumption that timber production is not compatible with urbanization and other noncommodity uses of land, foresters have often viewed the interface of urban development with forested land as a battlefield. From this perspective, land conversion is judged undesirable and action is aimed at slowing or preventing such conversion. From a different viewpoint, of course, land developers and sometimes urban planners see land conversion as representing the "highest and best use" of land. From that vantage point, an orderly conversion process should be promoted. Still other interests are caught in the middle, perceiving the benefits of both commodity and noncommodity values of the forest as well as the desirability of controlled growth—the best of all worlds.

Too often, when a battle develops between these different viewpoints about land use, the field for conflict is a government courtroom or legislative chamber. When one set of values is pitted firmly against another, both problem identification and problem solution are complicated. So it is important, before deciding that urban development and traditional forestry uses are incompatible, to look at the interface between these two uses in more depth.

THE INTERFACE CONTINUUM

To think of the urban interface with rural forests as only a contemporary phenomenon overlooks the last two centuries of settlement history in the United States, when almost every farm, town, and metropolitan area was carved from either forested or open and wild landscapes. Early settlements were established near natural water access points and were relatively compact. Over the years, development spread, overcoming the obstacles presented by wildlands—following canals, wagon trails, railroads, and eventually interstate highways.

Early settlers viewed wildlands either as a barrier to be conquered or a major source for commodity production. By contrast, today's settlers often move to wildland areas because of the attraction of rural landscapes and the appeal of a home on a large lot. Today, land use decisions are also guided by different and more complex laws and regulations than in the past. Some of these laws are national ones, some are state, and some local—the last is most often in the context of comprehensive land use plans. Some of this legislation clearly reflects nonmarket values of land and natural resources.

Rather than think of this new interface of settlement and traditional forestland as a simple dichotomy, it is helpful to think of it as a zone transformation that is a continuum. The zones, shown in Figure 23.1, suggest a decreasing degree of urban encroachment as one moves along the continuum from left to right. To the left of the development zone are intensely builtup city environments; to the right of the forest zone are remote wildland settings that are either inaccessible or designated for preservation.

It is in the four zones to the left of this figure that great opportunities and challenges lie for innovative thinking about the mix of activities.

The Development Zone Residential development in a forest environment—here called the development zone—is the popular image of the urban/rural forest interface. Of course, many other types of development occur in this zone, including commercial, recreational, and industrial activities. This zone is attractive for development because of potentially lower market prices for land as users move away from urban areas. In many cases, these less developed surroundings, still within easy commuting distance to cities, provide many amenities not found in builtup areas. Open space, trees, streams, and lakes are a few attractions that may lead developers and home buyers to the development zone.

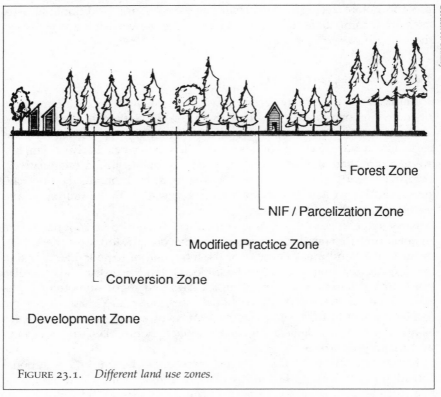

Gordon A. Bradley

Forest Zone

NIF / Parcelization Zone

Modified Practice Zone

Conversion Zone

Development Zone

FIGURE 23.1.   *Different land use zones.*

If these developments are carefully planned, many of the amenities sought can be realized with few problems. But severe problems may occur when developers or other buyers discover that insufficient buffers have been provided as part of the development. Suddenly, amenities thought to be a permanent part of the landscape are a component of another public or private owner's land use plan. Not only does the landscape take on a new and sometimes less attractive image, but many forestry development practices—such as the use of fire, chemicals, and heavy equipment—are in conflict with the new owner's perceptions of how adjacent lands should be used.

From the point of view of the forest, another problem in this zone is the impact of new uses on the forest environment. A forest stand is in a constant state of change, of biological succession. To fail to anticipate the effects of development on the management of the forest is to court disaster. Instances of trees blowing down on structures because of improper thinning and soil disturbance are all too common, as are problems with vegetation dying from overwatering, improper fertilization, and air pollution. Also, it is dangerous to suppress the natural forces of nature, such as the periodic occurrence of fire, without other mitigating measures such as brush clearing near structures, fireproof roofing, and easy access to fire hydrants. Recent examples of the result are whole subdivisions destroyed by wildfire, not only in the Northwest, but throughout the country.

The opportunities to mitigate negative effects of development on forestry and also enhance the quality of the living environment are also numerous, however. On such a site along a river in western Oregon, development units were clustered rather than scattered on ten-acre-minimum lots. Increasing densities not only consumes less land area but decreases the number of points of contact between the units and the forest. Open space lands can be designated for wildlife habitat. They can also be actively managed to produce firewood for residents, to reduce fire hazards, to increase aesthetic views, and to reduce the hazard of trees threatening structures.

Forest lands within such a development can also be managed for commercial timber production using modified forest practices, which makes harvesting compatible with the surrounding residential uses. Revenues from harvesting timber can offset maintenance costs for shared community and recreational facilities. Residential structures can be sited so that they are buffered from forestry activities on adjacent lands. If the development is on a scenic corridor such as a river, hiking trail, or highway, it can be buffered from the view of passing motorists.

The Conversion Zone This is land in forest cover that is expected to change to another use fairly soon. Conversion is usually prompted by an owner's expectation that a more profitable use exists for the land, whether that be urban development or agriculture. These decisions are often affected by such factors as zoning decisions or tax status changes which favor the new use or by a change in the use of adjoining lands.

Regardless of the motivation and intentions of the landowners, use conversions often lead to emotional debates. Local government and development interests may see opportunities for increased revenue through higher taxes. On the other hand, local government allied with environmental interests may view land conversion as creating additional financial burdens and diminishing an already scarce natural resource base near populated areas. The timber industry may question conversion because it diminishes the timber supply and may create nuisance conflicts in managing other lands for timber purposes.

A significant opportunity for better forest and development uses in this area could result from a better understanding of the requirements of the new use. Let us consider a negative example. In one such parcel located thirty minutes outside Seattle, Washington, a decision was made to convert the parcel from commercial forestry to residential use. Unfortunately, little consideration was given to that future use when roads were laid out and the site was harvested with clear-cutting methods.

As a result, no trees of any amenity value remained, and the site was significantly altered by the movement of harvesting equipment across the land. The site rehabilitation cost approximately $5,000 per acre before the parcels could be marketed. Improvement included grading, road redesign and construction, and the planting of native and ornamental trees to improve the site's visual character. Beyond the costs to the developer, better harvesting practices and planning would have resulted in fewer negative impacts for adjacent landowners.

Modified Practice Zone This is an area in which traditional forest land management practices are modified to allow for the continuation of forest uses while making them compatible with adjacent land uses.

An excellent example of such forest management is the Tiger Mountain State Forest, a 14,000-acre forest parcel administered by the Washington State Department of Natural Resources, located within a thirty-minute drive of approximately 1.5 million people in the Puget Sound region. Competing demands on the area include its use for hiking, for motorized vehicles, for hang gliding, and for communications facilities. In addition, adjacent landowners have come to view the mountain as an extension of their own backyard. Consequently, they are sensitive to aesthetic impacts and to some of the traditional practices in forestry, such as clear-cutting, spraying of chemicals, and the use of prescribed fire.

The area also includes the headwaters of Issaquah Creek, a prime salmon fishery; and it lies along one of the most heavily traveled corridors in the state, making the mountain a visual focal point for millions of passing motorists. The challenge for management is further complicated by a legislative mandate to manage state lands for the purpose of returning revenues to the various trusts for which the lands were set aside. So the challenge is to produce commodities while at the same time producing a variety of noncommodity benefits.

Given the sensitive nature of Tiger Mountain, the state Department of Natural Resources spent two years working with a citizen's advisory group to address the issues of competing demands and to make recommendations. The final plan, adopted in 1986, calls for modifications in harvesting techniques, in the shape and size of harvested parcels, in special treatments for riparian zones and other sensitive areas, and alternative road building and reclamation schemes. Some historic uses such as timber production, hiking, and horseback riding continue, while other uses such as offroad vehicles and target shooting are banned in their entirety.

In addition, a concerted effort will be made to use the forest as an experimental and demonstration forest where the surrounding population will have an opportunity to learn about the production of a wide range of forest benefits firsthand.

Nonindustrial Forest/Parcelization Zone This zone is distinguished from others by the fact that, within it, the owners of two distinct sorts of parcel sizes are seeking coexistence. The nonindustrial forest (NIF) landowner has a parcel ranging from five to 500 acres, on which the main objective is to grow trees. The second sort of owner has a "large lot," usually in a zone where the local jurisdiction has restricted minimum lot sizes. Typically such restrictions are for lots of five, ten, twenty, or even forty acres. In some cases, lot minimums may be as much as 140 to 640 acres. Often the landowners here are seeking an affordable place to live or a weekend retreat where they can enjoy the amenities of the forest.

Fewer problems usually exist here. Management practices of nonindustrial forest owners are less intensive and on a smaller scale that on industrial forest lands. If the second type of owner has a significant parcel of land but does not practice proper management of it, a second sort of problem arises, however. The productivity of the land for future timber resources may decline, but fisheries, wildlife, and aesthetic resources may also be involved.

Where urban and rural areas meet, conflicts often arise over land use policy.

Forest Service, U.S.D.A.

To prevent such problems, it is essential that foresters and other resource professionals become more involved in local land use planning debates. Land use requirements should ensure protection from fire, adequate access, buffers, appropriate water supply, and knowledge that landowners are living in an area where resource production is a primary use.

In addition, however, the area of landowner assistance needs rethinking. In the past several decades, foresters have focused their attention almost exclusively on trying to convince small landowners to grow trees for wood production purposes. But a decline in timber supply to an extent that requires production by such small landowners may not exist, and, in any case, numerous studies have found that the primary motivation of such small landowners is seldom growing trees for monetary return. So forestry efforts could be greatly expanded to help such small landowners with management plans that meet their desires to enhance wildlife habitat, aesthetic quality, fisheries, and recreation potential.

DEFINITIONS—AND REALITY

While the urban/rural forest interface continuum suggests a clear distinction between land uses and their associated opportunities and constraints, in practice the exact place of the interface is often more difficult to discern. If economic criteria are used to determine the area of interface, the boundary between traditional forest uses and urbanization is that line where the marginal value of land for urbanization is approximately equal to the marginal value of land for less intensive uses. If, by contrast, aesthetic criteria are dominant, the interface is a wide and sometimes fuzzy boundary, distinguished for the most part by the presence or absence of large blocks of trees.

From a jurisdictional perspective, the interface is sometimes thought of as either the boundary between public and private land or the place where parcel size begins to change from relatively small to relatively large lots. Where structures appear, the interface may be defined by a line drawn between the built and unbuilt environments. Finally, using physical and biological growth criteria, the interface may resemble a soils map where highly productive lands are distinguished from less productive lands.

Obviously, deciding on the appropriate uses for interface lands and on the mechanisms to achieve those uses without major conflict demands much thoughtful work. All relevant factors and angles of perception must be considered and made an explicit part of the strategies and policies for such transitions. With that work, however, we have the capacity to achieve new levels of integration of rural forest and urban development goals.

24

The Needs of Small Rural Communities

Gene W. Grey and
James J. Nighswonger

TREES ARE NO less important to residents of small rural communities than to people who live in large cities. A community forest provides the same physical and aesthetic benefits; it just does it on a smaller scale. The needs of trees—to be planted, watered and pruned, and otherwise tended—are also about the same. Again, only the scale is different. And if you think about it, the programs necessary to care for public trees in small rural communities require the same things as in large cities: (1) supportive and positive attitudes of municipal officials and residents, (2) legal sanction and authority, (3) a readily accessible source of accurate technical information and assistance, (4) projects that are practical and consistent with community abilities, and (5) consideration of the rights and wishes of individual property owners.

However, small communities, because of their generally small tax bases, must often rely on innovative funding for tree care programs. Some funding methods are given later in this chapter. Small communities also must rely heavily on local volunteers, not only to raise funds, but to provide program leadership and, often, even physical labor.

An approach that has worked well in many communities is setting up tree boards made up of volunteer community leaders. This approach has been particularly effective in Kansas, where 115 of the state's 618 towns of less than 10,000 population have formed such boards.

With assistance from the state forestry department, the tree boards begin work with surveys of public trees to determine overall program needs. Streetside and park trees are surveyed, primarily from a moving automobile, by species, size, age, and condition class. Species and tree condition class percentages are then computed, providing a planning base from which planting, tree removal, and maintenance needs can be determined. See Table 24.1, a sample survey summary.

When the program needs have been determined, priorities may be assigned and goals established. It then becomes necessary to identify what is needed to reach the goals. For example, if a tree board gives priority to a street tree-planting project, the following questions must be answered: (1) what species will be made available? (2) how will orders be taken? (3) how will the program be publicized? (4) how will payment be arranged? (5) how will planting spots be located? (6) how will trees be planted and maintained? and (7) what ordinances are desirable to regulate street plantings? Similar questions must be asked for tree removal and maintenance projects. The answers to these questions constitute annual or project work plans.

Ideally, the members of tree boards should serve in a planning and advisory capacity, with qualified city employees to physically implement work plans. Realistically, however, most communities do not have employees with either the responsibility or qualifications for such work. Hence, in most cases, tree boards actually administer and implement the program. Board members purchase and distribute trees, arrange publicity, mark trees for removal, stake planting sites, and the like. This approach has the obvious weakness of being dependent on the board members' interest. However, in small communities with limited resources, it is perhaps the most practical approach.

Technical service is vital to success. At the outset, few communities have the capability or available funds for the development of landscape plans, dead and diseased tree marking, planting site location, or insect and disease diagnosis. If work plans are to be carried out, these services must be made available. In Kansas, the urban forester who is also a landscape architect from the state forestry department provides such services. Area foresters located throughout the state also help.

Many communities give high priority to the development of park and recreation area plans or the landscaping of other public areas such as public squares, highway entrances, and central business districts. The first determination is whether or not funds are available to contract with a private landscape firm. If not or if the project is too small to be economically feasible for a private firm, the service is provided by the state forestry

TABLE 24.1

Sample Streetside Tree Survey Summary

Species	Number of Trees	Average Age	Average Diameter (in.) (2.54 cm)	Percentage of Species Total				Percentage of Total Trees
				Good[a]	Fair[b]	Poor[c]	D & D[d]	
American elm	2,158	60	19	31	25	24	20	33
Hackberry	1,090	60	16	59	31	10	0	18
Siberian elm	376	40	14	4	33	59	4	6
Hard maple (sp.)	328	10	4	74	5	18	3	5
Green ash	320	15	6	48	31	21	0	5
Pin oak	320	40	15	69	10	20	1	5
Sycamore/planetree	302	20	8	76	9	15	0	5
Honeylocust	288	20	9	71	8	20	2	4
Silver maple	280	15	10	39	13	48	0	4
Red oak	218	10	5	56	23	13	8	3
Redbud	138	10	4	78	2	20	0	2
Black walnut	130	55	15	34	54	12	0	2
Hybrid elm	82	15	6	7	56	37	0	1
Miscellaneous[e]	466							7
Totals	6,496							

[a] Healthy, vigorous tree. No apparent signs of insect, disease, or mechanical injury. Little or no corrective work required. Form representative of species.

[b] Average condition and vigor for area. May be in need of some corrective pruning or repair. May lack desirable form characteristic of species. May show minor insect injury, disease, or physiological problem.

[c] General state of decline. May show severe mechanical, insect, or disease damage, but death not imminent. May require repair or renovation.

[d] Dead, or death imminent from Dutch elm disease or other causes.

[e] Less than 1 percent each: bur oak, tree of heaven, flowering crab, sweetgum, basswood, black locust, Kentucky coffeetree, eastern redcedar, chinquapin oak, hawthorn, mimosa, catalpa, pine (sp.), cottonwood, willow, Osage–orange, purpleleaf plum, white birch, mulberry, fruit (sp.), Japanese pago-datree, shingle oak, English oak, Russian olive, ginkgo, boxelder.

Trees of small communities need the same administrative and arboricultural care as those of larger cities.

department. If funds are available, a list of private contractors is furnished to community officials.

Many plans are developed on site by simply staking planting locations. This is a direct and highly efficient way to get planting accomplished in situations where planting funds are available. If funds must be approved by a budget committee who need to see the planting plans, drafted plans are necessary.

Because tax revenues are not always available in small communities, programs sometimes must depend on other sources and methods of funding. Following are a number of fund-raising methods that have helped to build community forestry programs in Kansas, without the use of general tax revenues.

- A residential community neighborhood with a big investment in large American elms, which were vulnerable to Dutch elm disease, combined neighborhood fund-raising and volunteer efforts. The residents assessed themselves an amount to cover the cost of equipment and chemicals needed to treat elms, on a proportional basis. Some homeowners received training for elm disease prevention and control and donated their services in making tree injections.
- Another community assessed each property owner (residential, commercial, and industrial) an annual fee based on the footage of street frontage for tree planting and maintenance.
- Instead of burying dead trees in the landfill, some communities have turned them into income producers by converting them to wood chips, fuelwood, and sawlogs. Stump grindings were used as a soil amendment or compost material. A ready market for these products exists in most communities.
- One community used an ordinance to set aside twenty-five dollars from each building permit issued for new residences, with the funds to be applied toward a street tree planted in front of the new building after the owner moved in. If the owner preferred not to have a tree, it was planted in a city park.
- Some communities have established a nonprofit tree trust, which encourages residents to donate the cost of purchasing a tree in honor of special occasions such as birthdays, anniversaries, and holidays. Donations can also be sought from corporations, local businesses, and other institutions.
- At least one town established a memorial tree fund, through which friends and relatives of a resident who died could donate to the planting of community trees in the memory of the deceased person.
- The cost of a tree survey in one community was paid by a donation from the local chamber of commerce, which had an interest in an attractive

city. A power and light company or other public-interested groups may also fund such an effort.

- Neighborhoods have organized to raise matching funds for tree programs, thus supplementing scarce city monies.
- A specific area has at times been adopted for tree planting or maintenance by a civic organization, corporation, business, or volunteer group, which receives public attention for its effort. Its contribution can be in money, donated labor, or both.
- A new residential development published a homeowner's guidebook that deals with subjects such as protecting native trees during home construction, landscape planning, wildlife attraction, and maintenance of the community forest to enhance property values and climate modification. Each lot owner receives a copy of the guidebook at the time the building permit is issued. The homeowners association is in regular contact with the community forester who prepared the guidebook and can provide follow-up advice.

Another idea, which has not been directly tried in Kansas but which has promise, is that a community may want to consider a total forestry plan for its public lands—including harvesting some woods for fuel, growing Christmas trees, and so forth. Such sites can have educational value as well. Generally, the concept of community forest land management to produce income, while maintaining the more traditional recreational and aesthetic values, is usually popular with city administrations.

These are far from being a total list of funding ideas, but they provide some sense of the innovative approaches that can work in smaller and rural communities. Overall, one can say that it is organization, not money, that is the key to success. When funds are limited or nonexistent, the ability of leaders to organize, motivate people, and be creative will determine whether or not the town's forestry program will accomplish its goals.

PART SIX

TREES FOR
SPECIAL PLACES

From college campuses and historic parks to new greenways through our own backyards, each city has special places that can benefit from creative thinking about ways to bring trees and people closer together. This section describes how one college campus tapped its alumni to build a strong tree program. It analyzes the needs of city parks, reports on the fast-growing greenway movement, tells the story of a three-century-old community forest in Massachusetts, and ends with practical information on using trees to provide shade, food, and fencing around your home.

25

Reforesting the Campus

Josephine Robertson

WHEN THE UNIVERSITY of Colorado's one and only building opened for classes in 1876, it stood bleak against the sky without a tree or shrub to break its harsh silhouette. Only cactus punctuated the prairie—a place nature didn't intend as a tree-shaded campus with long shadows across green lawns.

Today, the Boulder campus is green and beautiful against a backdrop of Rocky Mountain foothills, with rugged old cottonwoods, elms, and maples. But there are serious problems. Most of the big trees were planted early in the century and are nearing the end of their lifespan. Some are succumbing to heart rot or disease.

Faced with the loss of more than 500 trees in the last few years, former grounds superintendent Mike Guthrie ruefully commented, "Unless steps are taken, the campus could revert to prairie." Since the university budget was too tight to keep up with the needed reforestation, landscape architect Dennis Haney, Guthrie, and three skilled trimmers—tree lovers all—decided to appeal to former students for help.

An article in the spring 1984 issue of *Colorado Alumnus*, detailing the threat to the campus trees, had surprising results—in both cash and sentiment. More than $40,000 was contributed, and along with checks came letters telling how much the campus trees meant during the donors' student years.

An initial gift of $2,000 came from the Directors' Club of the CU Alumni Association. Others came because graduates were distressed at the thought of a deteriorating landscape; many gifts were designated as me-

Boulder Historical Society

Old Main, at right, in this 1870s view of unrelieved prairie, was CU's only building.

morials. One woman wrote, "During my years in Boulder I received tremendous pleasure from the beauty of the campus. I have subsequently made my living in the forest-products business. How could I resist responding to your plea for help?"

A gift came as a memorial from the parents of a student who had died in a climbing accident. Contributions for three trees, a memorial to their parents, came from three children with the request that the trees be planted close together. All five members of the family were CU graduates. A check came from a man who had met his wife at the university and had "spent some enjoyable hours in the shade of the lovely trees."

The Bahai Community of Boulder sent $900 for white flowering cherries "in memory of the Bahai Martyrs of Iran." With a check for $102 came a letter explaining that it had been donated by a group of current and former employees in memory of Newt Bell, a construction worker who helped to build the University Memorial Center Building, with a request that the tree be planted nearby.

Surveys have shown that in addition to providing cherished memories, the beauty of the campus is a factor in attracting new students. Thus, it has an economic benefit. Many are impressed with the rugged, leafy trees at the foot of the imposing mountains.

WORKING WITH THE PRAIRIE

Planting trees in fertile areas is easy, but growing conditions in the high-elevation prairie are forbidding. Under a scant two to three inches of

A student perches in a huge cottonwood gracing Old Main as it looks today.

topsoil lies clay. Unless broken up and/or mixed with compost or sand, it becomes so compacted around a young trunk that water will not penetrate. The freeze-thaw cycle causes heaving and cracking. Winter can be long and bitter, downslope winds often exceed hurricane velocity, and the soil is full of large rocks. Annual rainfall averages less than nineteen inches, and its distribution is unpredictable; sometimes too much comes at once. Warm chinook winds may suddenly melt the mountain snowpacks, resulting in flooding. Summers are hot and dry.

But there are pluses in this high, dry climate. About 249 days out of the year are clear and sunny or only partly cloudy. Nights are cool in summer, and during the intense heat of midday it is almost as refreshing to step into the shade of a big tree as to take a cold dip. Growing young trees here calls for more water than the skies bring. Fortunately, the university in its early days bought many shares in a ditch company, an invaluable resource today. One of the picturesque features of the old Norlin Quadrangle—now designated as an Historic District on the National Register of Historic Places—is the rippling water in the old stone-lined lateral ditches. By inserting dams in the slots, water can be used to drench plantings and grass.

Mrs. Joseph Sewall, wife of the first president of the university, took the pioneer steps in beautifying the stark campus. The lone building was surrounded with rough dirt, which, during heavy rains, became "a sea of mud." With the help of the janitor and two students, she had four wagonloads of topsoil brought in, raked, planted with grass seed, and watered. But a typical Boulder high wind blew topsoil and grass toward Kansas. A farmer told her she needed fifty loads of topsoil, which she obtained, planted, and, this time, covered with old sheets held down with rocks. In late spring the covers were lifted and behold—an oasis of green grass!

As the university grew, students were encouraged to find trees to plant on May Day and Arbor Day. They brought in many cottonwood and willow saplings because the trees were plentiful along the nearby creeks. There was little overall planning in these efforts—or in the creation of assorted new buildings. The resulting haphazard planting and unrelated architectural styles were summed up wryly by President George Norlin in a public address in 1916 when he declared that the institution "looked like a third-rate farm."

He called for a long-range plan, and the challenge was accepted. The Philadelphia firm of Klauder and Day was consulted, and it was due to Charles Z. Klauder that an adaptation of the rural Italian style seen on Tuscan hillsides—native stone buildings with red tile roofs—became the motif of the campus. At the same time, more attention was paid to the value of large trees that softened the outlines and helped unify earlier diverse buildings while leaving the mountain vistas open.

PLANTING THE CAMPUS

Many a last glance backward from a June
Graduation remembers that the catalpas
Were in flower and the yellowwood
Beside the library, remembers the pointing
Of a particular dark pine as the sun
Of that afternoon mellowed between a stand
Of buckeyes spiring their clustered blooms.
Many a last bequest remembers to renew
The green, passing into the hands of the campus
Arborealist: Emeritus among the flora,
He remembers teaching the Latin names of trees
To those whose names have now pre-deceased
His own; and, lovingly planting the campus,
He chooses for each with care: for her
Who was Homecoming Queen a golden locust
Of extraordinary beauty; for another who led
His team to victory, a strapping oak;
A Chinese scholar tree to crown the achievements
Of an intellectual giant. Many a branch
Of learning in his planted avenues turns
Its remembering leaves in fall to colors
Like a doctor's hood, wreathing the shoulders
Of the boy and girl who pass beneath
With an eternal summer's degrees.

Nancy G. Westerfield

A detailed Campus Open Space Development Plan was produced in 1981 by architect William R. Deno. Though it covered many man-made features such as walks, signs, draining, curbs, and parking areas, an extensive section deals with "a palette of plant material" suggested as suitable for existing weather conditions. The lists included about forty deciduous trees, a quarter of them flowering, to add color as well as shade to the campus. Redbuds, hawthorns, and crabapples do very well. The palette includes more than eighty shrubs, some low and some tall, many native and many flowering. Lilacs do exceptionally well. Fourteen different evergreens are listed along with vines and ground covers. There are special grasses for lawns and recreation fields, and, for areas with little water, a dryland pasture mix of little bluestem, buffalo grass, and blue grama.

There are already many evergreens on the campus that relieve the winter bareness but do not provide the amenities of deciduous trees. The ultimate size of the new trees and staggered plantings will prevent future crises of simultaneous aging. There are already many spring-flowering trees, but new introductions will lengthen the flowering season. Now autumn reds, scarlets, and bronzes will enrich the native palette of golden aspens, cottonwoods, and willows.

Since that first call went out in 1984, more than 300 new trees twelve to fifteen feet tall have been planted. It has been determined that this size is more resistant to vandalism than smaller ones, which are more economical but don't quite look like "real" trees yet. Among the species planted are the autumn and summit ash, western catalpa, linden, ginala and Schwedler's maple, sweetgum, various oaks, yellow buckeye, black walnut, tuliptrees, and ginkgo.

Evergreens will include ponderosa, bristlecone, and limber pines; concolor fir and Douglas fir; baldcypress; Norway, Black Hills, and Colorado blue spruce. (The last, surprisingly, only flourishes close to buildings where it has shelter.) A few cottonwoods are being planted for auld lang syne, but as the rugged old original giants fall, the newer, varied plantings will give the campus a different look. There will still be abundant shade, but variety offers a form of insurance against devastating Dutch elm disease, spruce budworm, blight, and other fungal and bacterial infections.

When the first appeal was made, $100 was the suggested contribution for a 2½-inch-caliper tree. Today the appeal stresses that gifts of any amount are welcome but requests that the donation for a specific tree be at least $200. Originally, the possibility of individual plaques was mentioned, but as Guthrie said, "If we had a permanent plaque on each tree, the place would look like a cemetery! Besides, it would add something like $50 to the cost. Instead, we hope to have a master chart with numbers indicating the locations of the trees with the names of the donors."

Alan Nelson, the new grounds supervisor, is proud of the progress that is being made in stressing diversity. He told this writer that, considering all the hazards of Boulder's climate and unfriendly soil, 85 percent survival of new plantings is excellent.

The beauty of the old Norlin Quadrangle is a triumph of human struggle with a hostile environment. Architect Deno, in his introduction to the Campus Open Space Development Plan, comments, "The main Boulder campus was a treeless plain until the mid-19th century. . . . The barren hillsides coursed down from the flatiron rock formations over the mesas across the campus, and extended in waving prairie grasses to the east. . . It is here that pioneer people coaxed grass to grow and hardwood trees to shade the flowering shrubs. Growing plants was not easy then, and it is no easy now."

But enlightened tree planters are pulling it off again.

26

Restoring Urban and Historic Parks

Joseph M. Keyser

As I WAS leading a hike through a small national park in Washington, D.C., recently, the branch of an old white oak thundered through the dense hardwood canopy to our left and crashed to the ground. We had just gathered our composure and were about to move on, when a larger tree followed suit on the opposite side of the trail, raising our excitement level to anxiety. We were witnessing nature unbounded—the natural order of trees and forests. The crumbling giants and crushed undergrowth would eventually decompose and be replaced, but only after a great many years. Allowing nature to gradually replenish itself is part of the preservation policy historically upheld by the National Park Service, but that policy may need to change.

The aging trees in Washington's Glover–Archbold Park in the late 1980s mirror the condition of urban parks throughout the country. Unlike their larger country cousins, small urban parks are much more susceptible to the stresses of city environments, including dense air pollution, toxic runoff from automobile undercoatings, petroleum leaks, and heavy and increasing recreational use causing compaction of soil. All those stresses are compounded by the problem of aging trees not being replanted or maintained, with many parks having all or most of their trees within the same vulnerable age class.

Letting nature run its course in the urban park can only spell disaster in the not-so-distant future. Preservation as a uniform policy cannot compete with the negative effects of an expanding civilization. Since society must impact on the urban park, urban park supervisors must seek ways to minimize that impact—ways that include scientific forest management along with consideration for the human dimension: recreational use and aesthetics.

The philosophical conflict between park preservation and active forestry management is rooted in the clash between John Muir and Gifford Pinchot in the late nineteenth century. Preservationists like Muir argued for pristine natural areas untouched by human action, leading to what became the National Park System. Muir saw the hills and forests as natural cathedrals—sites for spiritual growth and the renewal of the human spirit. Pinchot, on the other hand, believed that the nation's natural resources should be managed scientifically for the benefit of human society, which

Gary Moll

The starkness of a bleak winter landscape whispers of a bleak outlook for many of our urban and historic parks—unless we take an active role in caring for them.

alternately led to the principles of sustained-yield management, multiple use, and active conservation. Pinchot's vision, though sympathetic to higher human needs, was founded on practical economics and utility. Today this philosophical dichotomy between protection and management continues, especially in the larger parks and forests of the Northwest.

As laissez-faire management of city parks becomes crisis management, however, the preservationist credo is coming under fire. Park commissioners—long accustomed to apportioning their budget to the glamour areas of recreation, acquisition, and development—are now finding their urban park forests in a serious state of decline.

In New York's Central Park, forester John Feith expects to lose most of that heavily visited park's 20,000 London planetrees within ten years. Tom Green at the Morton Arboretum in Illinois has conducted exhaustive inventories of forty-acre Reed–Keppler Park in West Chicago, finding that the mature oak forest there is at the end of its 150-year life expectancy. At the current 50 percent rate of decline currently experienced, Green estimates that the oak forest will be gone in twenty to forty years, noting that continued high recreational usage, damage by maintenance equipment (mowers), and related stresses on root systems will shorten that span considerably.

Baltimore's largest park, Druid Hill, shows similarly discouraging numbers as a result of public policy and limited funds. Most of the park's trees are old and dying prematurely, a condition compounded by the fact that over the last two decades, only one tree was planted for every ten lost. One-tenth as many trees are planted in parks as on the more visible street locations. And although the city has now stepped up its tree-planting program to help remedy this situation, the new plantings are creating another even-aged canopy—a problem that future generations will inherit.

A forest management plan prepared for San Francisco's Golden Gate Park indicates that the even-aged park's three major species (Monterey cypress, eucalyptus, and Monterey pine) have matured and are now in a serious state of decline. The trees mature at age sixty to ninety years and are now between 100 and 115 years old. While the level of decline is disheartening for park supervisors, there are more often cases like Philadelphia's Fairmount Park, where disease and mortality are noted but exact conditions are unknown and hard to assess due to funding limitations. For these parks, the crisis is hidden and can only intensify while remaining relatively unaddressed.

The urgent lesson being learned by cities everywhere is that their parks do not exist in isolation from the city environment and its population pressures, and that intensive management plans will be necessary to save the urban community from becoming wholly barren. Recognizing or quantifying the problem is perhaps the first step—"using inventory as a management and planning tool," as Tom Green observes.

ANDREA'S TREE

Situated in what is probably the poorest part of the city, Norris Square in the Puerto Rican neighborhood of West Kensington, Philadelphia, has become a symbol. No houses to deteriorate here, little enough space for graffiti artists, too open for the drug pusher, and soooo green!

Still, as elsewhere, this little pocket of urban forest has problems enough. Beetles, borers, bad tree varieties, and ozone aside, the problem here has always been vandalism and the tendency of some people to use the five-acre block of grass and trees as a dump.

It is the Norris Square Neighborhood Project, an urban environmental education center, whose work has saved the square from the plight of so many other urban parks. The goal of the center is to help local children better understand their environment. "Such an understanding comes to a child first through looking and studying, then by doing," says Carol Keck, the center's director.

Also important has been the work of remaining vigilant so that the square is not abused. This protection work often involves courage and, on occasion, high drama. Such was the case in 1987 when children rushed into the center yelling that a tree had

been set afire. Someone called the fire department while others rushed to fill buckets of water.

"Stand back," shouted the hoseman. "We gotta smash a hole in it."

Axes were being unloaded. It was a hollow tree, old but alive, roaring like a flue.

"No! Please!" This from Andrea Raffel, for ten years a teacher at Norris Square and author of all those workshops. "Use your short ladder. Put it out from the top!"

"Hey Lady! Will you please let us do our job!"

Three teachers, twenty-eight children, and assorted passers-by looked helplessly on.

"It's only about ten feet to the top of the hollow. Look! You do have a ladder." She ran to the truck and rattled it.

"Will someone get this woman away from me?" The beefy fellow with the helmet made his first swing.

Ducking beneath the axe, Andrea fell to her knees and with hands clasped, face upturned, implored the man to stop. In a trice, she had his left thigh and was tightening.

The spectacle, the embarrassment, the pure shock of the whole incident were too much for any of us. The fireman appeared to be suffocating, his face purple and swollen. He tried to

PATHS TO RESTORATION

Interestingly, this lesson has not gone unnoticed by the National Park Service. Although champions of the preservationist cause, the service boasts a nontraditional project developed during the Carter administration—the Urban Park and Recreation Recovery Program (UPARR), or Urban Parks Program, whose aim, according to outdoor recreation planner Ann Toole, is to systematically change the overall plans move but couldn't. When he finally spoke, it was awful what he said. But when he finished speaking, he threw his axe down. Three other firemen were already placing the short ladder against the tree.

The tree flourishes today, none the worse for its inner scorching. We like to think of it as Andrea's tree.

Norris Square needs to be replanted with large trees. In 1977, the children surveyed the trees in the square. There were eighty-seven. In the spring of 1988 there were fifty.

But in the neighborhood where a tree's value is demonstrated in everyday as well as extraordinary events, this city park refuses to die.

Peter A. Grove

Andrea and her students. Norris Square (in background) is their playground and learning center.

of municipal park and recreation systems to a holistic approach that recognizes the importance of forestry and horticulture as much as recreation space and development. Toole calls UPARR a problem-solving program, whereby grants are awarded city park departments to study why management plans are not working or how parks can be rehabilitated through innovative maintenance programs.

UPARR maintenance projects are in place in seventy-five locations in the

Northeast (which accounts for 80 percent of all national programs), with success stories coming from cities like Worcester, Massachusetts, and Baltimore, where urban forestry programs are introducing new management techniques. Elsewhere, monies are finally being shifted away from removal and recreation and put to work inventorying and studying the urban forest, replacing and maintaining trees, diversifying species, and planning for the future. Toole finds it ironic that although UPARR has less money than ever before, more projects are under way and enthusiasm is growing.

But the need for scientific forest management is not restricted to the urban park. National Historic Parks, which comprise 135 of the 334 units in the National Park system, are facing similar pressures from overuse, pollution, encroaching urbanization, and static management plans. As urban centers continue to expand, once-independent parks find themselves engulfed: historic battlefields are encircled by fast-food eateries, motels, and billboards. The wooded areas and forests traditionally associated with them become little more than buffer zones, aging and suffering from population pressures. The carrying capacity of these parks is also threatened by the large number of urban dwellers seeking recreational opportunities in green areas, trail systems, and natural/cultural landmarks. The Civil War clashes at Gettysburg, Harper's Ferry, and Antietam seem environmentally inconsequential compared with the many hundreds of buses and thousands of private automobiles depositing their hordes on these already abused ecosystems each day.

Acidification of water sources, storm and disease damage, and other natural elements also impact on these historic park forests. In this light, pure preservation attitudes may lead to even further deterioration of forest health. The desire to preserve a moment in time, although laudatory from a cultural perspective, overlooks the very dynamics of forest succession. Thick stands of pine that once concealed revolutionary militiamen from the British have grown old and died, replaced by hardwood forests that little resemble past scenes. Other woodlots have fallen victim to insect pests, disease, and ice damage. Paradoxically, active management may be the key to protecting the historic scene. As J. Douglas Wellman at Virginia Polytechnic Institute has pointed out, "If the overall objective of the park is to provide people with an undisturbed sense of the past, the National Park Service cannot allow nature to take its course."

Wellman and his colleagues have completed a forest management plan for Appomattox Court House Park that is now being implemented. The plan studies existing ground cover, examines the condition of the present forest and its state of disrepair, and recommends new management practices, including sanitation cuts that will allow long-term sustainable forest growth. The once-neglected and deteriorating buffer will soon become a vital part of the park again, adding to the recreational and cultural appreciation the site deserves.

Regarding the required salvage and sanitation cuts, Wellman notes that such actions no doubt alarm park visitors but can be turned into a positive experience through an educational program explaining how and why the trees are being removed. In fact, Wellman and his associates view such programs undertaken nationally as an excellent opportunity to make the public aware of the need for active management, turning preservationist alarm into conservationist support.

Marrying the two disciplines of park preservation and scientific management is perhaps the hardest job of all. It is easy enough to suggest that urban and historic parks should adopt forestry methods, but to do so ignores the fact that most forest management practices are directed toward production and profit. To truly restore our forest parks, we should consider a new order of management that borrows equally from the wisdom of Pinchot *and* Muir. After all, the park forest is a synergy of both worlds—part park, to be protected and preserved, and part forest, trees forming a dynamic ecosystem that needs to be managed. In dealing with the forest park, it will be necessary to manage with a sensitivity for basic, sustaining human needs beyond mere economics. Comprehensive inventories, silviculture, diligent maintenance programs, and genetic research and hybridization for disease and pollution tolerance are just some of the tools the urban and historic forest parks must employ.

Greenways or greenbelt parks are other options for urban areas to consider. Developing greenways—linear parks constructed along streams, utility rights-of-way, abandoned rail lines, and through lands set aside by conservation easements—may help take some of the pressure off our traditional urban parks. Small parks can be linked together, and urban and suburban areas can be joined with national parks and forests (and their extensive trail systems) to offer urban residents new recreational opportunities conveniently close to home.

City planners are just beginning to use open space in creative new ways to meet these present and future challenges. In the Winkler Preserve, in Alexandria, Virginia, the city worked out a compromise with developers to convey a natural area for public use. Without creative planning and negotiation, the city's budget would have been unable to create and preserve this valuable new resource.

But such incidents are still rare, and, worse, most people are still unaware of these new opportunities, so the more familiar park areas continue to be overburdened even if alternatives exist. Disseminating information about these new opportunities must become a greater overall priority.

There's much to be learned and unlearned if preservationists and conservationists are to work together to save our unique parklands and create new ones.

27

Greenways and the City

Charles E. Little

WHAT DO YOU suppose the young president of the Mad Dog Construction Company in Tallahassee, Florida, the owner of a string of pizzerias in Portland, Oregon, and a hard-cussing, retired state legislator in Denver, Colorado, have in common? The answer is not much, except for one thing: greenways. Or perhaps better put, the urban greenway *movement*, the leadership of which is as varied as it is inspired. At a time when the plight of cities is not even on the national priority list, much less near the top as it was only a decade ago, these leaders along with hundreds like them, have discovered a means to beautify harsh metropolitan landscapes, to provide a new kind of recreational amenity, to protect and enhance natural features, and in the process to rekindle pride of place by bringing citizens of all classes and cultures together to make greenways happen.

For those who are unfamiliar with the term, *greenways* are linear parks or open spaces that link existing natural and cultural features—usually, but not invariably, in or near cities and usually, but not invariably, with a trailway running through them. The term, though dating from the 1920s, came into common use in the mid-1970s, when federal money for high-ticket open space acquisition and recreational development projects started getting hard to come by. It was then that local leaders discovered, or rediscovered, open space resources they had earlier overlooked: underutilized riversides, often in industrial districts; abandoned railroad rights-of-way; semipublic lands, such as water company holdings; and scenic transportation routes.

But simply defining the term can scarcely convey how diverse and imaginative the greenway movement is when seen up close. During 1988 and 1989, in the course of conducting field research for a comprehensive book on greenways, I got in touch with over a hundred projects across the country. Doubtless, I hit only the high spots, but I was able to visit some thirty greenways. That's how I got to know Mad Dog Chuck Mitchell, among other colorful greenwayites.

A husky, athletic man, Mitchell and some counterculture friends from Florida State University decided fifteen years ago to build a group of houses cooperatively (i.e., do-it-yourself) after graduation and stay in Tallahassee rather than return to hometowns or go on to graduate school (Mitchell was bound for Yale). Their approach was so unconventional that the city building inspector started calling Mitchell and friends the "mad dog builders of Tallahassee." As it turned out, Mitchell got good at house building and decided to make it his career. Hence, the Mad Dog Construction Company—now a major contractor in north Florida. He recently received an award from the National Park Service for discovering and preserving a major archaeological site associated with Hernando de Soto (1499–1542) spotted in the course of excavating for a development.

When not mad-dogging, Mitchell works on a project of the Apalachee Land Conservancy to preserve Tallahassee's famed "Canopy Roads." The roads, which radiate outward from the city into the adjoining countryside, were the original routes used in pre-Columbian times by various tribes of the Creek nation. They were later taken over by the Spanish, and after that by plantation owners. Some of the roads are still dirt-surfaced and, through centuries of use, sunken several feet below the grade of surrounding fields. Lined with huge live oaks, the spreading limbs, dripping with Spanish moss, create an arboreal archway—a green canopy over the ancient avenues. They are splendid in their beauty. And yet, because they are narrow, without shoulders, and lined with a forbidding gauntlet of stout tree trunks, the roads are also unforgiving to motorists and deadly to bikers.

The transportation engineer's solution to this problem, which was getting worse as Tallahassee's population increased, was to cut down the trees and widen the roads. But to Mad Dog Mitchell that idea was truly crazy. Reduce development on them, he and his colleagues urged, establish alternate roads as through-routes, and acquire easements a hundred feet back on each side along the roads from the large landowners whose properties abut them. This would permanently protect the canopy as well as provide off-road pathways for hiking and biking.

Working in concert with the Trust for Public Land, the Historic Tallahassee Preservation Board, the engineering firm of Post, Buckley, Schuh, and Jernigan, Inc., and sympathetic public agencies (the cast of characters is abundant), Mitchell and his colleagues got their "Canopy Roads Preser-

CREATING COMMUNITY WITH GREENWAYS

Barbara Walker, a vital and articulate citizen activist who's worked for the Portland, Oregon, greenway since that effort got under way in 1968, is fond of short maxims. They let her capture years of experience and wisdom in capsule form. "Always work for mutual benefit," she says with a glint of energy in her eye. "That's different from compromise." It's a way to build community while you're building the greenway.

What does it mean? Instead of just opposing something—800 condominium units in a forested ravine, for example—"figure out the positive direction you want, and then talk to everybody involved about the advantages." Talk to landowners who neighbor the greenway space about the advantages of having a trail near their backyard accessible to toddlers and grandparents as well as regular

hikers. Talk to colleges and schools about how a greenway provides a living laboratory for study right outside their doors. Talk to bird-watchers about the value of a corridor wide enough to attract a diversity of species within its habitat. Talk to boy and girl scout groups about the opportunity for projects, to city councils about the economic advantages of an attractive city, to foundations about how the project can be a model for others, and to state departments of parks and resources about how it fits into their plans and needs.

Talk to business leaders. And, especially, talk to developers. Despite its phenomenal fund-raising record, the Portland greenway activists didn't always beat developers to the purchase of land they considered essential to the loop. "But in one case, we worked right with the developer to help him

vation Plan" adopted in concept by the Leon County Commission in February 1988. The commission also established a staff position to coordinate plan implementation. It is, in fact, a remarkable idea—building parks around a road rather than building highways through a park. Mad enough to be utterly sane.

Meanwhile, in Portland, Oregon, Al Edelman, architect, teacher, and former executive with the Nature Conservancy, now divides his time between the management of several small businesses in Portland (including the pizzerias) and leading the effort to complete the city's "forty-mile loop." One of the truly charming things about Oregonians is their way of being self-effacing. They delight in telling you how bad the weather is and how poor the salmon run this year. Accordingly, while you may suppose that something called the forty-mile loop will be forty miles long, you would be wrong. It turns out to be a *hundred* and forty miles long. The loop plan hasn't been forty miles since 1904, when John C. Olmsted (son of Frederick Law Olmsted) proposed a greenway running along the mountainside see that if he donated the lower third of the land as a greenway corridor, he'd receive a tax credit and other sewer and water advantages from the city. We showed them how being adjacent to the greenway was a terrific advantage for the housing they did build."

"Work constructively, not negatively" and "Cooperation is better than competition" are two more guiding maxims. "You can't go out and use devious tactics and then expect people to work with you in the long term," Walker says. "Citizen groups don't have direct power. We have to encourage people to want good things to happen."

Walker sees clearly how our society, not following these insights, tends to set people in opposition to one another. "Even hearings are usually set up so that people are divided into those opposed and those in favor of an action," she says. "I'd stand up and say 'I am neither opposed nor in favor. Here's what I'm for.'

"You need positive vision to sustain the effort," Walker emphasizes. "We got all sorts of people to invest in the greenway. People who gave two dollars—and a lot of our funds were made up of those small contributions—felt they were making a difference for their grandchildren. When people feel the greenway is theirs, they don't litter in it; they don't destroy and vandalize it. They take care of it."

Including people rather than excluding them, helping a whole community build a vision of itself for the future—these create legacies which go far past land purchase and the building of trails. They recognize the city for what it is: a living web of place and people.

Sara Ebenreck

to the west of the city, crossing the Willamette River, and then looping around again to where it started.

Actually, forty is a kind of mystical number for this greenway. It took over forty years for the first part of the loop to be preserved—the mountainside leg, which was the sin qua non of the project. Finally, after an inspirational mid-1940s visit by New York park builder Robert Moses, the 7.5-mile-long Forest Park segment was preserved in 1947. Then another forty years passed, or almost, without further action. At length, in 1981, Edelman and a number of other conservation leaders in Portland once again dusted off the old Olmsted dream, commissioning a major study and design plan for an expanded hiker-biker route that would link some thirty parks in the metropolitan area. It would require a cooperative effort by eight government entities, ranging from the city of Portland to the Corps of Engineers to various suburban municipalities, which were not famous for their ability to get along heretofore. But under the new 140-mile plan, the cooperation has been heartening. Today, the loop is about half finished (seventy miles). A key link remaining is an abandoned railroad right-of-way that in one fell swoop would add twelve miles of beautiful trail. Edelman is certain the circle will be closed by the mid-1990s—as complete and perfect as the most elegant pizza.

One of the earliest and certainly one of the most inspiring greenways is in Denver, Colorado. The city was, like many others, built alongside a river—in this case the South Platte. As the city grew, the river became a dividing line between the rich and poor sides of town, and a sewer for both. So things stood for a century on a river once described as too thick to drink, too thin to plow. Then in 1965 a devastating flood swept through Denver, sending the Platte over its banks and foul water throughout the city. The cost of damage was a third of a billion dollars. Everybody said something should be done. In 1973, another flood hit. An engineering report was prepared: the price tag for fixing up the river would be $630 million.

At that point, Denver had $1.9 million to use on the river. What to do? The answer was to call in Joe Shoemaker, hard-nosed Republican state legislator, a lawyer and ex-navy man, who, as he says of himself, doesn't take any crap from anybody. His idea was, instead of trying to pass a $630 million bond for flood control, which would probably be impossible anyway, why not set up a foundation and "return the river to the people"—not as a riprapped channel, but as a greenway.

And so it is today. Joe Shoemaker and a cadre of devoted young colleagues (now including his own son, also a state legislator) created the Platte River Greenway from one end of the city to the other (and nowadays, beyond) by assembling a foundation board of directors made up of powerful figures who might have been enemies, by resolutely avoiding the accession of any government trappings whatsoever ("to have no power is to have all power," says Shoemaker), and by piecing together from scores of public and private sources some $15 million to do the job. The result is a greenway that provides 450 acres of riverside parks, forty miles of interconnected hiking and biking routes, and a river that brings the city together rather than dividing it.

So there you have thumbnail accounts of just three of the hundreds of greenways developed, under way, or dreamed about in cities all across the country. There are a good many river-oriented projects, like Denver's. Others are based on converting railroad rights-of-way to hiker-biker trails, as in a part of Portland's forty-mile loop. Still others are meant to protect and enhance an historic amenity, like the Canopy Roads. There are, moreover, greenways which serve as ecological corridors to foster wildlife species interchange and genetic diversity; greenways that are meant simply to protect distant scenery; and greenways that operate on a grand regional scale, such as the Ridge and Bay trails in the San Francisco Bay Area and

205 of special places

the Hudson River Valley Greenway from Manhattan to Albany in New York state.

But there is one thing they all have in common: energetic, talented, and wonderful people who seek to build greenways in their cities and towns without a thought other than simply to succeed in bringing them into being. It is, withal, one of the most decent, heartwarming, constructive, democratic efforts in urban improvement seen in this nation for many a year.

28

Community Forests: An Investment in the Future

Robert Dyke

AT THE END of an abandoned military airstrip just outside the small town of Newington, New Hampshire, past the concrete and the grassy clearway, stands what is left of America's first community forest. The several acres of white pine are now home to picnic tables and playgrounds. On weekends, families come out to enjoy the shade of the trees and the pleasant woodsy smell of the outdoors. At night, teenagers sit on the tables and sip beer, talk about life, and listen to the gentle rustling of the summer breeze.

Once a 112-acre tract of forest set aside in 1640 for the good of the community, this area now stands as a reminder of the founders' ingenuity, foresight, and commitment to the future. The roots of these trees are steeped in the history of America's past.

THE BIRTH OF COMMUNITY FORESTS

To trace the roots of America's community forests, one must dig deep into the very roots of America's history and culture. Those roots lie, of course, in European soil. European towns and villages have been managing community forests to provide public commodities since before the Middle Ages.

Perhaps one of the earliest and most well known of these community forests is the Sihlwald of Zurich, Switzerland. Since the year 853, this 5,000-acre forest has been in continuous use, supplying the city with recreation, watershed protection, firewood, and timber. The funds gained from these resources helped pay for hospitals, schools, libraries, museums, and other communal needs.

Newington's forest has provided many of the same benefits. In 1713 its trees provided the materials to build and fund the town's first church. Further timber cuts were made from time to time to support the parsonage and to pay the minister's salary.

Gradually, the forest came to serve other community needs as well. In 1874, twenty-four acres were cut for timber, the proceeds of which paid the town's Civil War debt. Later projects funded by forest resources were the town hall, school, library, and, in 1912, a public water system. In 1915, Newington planted 10,000 trees to help speed the process of natural regeneration.

By this time, public interest in community forests was resurging throughout New England and other parts of the country. After World War I, prices for farm products dropped dramatically. The Great Depression hit agricultural communities early, and in the 1920s, New England farmers began to leave the stony, rolling hills of their homeland for more promising lands further west. After the stock market crash of 1929, national unemployment soared. Roosevelt's New Deal offered federal work programs putting unemployed men to work building roads, bridges, parks, dams, and other public projects. Community forests became an excellent means for utilizing excess land and labor. Men that were once unemployed were put to work planting trees for the public good. Farms with soil too tired and rocky for crops were planted with trees to provide communities with natural resources, funds, and employment.

By 1939, 1,500 community forests existed in the United States. In New York alone, 70 million trees had been planted on 579 community forests. Massachusetts boasted 177 community forests, New Hampshire 102, and Vermont 44. Wisconsin had 149 "school forests," with most of the trees planted by school children on unproductive farmland. The proceeds from these forests helped pay the cost of the school system. Wisconsin's northern counties held twenty-five county forests, ranging in size from 5,000 to 200,000 acres. And in Washington, Seattle boasted the largest city forest in the country. By 1939, its 66,000 acres had already paid back more than the initial $1 million investment.

But with the 1940s came World War II. Resources, labor, and national attention shifted to efforts overseas. Domestic projects not vital to national defense were put on hold while America's minds and muscles focused on the war.

In the postwar prosperity, community forests were often overlooked.

Industries turned their attention to producing automobiles, dishwashers, and other products. Forestry techniques and equipment were also improved. As forest management and harvest methods became more efficient, competition became tougher and profit margins became tighter. As the economy boomed, so did city populations. Suburbs expanded into outlying areas. Land and labor were no longer cheap, and development became more profitable than forest management.

In 1953 the Air Force paid $15,500 for 90 percent of Newington's town forest. Most of the 10,000 white pines planted by citizens and school children were cut and burned to make room for airstrips. The town council had voted 77–2 against the sale, but the land was acquired for "reasons of national defense." Today the airbase is abandoned, and the small stand of trees is all that remains.

THE REBIRTH OF COMMUNITY FORESTS

With the passage of time, the significance of community forests has re-emerged, albeit in a different light. The people who planted the trees did so with vision and commitment to the future, but the trees paid off in ways other than any of the planters anticipated. Rather than providing timber, firewood, or profit, the community forests of today provide clean drinking water, recreation, and peace of mind.

In Washington, D.C., Rock Creek Park runs north-south through the western part of the city. Its watershed is protected by national law. Bicycle paths and walkways run its whole length, and on a spring day one can see people hiking, running, fishing, picnicking—enjoying the great outdoors in the middle of the city.

In Chicago, the Cook County forest preserve provides 68,000 acres of hardwood forests, meadows, lakes, and rivers within the Chicago metropolitan area. Much of the reforestation work was done in the 1930s with labor from the Illinois Emergency Relief Commission, the Civilian Conservation Corps, and the Works Progress Administration. Today their efforts have paid off not in timber or other forest products, but in recreation and wildlife habitat.

With the restoration of the forests, wildlife on the preserve has flourished. Deer, foxes, and beaver have all returned and are thriving in their protected habitat. Deer have become so populous that herds of fifty to sixty animals are often seen grazing on several of the preserve's open meadows. Beaver populations have boomed, requiring planners to raise several roads to span their backwater ponds.

People have also made good use of the preserve. Authorities estimate they receive more than 31 million visitors per year. The preserve currently has 190 major picnic areas, with 202 shelters and 2,200 separate units. There are 90 baseball fields, 36 miles of paved bicycle trails, 175 miles of hiking and horse trails, 34 fishing lakes, 9 rivers and streams, 3 swimming pools, and five nature centers. The Chicago area is an excellent example of how an urban region can incorporate the benefits of forest recreation, health, and relaxation into the everyday lives of city residents.

Community forests are also used to protect water supplies. In West Springfield, Massachusetts, the town's 27,000 residents receive their water from Bear Hole Water Reservoir, surrounded by 12,000 acres of reforested farmland. Although the town sells occasional firewood permits to cut dead or diseased trees, the primary benefit of the forest is its ability to protect the reservoir. The trees blanket the ground with forest debris, which holds topsoil in place, protecting surface water from runoff siltation and algal growth. The forest also adds humus to the soil, enabling it to better filter the water as it drains into the reservoir.

The humus also allows the soil to act as a giant sponge, holding vast amounts of water and releasing it gradually into the runoff system. This helps to moderate the drought-flood cycle so common in many deforested areas.

Human activity at the reservoir is limited to hiking on area trails. Swimming, boating, fishing, camping—anything that might lead to contamination of the water—is not allowed.

In Baltimore, 18,000 acres of forests mantle the slopes of the city's three reservoirs. Officials allow hiking, horseback riding, picnicking, and non-motorized boating. Baltimore's six-phase water treatment system contributes to this human contact. The forests here provide a suitable setting for recreation and act as a buffer against future development.

THE FUTURE OF COMMUNITY FORESTS

Some community forests will continue to serve as sources of commodities. On Zurich's Sihlwald, timber cuts are still made, enough to provide the town with $80,000 a year. The people of Zurich still visit the forest to hike, picnic, and observe wildlife. This multiple-use management will most likely continue far into the future.

In Newington, the community forest has been listed with the National Register of Historic Places. The town's 833 residents intend to buy back the land from the air force and reforest the original 112 acres that served their town so well in the past. When the trees come of age, the town members will resume the forest management practices carried out by their ancestors.

The Zurich and Newington community forests are exceptions rather than the rule. It seems clear that few municipalities will utilize community

forests for commodities and revenue. But as development continues un-
abated, Americans are turning more and more to the outdoors for a re-
prieve from the pollution, noise, and tension of urban areas. Community
forests provide an ideal opportunity for cities and towns to incorporate
forest recreation, watershed protection, and peace of mind into the everyday lives of community residents.

29

Shading Your Home

Gary Moll

PLANTING TREES AROUND your house can lower your energy use, save dollars for your home budget, create a more pleasant home and yard—and make a small contribution to the global problem of air pollution and the greenhouse effect. It's hard to go wrong planting a tree, so we encourage you to plant at least one and encourage your friends and neighbors to do the same. A large tree supplies more shade and uses more CO_2 than a young one. So it's wise to take advantage of existing trees by maintaining them in a state of good health.

The following is my best, brief information on how to select a good tree and plant it in the right place.

WHERE TO PLANT

The central idea is to plant a tree where it will shade your home as it grows or where it can block the wind or control air flow patterns around the house. Any tree that shades a building or concrete will contribute to reducing heat around the house, but more thoughtful plantings have a bigger effect. Knowledge of local climate conditions, combined with your ability to control the growth habits of trees and shrubs, offers a wealth of opportunities that go far beyond the simple shading and blocking of the wind.

Start with a sketch of your house and yard. The location of trees in relation to the house and sun are important, so determine which way is north and place a directional arrow on the sketch. Plantings on the southeast or southwest offer the best shading in most locations; however, the best planting spot will vary depending on your geographic location.

Trees planted on the south side of the house should grow tall enough to shade the roof. Summer sun is at a high angle and heats the roof much more than the south wall of the house. If you live in the South, south side plantings can be thick and effective at shading all year round. If you live in the North, leave the southern exposure more open so the sun will help warm your house in the winter. In the North, also be sure to use deciduous trees.

If you live in a warm climate, maximize the shade by planting at least three trees on the south, southeast, and southwest sides of the house. The more you shade the better. Studies show that cooling costs in some of the warmer areas can be reduced by as much as 50 percent by planting and using vegetation. You can maximize summer shade without having to worry about any detrimental effects of shade in the winter.

Since sun angles are high in the summer, shading on the east and west walls of the house are perhaps even more important than trees on the south side. Trees supply a major benefit when they grow over the roof and shade it. Shading an outside air-conditioning unit can also improve energy consumption. Shrub planting can be added to the planting scheme to help shade walls and windows. Shrubs then can be pruned seasonally to shade windows in the summer and open them to the sun in the winter.

For protection from winter winds, plant a row or group of trees in the pathway of prevailing winds. They'll grow together as they mature, and as the branches start to interlock, the effectiveness of the planting improves. If you don't know prevailing wind direction, the northwest side of the house is a good bet. (Information on prevailing winds can be obtained from the National Climatic Data Center at the Federal Building, Asheville, N.C. 28801. 704–259–0682.)

Trees are effective windbreaks for a distance of about four times their height. If your trees will grow thirty feet tall, they will eventually block the wind for a house 120 feet away. Trees will block the wind from more directions if planted closer to the house. For best results, we suggest windbreaks be planted fifty feet from the east or west sides of the house and even closer on the north side.

If you live in the South where hot temperatures lead to using air-conditioning almost all year round, wind breaks that will stop breezes from striking walls are a very energy-efficient planting. This is a surprise to most people because we usually associate air movement with cooling. However, when very warm air moves past the walls, it takes the coolness from the building. Blocking the wind in these conditions saves energy use.

The opportunities to modify air movement through vegetation offer a skilled gardener even greater energy savings. Experiments in Pennsylvania by researcher Gordon Heisler showed yearly energy savings as high as 75 percent when trees and shrubs were used to control wind as well as to shade houses. The key is use of shrubs, which grow fast enough to accommodate seasonal trimming. When the temperatures are moderate, prune the shrubs back and allow the wind to move to the house. Leave them untrimmed to block the wind when it is very hot. The greatest savings come when cool breezes can be funneled to the house by the tree-shrub combination, extending the periods when no air-conditioning is needed. (See Figure 29.1.)

WHAT TO PLANT

The tree you select will need to grow tall enough to shade the roof of your house, so some of the smaller species will not be good choices. Broad spreading, deciduous trees are usually the best choice for shading, while pines, spruces, and other evergreen are best for windbreaks. You will want to select trees that have a desirable growth pattern and will live a long life on the site you select.

What trees are best for your site? Before that question can be answered, information is needed on site conditions. Is the soil sandy or is it clay? Is it wet, dry, or lightly moist? Go out to the planting area with a shovel and

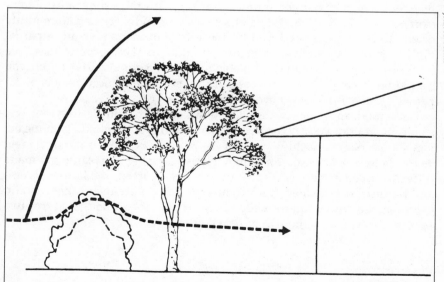

John H. Parker

FIGURE 29.1.   *Seasonal prunings allow breezes in during mild periods, but block them during periods of air-conditioning.*

answer questions about the soil before you visit a nursery or garden center. Checking both before and after a rainfall is helpful.

We can give only general advice about which trees to plant since the local conditions are one of the most important considerations in plant selection. Our advice is to look for a tree that will benefit your yard over a long period of time and supply other values along with shading and diminishing air pollution. It is tempting to plant a fast-growing tree because that will supply shade sooner. But fast-growing trees usually need more mainte- nance than slower-growing species, and they also live shorter lives. Fast- growing trees also often have brittle wood and fragile branches that litter the lawn whenever the weather gets a little rough.

Surprisingly, native trees are not always the best either. Once land has been converted from farms and forest into residential communities, they are usually no longer in their natural state. The trees that used to grow on or near the site may no longer be suitable to the soils remaining and the new conditions of heat or water availability. Generally, trees that can toler- ate soils with minimum air space (species used to growing in swamps) and those that can handle dry conditions are often the best choice for urban areas.

Because many species of trees fit this description and, once planted, you will need to live with the tree for a long time, it is wise to do a careful check on the best varieties for your location. Ask a local expert about recom- mended trees for your community, starting with the Cooperative Exten- sion Service, the State Foresters office (see Appendix H), or a community or city forester. Lists produced by these organizations give an impartial evaluation of trees and won't be influenced by market opportunities. The local nurseryperson will also be able to give some good advice, but you should be aware that, in some cases, their recommendations may be sym- pathetic to the stock they have on hand.

The American Forestry Association suggests you buy a tree that will shade the roof of your house within seven years of planting. That means you should plant a healthy tree that has been grown in the nursery a few years—a tree that has some size to it, but is not so big that planting is made difficult. If you are going to pick up the tree yourself, the largest balled- and-burlapped specimen we recommend is 2- to 2½-inch caliper (six to eight feet tall with a full-formed crown). That is about the largest tree two people can handle without very heavy lifting.

PLANTING

Here is a simple, ten-step list of planting instructions.

1. Locate a site that will provide adequate space for the tree at maturity and ample sunlight and drainage throughout its life. Check for over-

head and underground utility lines, and avoid conflict—present and future—with them. The choice of steps 2 or 3 depends on the quality of soil on the site.

2. If the soil is good (high in organic matter and porous), dig the planting hole at least as wide and deep as the roots themselves. Roots should not be forced into a limited space or be allowed to wrap around themselves.

3. If the soil is poor, get out a rototiller or use a shovel to work organic materials such as peat moss and topsoil into the soil in a large circle around the tree—the larger the better.

4. Remove the tree from the container and place it in the hole so that the root collar (the point at which the tree's main stem meets the root) is at ground level, not below or above.

5. If the plant is bare-rooted and the roots appear tangled, gently separate them and spread them in the planting hole.

6. Tamp the soil into place around the tree.

7. Place mulch around the base of the tree. The mulch area should extend at least as far as the longest branches of the seedling, further if possible.

8. Water the new tree.

For follow-up care, we recommend that you:

9. Water the planting once per week and more frequently during severe dry periods.

10. Check your tree for signs of insect, disease, or animal damage. Protect it as needed.

That's it! With one or more trees in place, you can take on the role of watching them grow, measuring your savings, and taking a quiet pride in your own special contribution not only to your yard, but to the global environment.

30

Creating a Backyard Orchard

Gene W. Grey

THE IDEA OF planting fruit and nut trees as a part of the home landscape is not new. There are many of us, even some with urban backgrounds, who can remember backyard fruit trees. There may even be those among us who can remember the taste of someone else's apples or pears that just happened to be within reach from an alley fence. If the thought of crisp apples, juicy pears, or crunchy nutmeats fresh from your own tree appeals to you, please read on. There are some things you should consider before and after you plant your trees.

BEFORE YOU PLANT

Backyard fruit and nut trees can do more than just bear fruit and nuts. They can serve your landscape as well. Fruit trees come in several forms, sizes, leaf colors, textures, and other landscape qualities. Thus, you can choose one that not only produces fruit but also screens, complements, contrasts, or does something else positive. An excellent use of fruit trees in the landscape is for borders—those plantings that separate one use area from another in your lawn. Dwarf apple, peach, or cherry trees, rather than crabapples, could be planted in a border. Generally, it is better to have groupings (depending on the space) rather than single trees. If border space is extremely narrow, an apple or pear "fence" might be developed by training branches to grow along wires (espalier). More about this tactic later.

You've got to give them enough space. For best tree growth and fruit production, full sunlight is needed. Choose a tree that will fit your space, rather than attempting to make it conform by severe pruning. Fortunately, fruit trees come in three sizes to make this chore easier for you—standard, semidwarf, and dwarf. Dwarf and semidwarf trees, by the way, have standard-size fruit. Dwarf trees are produced by grafting or budding a desired fruit variety onto a dwarfing rootstock. Several rootstocks are available for dwarfing apples. Named after the East Malling Research Station in Kent, England (for you Trivial Pursuit buffs), these are given the prefix EM, and include EM IX, EM 26, and EM VII.

Since each rootstock will produce a different size tree and since you want your tree to fit its space, you should know which rootstock is on the variety you are buying. This may take a bit of doing. If your retailer does not know, ask him or her to check with the supplier. For other kinds of fruits, the variety of rootstocks is not as great. Hence, you won't have as many size choices in peaches, plums, or cherries.

Semidwarf trees are simply smaller strains of standard fruit trees. Mainly apple varieties, they are usually about 80 to 90 percent as large as standard trees.

Nut trees vary greatly in size and species. Pecan, hickories, and black walnut grow ultimately into large specimens and thus must be considered as major shade trees on your lawn. Almonds and English walnut trees are smaller.

What will grow in your area? Now that you have thought about landscaping with fruit and nut trees and considered the space that you have, it is time to look for species and varieties that will grow best in your yard. Obviously, you should eliminate those that have no chance. If, for example, peaches or English walnuts invariably freeze back in the winter and do not bloom in your area, don't fight it. Plant another species that will produce. I will not attempt here to list varieties for all parts of the country, but I will recommend, urge, admonish (order, if I could) you to seek the advice of local experts. Go to a local nursery, orchard, or your county extension office. I doubt there is a county extension office in the nation that does not have a brochure on recommended fruit varieties.

Fruit and nut trees can have many maladies, but don't let that discourage you from planting them in your yard. It is simply a warning that you may have to deal with some problems. The varieties in the brochure that you pick up from your county extension office will be recommended because they are adapted to your climate and also because they may be less susceptible to insects or disease. That doesn't mean, however, that there won't be some bug or blight at some time during the tree's life. So pick up

Children often have a special knack for discovering and enjoying the finer things in life.

another brochure about insects and diseases so that you will know what to do about them. Also, birds and squirrels love fruit and nuts and have an uncanny ability to sense when things are ripe; they are sure to begin harvesting before you do. Depending on your definition of a fair share, it isn't all bad to let them have some.

Some kinds of fruit and nut trees take two to tango. For example, apricots, sour cherries, nectarines, and peaches can self-pollinate, meaning that one tree will produce fruit. Some apples and European plums will pollinate flowers on the same tree but generally have heavier fruit crops when two or more varieties are planted together. Sweet cherries, pears, and Japanese plums are self-sterile and must have two varieties for pollination. Again, check with your local authority. Your extension brochure will probably discuss this.

Don't forget the roots. Fruit and nut trees grow best in soils that have good surface and internal drainage. Roots of fruit trees require oxygen, and wet soils exclude oxygen. Yards are often difficult planting sites because of soil compaction and other disturbances that occurred during home construction. Surface drainage can often be improved by elevating the planting bed with railroad ties, rocks, or other retaining-wall materials. Internal drainage can be helped by replacing poor soil with better soil or incorporating sand, compost, or other organic matter. It is also a good idea to incorporate some nitrogen fertilizer to speed decomposition of the organic matter. Your fruit tree roots will like this too.

AFTER YOU PLANT

1. Check the root graft. Make sure that the lower part of the graft union of each dwarf tree is above the ground. Keep the soil from building up in this area as you cultivate around the tree. Otherwise, roots may grow from above the graft and eliminate the dwarfing effect.

2. Stake dwarf apple trees. Apple trees on certain rootstocks do not have large enough root systems to hold them upright when heavy with fruit. Such trees need to be supported by staking and tying. Be sure to locate stakes in order to avoid rubbing, and pad wires to prevent their cutting into the trunk.

3. Cultivate. Keep the area immediately around the trunk free of grass and weeds. This simple practice takes only about five minutes per tree per year and pays a higher proportionate dividend than anything else you can do for your tree. It promotes growth and vigor, and eliminates the necessity of running your lawnmower close enough to bump the tree. Lawnmower blight is an all-too-common disease, causing bruised and broken bark and subsequent entry of insects and decay.

4. Fertilize. Fruit and nut trees require generally the same nutrients as

does your lawn grass. Hence, in most cases they get at least minimum amounts of required nutrients as a result of lawn fertilization. However, if you want to pamper them, give them a bit extra by simply broadcasting lawn fertilizer on the cultivated area around the trunks of small trees or by putting it in holes beneath the crowns of larger trees. Use about a pound of active ingredient per inch of trunk diameter per year. I realize that these recommendations are quite general, and there are situations in which more precision is required. In those cases, get a soil test and consult a local expert.

5. Prune. Landscape fruit trees need to be pruned to help them produce more fruit and to better serve their landscape purposes. You should do a little pruning each year, starting at planting time. Fruit trees have natural growth forms, and pruning to enhance the natural form allows stronger, better-bearing trees. Generally, apples, pears, and sweet cherries are upright growers, while peaches, plums, apricots, and sour cherries are spreaders. Thus, apples, pears, and sweet cherries are often pruned to favor a main upright leader, while peaches, plums, apricots, and sour cherries are pruned into a modified leader or spreading form.

Pruning to establish the basic framework of a tree is called training and is done during the early years of the tree's life. Training begins at the time of planting. Your new tree will probably be a "whip" or unbranched tree about four or five feet tall. Cut it off about thirty inches above the ground. You won't need to do much the rest of the year except clip back any abnormal growth. Most pruning from now on should be done during the dormant season—late winter or early spring is usually best.

Second-year pruning involves selection of the leader and initial scaffold (structural) branches. Scaffold branches should be about six to ten inches apart vertically. They will be the tree's main framework, on which will be produced secondary branches, so they should be trained to grow outward. Years two through four are best for this growth. You can use spreader sticks (small pieces of wood with nails in each end) to hold the branches until they grow strong enough to hold their positions.

Third-, fourth-, and fifth-year pruning, in addition to outward training, should be aimed at maintaining symmetry and balance between parts of the tree. Thin the upper branches a bit to avoid heavy shading of lower branches. Don't cut off the spurs, as these are the short branches upon which fruit is produced.

If you have limited space or want to do it just for the fun, consider espalier—training trees to grow in a flat profile. Stretch some heavy-gauge wire between posts set about twelve feet apart. Plant an unbranched young seedling (an apple or pear is best) midway between the posts. Cut the seedling off just above a bud a bit taller than the first wire. This bud will be the leader to grow up to the second wire, and the first buds beneath it will become the lateral branches to be trained onto the wire. During the first year, do not allow any other shoots to develop, and force all growth into the terminal and the two lateral branches. This process can be performed on the second, third, and additional wires if desired. Lateral branches should be tied to the wires with willow or plastic ties or other material that will not damage the bark. As the lateral branches grow, be sure to prune back side branches, but do not cut fruit-bearing spurs.

Dwarf trees often bear fruit in the second or third season after planting (standard-size trees take a bit longer). At this point, all you have to do is enjoy them—and perhaps share with neighborhood birds, squirrels, and small children.

31

Living Fences

Deborah B. Hill

WHY BUY CHAIN link or stone for a fence when the possibilities for growing your own fence are limited only by your imagination? From simple fences like a privet hedge to evergreen walls of native pine or exotic Leyland cypress that reach forty to sixty feet into the sky, living fences can enclose your yard, filter a less-than-desirable view, or just complement the architecture of your home.

In rural Kentucky where I live and work, farmers have traditionally established living fences as boundary markers along roadways. Common species incorporated in such subtle barriers are osage orange and black locust—used because their thorns would turn anyone away, especially after a few scrapes with the trees—and hackberry and multiflora rose, because no one would want to get tangled up in their denseness.

These same trees can be used in your backyard for the same or additional purposes. Dense trees and shrubs, for example, not only discourage access when situated on a boundary line, but also can be used to divert foot or vehicle traffic away from certain areas in your yard. They will function as a visual or noise screen and can attract wildlife as well. A row of evergreen trees on the windward side of your home can reduce heating bills in winter and shade you in summer. Although it may take longer to establish a living fence than it does a stone or wooden one, once it's done, living fences require less time and expense in care and maintenance and may never need to be replaced.

Planning ahead is in order, however. First, as with any other project, you should determine your objectives. What exactly is it that you want a living fence to do in your yard? Do you want a tall screen between you and your neighbor, or would a short hedge be more appropriate? If you want a boundary fence to act as a noise buffer, a windbreak, or a wildlife haven, select species that will help you attain these benefits.

Perhaps you want to block your view of a neighbor's shed and his view of your patio. A living fence could solve the problem more aesthetically and tactfully than a stockade fence, will require less maintenance (plants don't need repainting), and will not require a building permit as standard fences do in many communities.

On the other hand, maybe you'd rather not put any walls between you and your neighbors but can think of some ways that living fences could be used within your yard to add dimension and beauty. The combination of a standard fence with a living one—called a *fedge* for fence and hedge— makes an attractive setting for the home landscape. A fedge could be a wooden fence onto which climbing vine has been trained to twine or a hedge growing over a stone wall. Rose-covered fences and trellises are typical fedges.

PREPARATION, PLANTING, AND PRUNING

Once you've decided on objectives for growing a fence or two in your yard, you must determine your climatic zone and what plant materials are best to use in that zone for the purposes you have in mind. Work with a reputable nursery to obtain your planting stock, and make sure it is appropriate for your needs. If you want a small hedge to set off your garden, look into dwarf species or low-growing shrubs rather than tree species. If you want a fence that will provide screening, ask the nursery about fast-growing columnar trees.

Commercial nurseries offer a great variety of species and sizes, but if cost is an important consideration, many broad-leaved and coniferous seedlings are available for nominal cost from state nurseries. When planting such small plants, however, you must think about the size the plant will be when full grown and be willing to wait for your fence to grow to that size.

Planning ahead for the expected final heights and widths of any size stock is essential. For example, if you want a hedge that will ultimately be only three feet high, then you need only a three-foot planting strip; but if the final height will be twenty feet, you may need as much as fifteen feet in planting-strip width. For windbreaks and screens, plant trees separately— rather than together in a strip—in a pattern of predetermined spacing (e.g., 2 × 4, 4 × 8, 6 × 12) between trees within a row as well as between rows.

For hedges and certain other kinds of living fences, dig a trench about ten inches deep and a foot wide, and place the plants about one and a half to three feet apart. Choice of spacing depends on how fast you want an effective barrier. Closer spacing gives more rapid results, but wider spacing may make a healthier barrier in the long run.

It is best to have the ground or planting strip prepared—cultivated and fertilized—before the planting stock arrives. Make sure the stock is dormant (not budding) when planted. Plants transplant better when dormant because they can put all their energy into adapting to a new environment instead of putting on new growth immediately. Most deciduous varieties can be planted in either spring or fall in the temperate zone (even in winter in the deep South); conifers other than arborvitae, yew, Austrian pine, mugo pine, or white pine should be planted only in the spring.

Keep the roots damp before planting, and, if possible, plant on a cool, overcast, or misty day. If you can't avoid planting on a hot or sunny day, try to do the job in early morning, late afternoon, or evening to minimize the extra work a just-planted plant will have to do under hot, dry conditions.

When planting balled-and-burlapped stock, make sure the hole is as deep as the ball is high and one and a half times the width of the ball. If the binding material is organic (untreated, undyed) burlap, it can be slit around the base of the tree and left on to rot. If it is plastic or treated burlap, it should be removed.

From hedges to windbreaks, living fences can be used in a variety of ways in your front or back yard—to save money, ensure privacy, and brighten your landscape.

Unless the whole planting area has been worked up and adjusted with fertilizer, lime, or organic material, the backfill around the root ball should be the same material that was removed, without alteration. The soil should be tamped firmly down around the ball and, if possible, the base of the tree left in a slight well so water can accumulate around the tree.

If the planting stock is bare-rooted, trim roots to fit the opening intended for them, and loosen the roots so that they can occupy the space available. If you are filling a trench in a planting strip, pack soil firmly in stages so that the bases of the roots are not caught in an air pocket.

Once in the ground, all new plantings should be watered thoroughly and, if possible, mulched to about two inches depth with some well-rotted organic material—sawdust, leafmold, compost, or manure. Mulches serve a dual purpose of retaining moisture in the soil and providing some extra nutrients for the plants as the mulch decomposes. Sprinkling the foliage of these young plants with water during their first year of growth (in early morning or after sunset) will also keep them healthier and more resistant to drought.

Even though living fences do not have to be painted or maintained in the same way as standard fences do, they need some special care. As soon as deciduous plants are in the ground, as much as one-third of their branches should be pruned back to discourage sprouting. Hedges that are up to three feet tall when planted, for example, can be cut back to less than a foot to foster low branching.

Once the hedge begins to attain the desired height, maintain it with regular (at least annual) cutting. For this purpose you can use hand pruners (either anvil or scissor-type), two-handled lopping shears, two-handled hedge shears, or a variety of electric or gasoline-powered shearing devices. Pines should be pruned only when they have just completed branch and needle elongation that has not yet hardened into woody tissue. Trimming of both broad-leaved species and conifers other than pines can be done during the growing season, like cutting the grass. Major pruning (branch removal, etc.) should wait until the dormant season, preferably fall or winter.

LIVING FENCES: OLD AND NEW

The idea of growing a fence is not new. Shelterbelts planted during the 1930s dust bowl helped combat soil erosion on the great plains. As boundary markers, hedges were first introduced in Great Britain with the Land Enclosure Acts of the eighteenth and nineteenth centuries. Hawthorn and hazelnut were species of choice because of their naturally dense growth and, in the case of hawthorn, its thorns.

Today's China's "four-around" policy (around houses, fields, factories, and along roads and railroads) has established rows of trees and shrubs in locations not required for crop production. In the Dominican Republic, trees are planted along diversion ditches in sloping cultivated fields and along land borders to define boundaries and alleviate erosion. In Africa, cut poles are placed in the ground—sometimes outside a wooden fence— and allowed to root and sprout. When the sprouts grow big enough, they are in turn cut and placed as additional poles between existing ones. This process is repeated until a palisade of living trees is formed; then the original fence is removed.

Living fences do take time and some effort, but the results are worth it. Once you've set your objectives, selected your planting stock, prepared the site, planted the fence, watered and mulched it, and set up a pruning schedule, you can sit back and watch your fence grow. Each year the trees or shrubs will reach a little closer to your goal, weaving their branches together and stretching closer to the sun. Before you know it, that ugly shed next door will be invisible, and your neighbor will have to resort to cleaning out his gutters if he wants to gaze onto your patio.

PART SEVEN
CITIZEN ACTION AND EDUCATION

In almost every city with an outstanding urban forestry program, powerful citizen action is an essential element. For the long term, citizens need to be committed to their trees, using the strength that comes from personal investment to plan, plant, and maintain them. That is the only assurance that city forests will thrive. Education about trees, on all levels, both formal and informal, also needs creative attention in a strong forestry program. This section describes action ideas that are working in cities both large and small.

32

Citizens with a Vision

Nancy A. Dawe

WHEN PILGRIMS JOHN and Priscilla Alden of Mayflower fame moved a few miles north from Plymouth in 1627 to settle the seaside town of Duxbury, Massachusetts, they found emerald-green salt marshes that shimmered to wheat in autumn and an upland clothed in maples, pine, and oak. Through the generations, Duxbury evolved from a sleepy farming community to one of the nation's busiest shipbuilding ports. By the early 1800s, its 600–700 barques and brigantines were seen on every ocean—but the cost was a Duxbury landscape stripped clean of its trees.

That wealthy heyday ended with the advent of the larger clipper ships, the Civil War, and railroads. From the late 1800s until after World War II, Duxbury existed on farming, fishing, and the summer visitors it drew to its shores. And through those years, its forests regenerated.

The next major threat to the town's trees came in the mid-1960s, with the opening of a major expressway that joined Boston, thirty-five miles to the north, and Cape Cod. It put Duxbury within easy commuting distance of the city, subjecting it to heightened development. That fact galvanized Dr. Lansing Bennett, a local physician and chairman of the Conservation Commission, into action.

Under Bennett's guidance, the idea for a greenbelt built around Duxbury's wetlands and eastern and western forests was devised, and plans were made to acquire as much of that property as possible. A slide presentation was created and shown during a year he spent talking "to anybody who would listen." At the 1970 Town Meeting, "with not a nay in the place," Bennett got the town's commitment to conservation, $800,000 for land acquisition (to which more funds were later added), and a standing ovation.

The Conservation Commission ultimately bought over 1,800 acres in the twenty-five-square-mile town and was instrumental in passing the first protective wetlands bylaw in Massachusetts.

Bennett was helped in all this work by other commission members, members of town boards, the Duxbury *Clipper* newspaper, and a volunteer group, the Friends of Conservation, founded by Donald L. Connors, a Duxbury citizen and attorney whose specialty is environmental law. Together, they mapped the wetlands and fought wetlands development in court, cleared walking trails and conducted tours in the forests, and educated the town's children through a summer nature study program. It was citizen involvement at its best, and, says Connors, it "preserved for generations a sense of security and identity with the land and the earth."

What Duxbury accomplished twenty years ago is being repeated across this country, from Minnesota to Mobile, from San Francisco to New York City, in programs large and small, with citizens of all ages from every walk of life. What motivates them seems to be a "spiritual sap," a feeling that trees—like cathedrals of the Middle Ages whose soaring spires were "faith flung toward Heaven"—appeal to what is stately and sublime in our nature.

But practical motivations impel the work. In Mobile, Alabama, when hurricane Frederic struck in 1979, it devastated many of the city's ancient trees, from which would ultimately come an action program called Streetscapes. Tree-killing smog in Los Angeles was the original impetus for TreePeople, while the New York Street Tree Consortium was born from the knowledge that city government could no longer fund and maintain all the city's trees. And in Atlanta, the fact that the most heavily forested urban area in the country had a treeless downtown gave birth to Trees Atlanta.

CITIZENS WHO ARE DOERS

Tree programs involving citizen action have various aspects in common. Citizens plant, preserve, prune, and maintain trees; educate the public; advocate for tree issues; and provide technical assistance. But two elements are essential to all such programs: fundraising—through grants, foundations, private and corporate donations—and media attention. You can't get your message across if no one knows about it.

To address this need for communication, many citizen tree programs have newsletters; some have public service announcements on radio and television. Feature articles, editorials, op-ed essays, and letters to the editor appear in many city and town newspapers. Occasionally, there are features in major magazines, and, in the case of Andy Lipkis, founder and director of TreePeople in Los Angeles, an appearance on the Johnny Carson Show, as Lipkis was striving—successfully—to get 1 million seedling trees planted before the 1984 Olympics.

Not all tree programs are of that scale, but all are important. In April 1987, Jonathan Steigler, coordinator of Forestry and Environmental Services for Robbinsdale, Minnesota, planned a special event for the Arbor Day and Arbor Month celebration. Called "I Helped Plant Sochacki Park," it drew 300 volunteers who planted 5,000 trees on four different Saturdays. The thirty-seven-acre park, largest in Robbinsdale, is dedicated to being a place to watch wildlife in the marshes and walk among nature prairie grasses and wildflowers. "I wanted to introduce people to the park and involve as many kids as possible," says Steigler. "It gives them 'roots' when they return to check on 'their trees.' "

James Nighswonger is a Kansas forester who works closely with citizens in establishing community forestry programs. As an extension specialist in Environmental Forestry, located at Kansas State University, Nighswonger has a statewide vision. "Ninety percent of Kansas towns operate with a volunteer tree board," he says. "They are appointed by the mayor or other appropriate official, approved by the city council, established by ordinance, and staffed by unpaid citizens." Once set up, tree boards conduct tree inventories, define priorities and long-range goals, recommend legislative and policy changes, prepare annual work plans, and see that those plans are carried out. They get assistance in all stages of the program—from development to implementation—from forest experts like Nighswonger.

"These citizens are doers," he says proudly. They are doctors, lawyers, secretaries, young business people, retired persons who have time—and they have totally reforested some towns." Statewide, he points out, 36 percent of the 300 communities that have realistic potential for operating successful urban and community forestry programs have done so.

Elsewhere in the country, citizen action programs reflect the needs and ambiance of individual cities. Mobile, Alabama, was known to airline pilots as "the city under the trees," its magnificent live oaks speaking of its history and charm. Hurricane Frederic was a turning point, a time of insight, when Mobilians realized they now had to recapture that past glory.

Streetscapes, a self-sustaining, nonprofit organization, grew out of the regulatory Mobile Tree Commission and is headed by activist Anne Wright. She, along with her board, works with wit and wisdom, alerting citizens to the needs of the city she loves. Streetscapes' first project of many was to help restore historic Bienville Square in the heart of downtown Mobile. The square was suffering from neglect—its trees victims of urban stress, its once beautiful flowers dead, and its ground covered with litter. That area now has a caretaker, and the city has its first arborist to boot.

Beautiful San Francisco has been made even more attractive by the addition of over 7,000 street trees, thanks to San Francisco's Friends of the Urban Forest. This private, nonprofit group was started by five citizens in response to California's Proposition 13, which included cuts in funds for urban forestry.

Friends of the Urban Forest (FUF) assists any neighborhood group that wishes to plant a minimum of twenty street trees. The group acts as a consultant for the neighborhood's tree-planting project and offers financial, technical, and practical assistance. An interested group participates in the planning and planting process, each individual paying $95 per tree, approximately half of FUF's costs. Each person also agrees to maintain the tree. Says the program manager, Cheryl Kollin, "We celebrate the completion of each tree planting with a potluck lunch, a time for everyone to come together, admire their work, and acknowledge the project organizers and FUF volunteers."

There's lots more to admire about FUF: their guided Tree Tours, where participants discover the relationships between the natural, historical, and cultural character of a neighborhood, while learning about the history and future of San Francisco's urban forests; its classy, award-winning manual "Trees for San Francisco;" and for young people, grades K–12, a newly developed curriculum guide called "City Trees." By using the urban forest as a textbook, teachers provide a fresh approach in a variety of disciplines, using a tree-planting project and then the maturing trees as an ongoing laboratory.

Across the continent, another kind of education is offered, courtesy of the New York City Street Tree Consortium. Like FUF, a fiscal crisis led to its establishment by an ad hoc group in the mid-1970s. The group responded to a New York City parks system that simply didn't have enough staff to regularly care for or even inspect the 600,000 street trees. Moreover, while those trees were dying at a rate of approximately 13,000 a year, the city was replacing only 4,500 a year.

Overseen by its dynamic executive director, Marianne Holden, the consortium offers courses in basic street tree care and pruning techniques. Through illustrated lectures and fieldwork, participants learn how to save trees through soil conditioning and pruning techniques and by identifying various problems affecting trees.

Participants who pass an examination are certified by the city's park department as Citizen Pruners, a corps of more than 1,300 neighborhood volunteers. Said one course instructor, also a forester with the New York State Department of Environmental Conservation, "Citizen awareness is probably the single most important aspect of street tree care. It never ceases to amaze me who shows up to take classes." Said one participant, "It provided me with the means to give a little something back to my hometown."

Actually, a lot is given back, with the Citizen Pruners not only tackling tree maintenance but also underscoring a spirit of unselfish involvement and civic responsibility.

This is symbolized in Sam Bishop, a resident of Stuyvesant Town, who after completing the course conducted on his own a comprehensive survey of his neighborhood. He found more than 150 trees either missing, dead, or in need of replacement. Copies of his detailed report were presented to the Manhattan parks commissioner and numerous civic and neighborhood groups. The local newspapers chronicled Bishop's efforts, and not only did the parks department replace many trees; its officials lauded Bishop, whose survey became a model for other Manhattan neighborhoods.

There's something wonderfully human in all this, its roots going back to colonial times. When a thoughtful William Penn conceived his original plan for Philadelphia in 1681, it was for a "Green Countrie Towne," with "care to be taken to leave one acre of trees for every five acres cleared." That plan fell by the wayside as the years progressed, but today, thanks to the Pennsylvania Horticultural Society's "Philadelphia Green"—an outreach horticultural program begun in 1978—the city boasts the most concentrated community greening movement in America.

Philadelphia Green works with organized blocks in the city's low and moderate-income neighborhoods to plan and implement greening projects. "Ours is a comprehensive program," says the society's Patricia Schreiber. "We plant window boxes, street containers, vegetable and flower gardens, and have installed approximately 2,000 trees in the last ten years." Funding is provided by grants, the city's Office of Housing and Community Development, and the society's Philadelphia Flower Show.

The effect of Philadelphia Green was eloquently expressed in a society publication by Willie Mae Bullock, who, with her neighbors, wanted to fight urban decay in their North Philadelphia neighborhood. "We started by planting window boxes and tire urns with flowers," she said. "Then we planted our first vegetable garden on a vacant lot and called it 'Hope Springs.' Later we developed our wild garden. Next came twenty Callery pear trees on our street, and then we tackled a corner lot that was an eyesore—that became an herb and vegetable garden. Finally, five years later, we transformed the last vacant lot into our pride and joy, the sitting garden. We also named it 'Hope Springs.' I'm proud to say that now, in our whole community, hope springs."

If beautification is integral to any urban forestry program, so too is advocacy. And no one is better at it than Trees Atlanta's executive director,

Marcia Bansley. For the last two years, while planting willow oaks and Bradford pears along busy Atlanta thoroughfares, she's also acted as advocate for tree-related issues citywide. In 1987, she was able to get the Georgia Department of Transportation (DOT) to change a longstanding guideline that was ruling out many downtown trees.

"It said that no tree could be planted within thirty feet of a state route, but this was based on high-speed roads," she says. "We felt it was being applied incorrectly to downtown streets, prohibiting developers from planting near rights-of-way." Bansley, who has a law degree, gathered relevant people, data, and facts and went to see the DOT commissioner. He agreed to lift the restriction.

Imagination, too, is a component of citizen action, exemplified in Andy Lipkis of TreePeople in Los Angeles. "My strength has been as a trailblazer—to see a problem, hear other people say it can't be solved, and find a way to do it," he says.

That trailblazing literally began on the trail. "I grew up in Los Angeles and in the summer escaped the smog at a camp in the mountains 100 miles away." When he was fifteen, a counselor predicted that in twenty-five years most of the trees on the mountains would be dead from smog, so Lipkis and several friends got permission to plant trees on campgrounds. From that seed, TreePeople grew and is now an eleven-year-old nonprofit organization with a full-time staff of ten, plus four part-timers.

Although the campaign for a million trees was one of its biggest and most difficult tasks, TreePeople is still rising to challenges. One of its latest projects has been raising and shipping seedlings to fire-ravaged lands in Northern California in cooperation with the Forest Service. In 1986, TreePeople airlifted 5,000 fruit trees and planted them in African villages hit by food shortages.

Education is important to TreePeople too. About 150,000 children have attended assemblies on trees and have been given saplings by TreePeople. It also maintains a federally owned ten-acre park, "visited by a lot of kids from the inner city that never knew there were woods in Los Angeles," says Lipkis. "Many kids come back with their parents, and it opens up new worlds of possibilities. The deer, the trees . . . it's such a contrast from the concrete."

Lipkis is visionary about citizen action. "If we invite people to share their dreams of what a city can be, if we give them the tools, teach them the process, they can cross the bridge from dreams to reality. We're at the dawn of a new era . . . people want to get involved, and the tree is a meeting ground where everyone can gather."

What would those Mayflower visionaries—John and Priscilla Alden—think if they came back today? They might be surprised to learn that their direct descendants now number in the millions, and that they include poet

Henry Wadsworth Longfellow ("Under the spreading chestnut tree . . ."). They would be pleased to know that their modern pioneering counterparts—those who seek to better society—are busy planting, preserving, pruning, and maintaining trees. They would be happy to discover that Duxbury is still a jewel by a shining sea—with forests much like those they trod.

33

Kids and Trees for a Cleaner Chesapeake

Robert L. Rose

TWENTY-FOUR SCHOOL CHILDREN—costumed as trees, with dark brown trunks and huge green leaves, or dressed as pink-and-yellow flowers—sang and danced under a blue sky and bright sun, celebrating the joys of nature, or rather of nature returned. Some 1,200 schoolmates, watching the show on a grassy field alongside a slow-running Baltimore stream, joined in the celebration, applauding, screaming, and shouting. A five-piece band belted out jazzy tunes as background for the ceremonies.

The mayor was there plus a man from the governor's office, plus an assortment of other city, state, and school officials. But it was the kids' day, a landmark day for urban forests, for starting to turn a tiny piece of Chesapeake shoreline back to the way it looked almost 400 years ago.

In those discovery days, English explorer John Smith wrote enthusiastically that "Heaven and earth never agreed better to frame a place for man's habitation" than the Chesapeake Bay. Thousands of settlers yet to come couldn't have agreed more.

By the time of the Revolutionary War in 1776, a quarter-million immigrants, mostly farmers, had come to Maryland, stripping forests and planting wheat, corn, and flax along the bay and its tributaries—including Herring Run, the scene of the children's day celebration in Baltimore on May 12, 1988.

Today, metropolitan Baltimore has grown to 2.3 million residents. Herring Run is surrounded by apartment complexes, private homes, industry, and shopping malls. City officials established the 500-acre Herring Run park, along with other city parks, when the post–World War II building boom began.

Though the park was saved from development, nothing much else was done, except for putting in some paved bike and hiking paths. "Basically, what we had was nothing more than an old farm," says James H. Himel, environmental liaison from the Baltimore mayor's office. "The city maintained the site just by a little mowing."

All that took a change for the better in December 1987, when Governor William Donald Schaefer announced a Green Shores program to encourage Maryland communities to help save the endangered Chesapeake Bay by planting trees along watercourses throughout the state. The forest buffers, in addition to enhancing a stream's beauty, reduce pollution and sedimentation by filtering soil and reducing runoff of harmful phosphorus and nitrogen.

Baltimore quickly took up the challenge from its former mayor, leading the way in a project that not only has local and statewide implications but sets a nationwide model as well.

It turned out to be a race for time.

"The city wanted to do something this year," Himel explained. Almost as a coincidence, people from the mayor's office, the Baltimore City Forestry Board, the Maryland Department of Natural Resources, and the American Forestry Association (AFA) began talking up the idea, and all got together in January to make plans.

"We decided we should fast-track everything we could. But we had only three months to plan the project and get it in the ground. We had to hit that one-month planting window before May 1," Himel said. "It worked, quite frankly, only because of the dedication of the people working on the project, working together with just one goal." That plus the all-important help of the school kids after the aid of the city schools had been enlisted.

The AFA's job, as assigned to the marketing vice president, Richard J. Crouse, was to supply staff help in planning, fundraising, and other chores. The AFA also pitched in with an up-front loan fund to get the project under way.

With the pilot Green Shores program officially under way, the Herring Run site was picked—a long, narrow strip of park land with widths of 150 to 400 feet, extending 1,600 feet along the stream. It was decided that 6,000 trees would be planted on the five-acre site.

Jeff Horan, a bay watershed forester for the Maryland Forest, Park, and Wildlife Service, and Myra Brosius, landscape architect and planner for the city of Baltimore, decided to do something unusual. Instead of choosing trees of one size and one type for the job, they chose eighteen varieties ranging in size from one to fourteen feet, in an effort to restore the looks of the area as it was four centuries ago. The species list includes red maple, ash, tulip poplar, sweetgum, black locust, black willow, baldcypress, Virginia pine, winterberry, silky dogwood, flowering dogwood, red oak, alder, sawtooth oak, loblolly pine, bush honeysuckle, bicolor lespedeza, and crabapple.

Then came the planting. The city usually plants some 1,500 trees a year. So 6,000 was a big order for the forestry staff. To the rescue came more than 500 youngsters, ranging in age from five to seventeen, all dubbed official Baltimore Forest Rangers.

The ranger program, funded through a grant by the Weyerhaeuser Company Foundation, recruits students who have already shown an appreciation for urban green areas and then gets the young Baltimoreans involved in maintaining the city forests. Students are nominated for the program by a parent, teacher, or neighbor. The schools are assisted in finding projects that meet the particular needs of their students, with teachers invited to attend monthly meetings where curriculum and strategies are discussed.

Through classroom instruction, field trips, and a two-week summer program, the Forest Rangers deepen their appreciation of the outdoors and pass along their tree ethics to family and friends.

For the planting, the city also provided its own foresters and some jailhouse inmates who volunteered to help out. "It was quite a scene," Himel said. "You'd see school kids showing prisoners how to plant the trees—under the supervision of the foresters, of course."

Everybody got the job done, and on time.

At the ceremonies, Ralph Jones, director of the Baltimore Department of Recreation and Parks, boasted that Herring Run had become the "first large-scale community response" to Governor Schaefer's Green Shores program. He also praised the hands-on effect of the program on the school children involved. "This is learning by doing, folks," Jones said. "We can draw a tree. We can draw a leaf. But to feel that leaf is of the utmost importance."

David Carroll, the governor's Chesapeake Bay environmental program coordinator, promised that Herring Run would be the starter for fulfilling the state's determination to get the entire bay shoreline planted with trees.

Mayor Kurt L. Schmoke told the school children they had revitalized a park that one day "everyone will enjoy. People will delight in walking through your park, breathing the clean air, and enjoying the shade. Herring Run will be helped because its water will be cleaner and purer." The students themselves will profit by becoming aware of the environment, "seeing the need for helping and acting on that need, setting an example for other students by working with your teachers and each other. I want you to know your city is very proud of you."

Schmoke noted that Herring Run was the largest state-local-private sector tree-planting project in the state and nation in 1988.

"I hope you will one day walk beneath the trees you have planted here and remember the day we gathered to celebrate this new forest," the mayor said.

Schmoke wound up the ceremonies by planting one more tree at the site, aided by the AFA's executive vice president, R. Neil Sampson, and sixth-grader Eugene Foster, 13, one of the Forest Rangers. "You can bring your kids back here," Sampson told the applauding children. "You can have a picnic under a great big tree and tell them 'I planted that tree when I was in school.' "

Freckle-faced Julia Johnson, 14, who introduced Sampson to the crowd, said she really enjoyed taking part in the tree-planting project. "It's something you do for your country, or something like that," the perky eighth-grader said with a grin. "Besides, you don't have to go to school."

There were several postscripts to the event. About two weeks later, more than 50,000 people walked across Baltimore's Chesapeake Bay Bridge in the annual event designed to mark the bay's impact on recreation, tourism, and the seafood industry. This year Governor Schaefer aimed the event at fighting pollution. He helped plant a fifty-tree demonstration project, as a follow-up to Herring Run.

Schaefer then announced that his Green Shores program would be financed by $400,000 in state funds, targeted at planting trees and other vegetation in marsh and tidewater areas to stabilize eroding shorelines. "We face an immense challenge in order to clean up the bay," he said. "Over 95 percent of the land in Maryland drains into the Chesapeake Bay."

In Baltimore, James Himel said the city was so pleased with its pioneering efforts at reforesting a city park that even more will be done next year. Included is a plan to invite businesses to buy trees to reforest their own private lands, with the city and schools helping out in planning and doing the actual work. "Of course, we'll involve the kids again," Himel said. "It should be very exciting."

34

Profiles of
Citizen Action*

Sara Ebenreck

WHILE THE ACTUAL process of planting a tree follows a very similar pattern in almost any part of the country, the process of organizing citizen action groups in support of tree planting usually takes on a flavor that reflects the particular needs of a community and the people involved in the founding of the group and the work it does. The following five profiles of groups from across the nation reflect outstanding approaches to the urban forestry issues they faced.

PLACE: Los Angeles, California
GROUP: TreePeople

Major Action
Planting 1 million trees in the three years prior to the 1984 Olympics in Los Angeles. Now involved in local effort to plant 2 to 5 million trees by 1992 and also a statewide consortium to plant 20 million trees by the year 2000.

Action Steps
TreePeople based its 1-million-tree goal on Los Angeles City Planning Department figures that claimed that 1 million trees, when mature, would

---

* This chapter was compiled with information and assistance from Cheryl Kollin of the San Francisco Friends of the Urban Forest, Kirk M. Brown of the Twin Cities Tree Trust, Marcia D. Bansley of Trees Atlanta, Andy and Kate Lipkis of TreePeople, and the staff of the New York Street Tree Consortium.

be capable of filtering up to 200 tons of particulate smog from the air every day. The figure sounded both solid and inspirational. The city projected it would take twenty years, and TreePeople leaders Andy and Katie Lipkis decided to do it in three.

An advertising group contributed a public relations campaign with theme materials and artwork. The tag line was "Turn Over a New Leaf, L.A.—Help Plant the Urban Forest." A one-liner for posters was "Urban Releaf." The campaign included television spots in which Gregory Peck had agreed to be spokesman. General Telephone provided a video camera crew. A billboard company posted 800 billboards at no charge. TreePeople paid for 400 bus signs. Radio spots from the advertising group used a local radio comedy team; tapes were delivered to over seventy-five radio stations. TreePeople followed up with live announcer scripts written by their own staff.

Print ads were run by companies who helped sponsor the campaign; the ads highlighted the campaign but also included note of the individual company efforts. A brochure, "Help Plant an Idea," explained the campaign. A bumper sticker, "I Brake for Trees," was given to all members of TreePeople. Selling the bumperstickers underwrote their cost.

TreePeople learned to get a fresh twist into every media event. One local television station got involved in providing regular updates on the campaign and a "tree-mometer" to measure progress toward the 1-million-tree goal.

TreePeople recruited and trained staff and volunteers for a speakers bureau that appeared on television and radio interviews, at Rotary and Garden clubs, or at any other opportunity. A presentation to the Inter-Religious Council of Southern California inspired leaders of other religious groups to get involved. A few congregations organized seedling distributions.

General Telephone's (GTE) vice president joined the TreePeople Board of Directors. He invited GTE people to become "Urban Forest Rangers" who visited elementary schools with seedlings for children and curriculum packets for teachers. Almost 700 people volunteered, and GTE underwrote the entire cost of that program for 70,000 kids. Many schools took on plantings, and children took home trees they'd grown in the classroom. Scouts and other youth groups got involved. A door-to-door effort was tried but was eventually discontinued because it got too labor-intensive.

Underwriting of a major planting effort by Southern California Honda Dealers and an Urban Forest Run sponsored by May Company, Louisiana-Pacific, and other companies brought more attention and achievement.

After three years, four days before the lighting of the Olympic Flame, TreePeople received word that an apricot tree in Canoga Park had just been planted—the one-millionth tree.

Publications and Other Resources
- "A Planters Guide to the Urban Forest"
- "Taking It to the Streets" (public education how-to paper)
- Seven-minute historical video
- Seven-minute citizen forester promotional descriptive video
- Plan for a Global ReLeaf campaign of 2 to 5 million trees

Other Activities
- The 1989 campaign for 2 to 5 million trees by 1992
- An environmental leadership program for 50,000 schoolchildren each year
- Citizen forester training for residents (with workbook)
- An overseas project involving planting 6,000 food trees in fourteen villages in four African countries
- Running an educational center with recycling and composting displays as well as nature trails in Coldwater Canyon Park
- Selling drought- and smog-tolerant seedling stock in a retail nursery
- Ongoing urban and mountain planting and maintenance events

PLACE: San Francisco, California

GROUP: Friends of the Urban Forest (FUF)

Major Action
Assistance to any San Francisco neighborhood group that wishes to plant a minimum of thirty street trees. FUF offers financial, technical, and practical assistance.

Action Steps
An eight-week process involves two community meetings. At first, a slide presentation on tree planting is followed by work to organize the group's tree-planting campaign. FUF recommends tree species. Property owners sign agreements to help plant and maintain trees. Property owners pay $135 per tree, which includes all site preparation and materials.

After the first meeting, FUF contracts for sidewalk cutting and soil augering. It also selects and orders trees and supplies. At the second community meeting, the group goes over details. On the day selected, everyone gathers to plant, led by FUF staff and volunteers.

The remaining maintenance costs are subsidized through the group's Tree Trust (see below).

Publications and Other Resources
- Organizer's handbook, which explains how to get neighborhood groups together to sponsor a project
- "Trees for San Francisco," an award-winning guide to tree selection and planting

- Educational exhibit for fairs and shows
- "City Trees," a K–12 curriculum guide of seventy-five activities to teach students about urban forestry in their community

Other Activities
- Monthly walking tours to explore historical, cultural, and horticultural aspects of city neighborhoods
- Program for school tree plantings with "City Trees" guide
- Tree Trust, a nonprofit program to accept donations from corporations, foundations, private individuals, and members; the trust funds the tree-planting program
- Advocacy of a city tree ordinance
- Technical assistance to share community tree planting model with other cities

PLACE: Minneapolis–St. Paul, Minnesota
GROUP: Twin Cities Tree Trust

Major Action
Urban reforestation and park construction with job employment and training programs for economically disadvantaged and disabled youth and economically disadvantaged adults.

Action Steps
Tree Trust, a nonprofit, organization, was founded by two men who combined the need for urban forestry (Donald C. Willeke) with the employment of disadvantaged youth (G. Rolf Svendsen). Start-up costs came from foundation grants.

The first project combined the reforestation needs of the Metropolitan Waste Control Commission with the need for quality work experiences for youth in the Anoka County Summer Youth Employment and Training Program (SYETP). The program has now expanded to cover five counties and employs over 900 youths each year.

As the program grew, it expanded beyond reforestation to include park construction and landscaping projects. Over 13,000 economically and disabled youth (60 percent disabled in 1988) and 1,600 hard-to-employ adults have been trained. As of 1988, over 27,000 balled-and-burlapped trees and 300,000 whips and seedlings have been planted. In addition, more than 12,000 diseased trees have been removed, and numerous park construction and landscape projects have been completed.

A typical SYETP program involves crews of ten to twelve youths aged fourteen through twenty-one, who work for ten weeks during the summer. The youths are under constant supervision of a Tree Trust crew chief, who works directly with the youth. A Tree Trust site supervisor directs three to four crews and coordinates the projects with the municipalities. Each crew member is paid a minimum wage and receives transportation and lunch. Youth are hired on a first-come basis after they meet the SYETP eligibility requirements (economically disadvantaged and/or disabled). No job skills screening is done prior to employment. Municipalities specify the projects and provide the financing for materials. The Tree Trust program stresses basic job skills: attendance, working with others, and the importance of a job well done. Projects must meet high professional standards.

The Tree Trust has four professional staff members. The forty to fifty additional staff members are college students and teachers hired and trained for the summer.

The Minnesota Youth Program and the Federal Job Training and Partnership Act's SYETP provide the funding for the youths' wages and supervision. Private donations help fund administration, supervision, and other expenses to ensure a successful program.

Publication
• An annual report

Other Activities
• Annual awards ceremony and picnic
• Coordinates/participates in school and neighborhood plantings and Arbor Day activities
• Landscaping, park construction, and park maintenance
• Employment program for hard-to-employ adults

PLACE: New York City, New York
GROUP: New York City Street Tree Consortium

Major Action
Citizens' training program for planting and care of the city's street trees. A corps of trained Citizen Pruners work with city trees.

Action Steps
The stimulus for founding the consortium was the fiscal crisis in New York City in the mid-1970s, which cut funding for street trees. An ad hoc group formed by concerned individuals evolved into the consortium, which now represents a broad variety of environmental, horticultural, landscape, and park groups, both public and private.

The consortium has focused civic attention on the importance and needs of New York's street trees. It produced a one-page fact sheet, "Tree Tips," which listed activities that anyone can do to help trees. The publication was issued in both English and Spanish, and the consortium has distributed over 75,000 copies since 1986. The group also produced a companion illustrated fact sheet called "Tree Tips for Kids" and distributed it widely.

Next, a course on street tree pruning and maintenance was offered to teach tree identifications, recognition and treatment of diseases, understanding of the stresses on urban street trees, the art of basic tree pruning and general maintenance, as well as how to involve a community in these activities. Graduates of the course, called Citizen Pruners, are certified by the Parks Department for their work with trees. Over 1,500 New Yorkers from all five boroughs have graduated from this course.

The course is now given twice a year in all five New York City boroughs. When funds have allowed, the consortium maintains contact with Citizen Pruners by a newsletter; it has also compiled a directory of Citizen Pruners organized by zip code for neighborhood accessibility. Active pruning groups such as the Cobble Hill Tree Association in Brooklyn and the Down-to-Earth Beautifiers in Queens have grown to administer their own planting and adopt-a-tree programs.

To broaden and strengthen the city's stock of street trees, starting in the spring of 1986, the consortium introduced experimental trees—including Amur, English hedge maple, and American hophornbeam—to selected urban sites. The experimental trees were cared for and monitored by Citizen Pruners. The consortium hopes, in this way, to reduce the potential loss threatened when disease strikes a monoculture in the city.

Publications and Other Resources
- "Tree Tips"
- "Tree Tips for Kids"
- "Citizen Pruner Directory"

PLACE: Atlanta, Georgia
GROUP: Trees Atlanta

Major Action
Building a public-private partnership to plant large shade trees along the concrete sidewalks in the barren areas of downtown Atlanta.

Action Steps
Trees Atlanta was formed by Central Atlanta Progress, the Commissioner of Parks, and the Junior League of Atlanta in 1985 to respond to the problem of a downtown barren of green trees—despite the fact that, overall, Atlanta is a heavily forested city.

Executive director Marcia Bansley carefully built a board of directors composed of business, industry, government, and other leaders in the city. The board includes Atlanta's commissioners of Parks and of Public Works, a representative of the Junior League of Atlanta, the executive vice president of a major wood products corporation, senior executives of major companies, including utilities, banks, and newspapers, and directors of the botanical garden and the historic preservation organization.

In support of the tree-planting effort, the wood products company funded an executive director's salary for one year; another company provided a free office.

Planting projects were planned and budgeted in detail before the fundraising was begun. A landscape architect enlisted help from three major Atlanta firms to design planting plans. Tree grates, which allowed the inscribing of donor names into the grate, are used to help fundraising. For a lesser donation, a plaque is attached to a planted tree.

The Trees Atlanta's planting program includes funds for professional planting and maintenance. Over 200 large (four-inch caliper) trees have been planted in downtown Atlanta since 1985. Among other successes is the saving of some 120-year-old trees along Peachtree Street by showing a developer how to build a needed parking lot in a way that let the trees still get enough oxygen and water to survive.

Over 550 people, many of them professionals, have given volunteer help to the programs, and in 1988, the group developed a membership program.

Publication
- A newsletter

Other Activities
- Seminars for developers and builders on preserving trees on construction sites
- Reclamation and transplant of trees that had to be moved in road-widening projects
- Support of tree protection/preservation ordinances in the counties of the metropolitan areas
- Distribution of 35,000-year-old seedling trees grown by the Georgia Forestry Commission
- Pruning of the 100-year-old champion trees in the Atlanta area
- Development of a grove of champion trees in Piedmont Park
- Measurement of tree loss in the metro area for the period 1975–85, the first such study in the region

35

Public Awareness and Urban Forestry in Ohio

Ralph C. Sievert, Jr.

SINCE 1981, OHIO has had the most Tree City USA awards—granted by the National Arbor Day Foundation—in the nation. One reason is a commitment to public awareness of trees. In the past a shade tree commission or municipal forest manager would often concentrate solely on the planting, maintenance, and removal of public trees. Now they recognize that a portion of time must be directed toward forming a positive public image of a community tree program.

The uniting component of public awareness is media coverage. Newspaper, radio, and television exposure all serve to maximize the results of positive action. When these media are used in combination with individual and group meetings, it is possible to target virtually all benefiting taxpayers.

The following are some of the successful public awareness methods in use today in Ohio.

Planting new street trees is the most visible way of demonstrating the benefits of a tree program. Often a city will install new trees without informing the adjoining property owner. Since the early 1950s, Wooster has held neighborhood meetings to let property owners express their tree preferences within the parameters set by the Shade Tree Commission. Residents gather at a neighbor's home to hear a presentation by the Shade Tree Commission on choosing a suitable tree for their street. This not only involves participants in the decision-making process but develops a sense of unity among neighbors about the trees that are planted.

It's a well-known fact that homeowners will care for trees more if they have an investment in them. Findlay uses an adopt-a-tree program to encourage participation in its street tree-planting program. The process begins with the homeowner's filing an application at city hall. The tree commission purchases the tree and approves the planting site. In the spring homeowners can pick up their tree for planting, paying a minimal administrative fee. The combination of a financial investment and a labor investment results in the participant providing extra care for the growing tree.

Community involvement also occurs in Wadsworth. Citizens may request trees on their street by obtaining a petition from the service director. The residents then canvas their block for signatures. A majority of signatures on the petition assures that the area will be considered for planting by the Shade Tree Commission. Because participating residents are assessed according to the frontage of their property, there is a financial commitment as well as a genuine desire for trees.

If such intensive public contacts are not possible, a letter can help. In Dover residents are informed that trees will be planted on their street and are provided a description of the tree species. After the trees are planted, another letter encourages watering and seeks support in the form of contributions or letters to the council.

Often cities find creative ways to encourage tree planting. In Hudson contributions may be made for a memorial tree to be planted on the village square. To celebrate their one-hundredth anniversary, the Sugarcreek Shade Tree Commission used boy scouts to plant a tree at the local high school.

"A Christmas tree for a park" is one way that Delaware obtains trees to plant. In exchange for a tax-deductible donation, a potted evergreen is delivered for use as a Christmas tree. After the holidays, the city plants the trees in their parks for all to enjoy. Residents are pleased to know they have helped beautify their city in this manner.

A cooperative tree-planting project has proven quite successful in Sugarcreek. Using a local club called the Swiss Wheelers, trees that would have been planted by a financial contract were installed by volunteers. This resulted in considerable savings and, in effect, allowed the Shade Tree Commission to plant more trees throughout the town.

It is not uncommon to find a civic or service organization that is willing to take on such a project when they recognize the benefits. The Kiwanis Club in Navarre not only purchases seedlings each year for the town nursery but takes an active role in planting and caring for trees on the streets. Using these dedicated individuals saves the town money and fulfills the club's responsibility for civic service.

Public awareness can even be used to accomplish necessary maintenance. Many towns organize pruning parties to spruce up overgrown
trees. In downtown Delaware merchants joined in to remove lower limbs
that were interfering with pedestrian traffic.

Community services are an integral part of public awareness. Sandusky
takes an additional step by preserving several overgrown American holly
trees in a nursery, thereby providing a source for decorations during the
holiday season. Sugarcreek's Shade Tree Commission updates urban forestry information at the local library for any interested citizens.

The high cost of energy has made wood-burning stoves popular in
Ohio. To aid residents, some cities are providing firewood to interested
citizens. Orrville and Cambridge allow interested citizens to remove fallen
park trees for a nominal fee. This service has proven very popular with
homeowners and saves the city the cost of disposal.

Occasionally, a municipal forestry program will do something totally
unique to develop public support. In Sandusky floral displays are constructed on the square to commemorate community events and organizations. They not only attract attention during the summer but provide an
added benefit at the end of the growing season because residents are
allowed to take cuttings from the displays before they are dismantled. This
provides direct contact with a city service.

Cincinnati started its street tree program in 1978, with excellent results.
This is partially due to the use of two promotion ideas developed by the
city forester. "Mr. Tree" is a fictitious character who promotes city trees
through a unique appeal to both children and adults. He has become
popular at parades, festivals, and at Arbor Day celebrations. The second
promotional device, a column called "Tree of the Week," has been a regular
part of the local newspaper. This informational piece helps increase people's awareness of many native trees and creates an interest in the city's
street tree program.

As a pesticide substitute, ladybugs were released in Toledo to combat
specific tree pests. A quick-thinking city forester expanded this appealing
program into a cooperative effort with local schools. Children, dressed as
ladybugs, took part in a citywide celebration to help select planting sites
for the following year. The resulting success showed the city's sensitivity to
controversial issues and its ability to deal effectively with them.

To demonstrate an ongoing street tree program, Westerville utilized the
bicentennial celebration by involving residents in a contest to choose a
favored tree for the city. The winning species has since been promoted as
an example of community commitment to its tree program. This is supple-
mented with slide shows and public speeches to any interested group in
the city.

School children were involved in the development of Chardon's street
tree brochure. A logo contest was held to obtain a design for the brochure

and for stationery for the Shade Tree Commission. Winners received prizes from local merchants, and the media provided coverage of the event.

Tree planting can even become a matter of pride in one's ancestry. Heritage Park in Lakewood has planted a tree for each nationality in the city. This provides a positive awareness of the cultural differences that exist among neighbors.

With the continual turnover in the population of a city, it's not surprising that many residents are unaware of the laws relating to trees. By consolidating tree policies into a brochure, the city informed residents of these laws. Salem paid for a tree brochure by obtaining contributions from local nurseries and garden centers, thus saving many tax dollars. By adding a list of trees by street to their brochure, Wadsworth created a self-guided tour of city trees.

Probably the best rallying point for a municipal forestry program is Arbor Day. Every spring, Ohio cities and towns use a variety of methods to capitalize on this annual event.

The most successful Arbor Day programs involve school children. In 1956, the Wooster Shade Tree Commission, in cooperation with service groups, began distributing potted dogwood trees to all first-graders. Since then, over 12,000 have been planted throughout the city. It is not uncommon for youngsters to plant new trees next to ones planted by their parents years ago. The program has since been expanded to include fifth-graders too. School officials enjoy the favorable image provided by such programs, but, most importantly, the public views trees as positive and beneficial.

The distribution of seedlings for Arbor Day can be successfully done on a large scale. Operating on a grant from the Cleveland Electric Illuminating Company, the city's Division of Urban Forestry and the city's schools distributed 5,500 trees to the city's fourth-graders in 1986. It is anticipated that vandalism will decrease over time because students will come to value the trees they have actively participated in planting.

In order to recognize those who have made significant contributions to the beauty of Salem through tree planting, the town's Shade Tree Commission presents an annual Arbor Day award. During a ceremony at city hall, a personalized certificate is presented to a worthy recipient. With proper radio and newspaper coverage, such recognition serves to perpetuate an appreciation of trees.

A variety of events are used to celebrate Arbor Day in Dover. Local merchants display Arbor Day messages in their windows during April. A display at the local supermarket helps to demonstrate the accomplishments of the program. New parents can receive a seedling to commemorate the birth of a child. A free tree drawing is held at all home football games.

Lisbon holds an annual essay and poster contest as part of its Arbor Day celebration. The Shade Tree Commission and school officials organize the event, and merchants fund the prizes. Children receive either a potted seedling or a Tree City USA T-shirt, depending on their level of achievement.

When used in conjunction with an Arbor Day program, the Tree City USA award can be the crowning jewel of a municipal forestry public awareness program. This award from the National Arbor Day Foundation recognizes those municipalities that have reached a predetermined level of competency. Official recognition materials and a meaningful ceremony are ready-made for media coverage. It is quite typical for such cities to proudly fly the Tree City USA flag above city hall.

Nine Ohio communities were so recognized in 1980. This figure grew to eighty-six in just six short years. Earning this award gives residents a source of pride and provides shade tree officials with strong grounds for advocating their programs.

There are many other public awareness ideas that can be used. For example, a fun run is an excellent way of turning the jogging craze into a tree-planting event. A calendar, displaying street tree scenes, can be sold as a money-making project. Renting a sugar maple can develop interest in syrup production while supplying added income.

Gary Moll

Arbor Day races are only one way to increase citizens' awareness of park problems and raise funds for park maintenance.

With the economic constraints facing cities today, urban forestry officials need a guaranteed financial commitment from their municipality in order to maintain a beneficial tree program. In Ohio and elsewhere, public awareness has proven to be a valuable tool in the justification of tree activities because it develops a public interest group that helps to lobby for support.

The possibilities for creating public awareness in any town are virtually endless. While public awareness techniques that are successful in one town may not be so elsewhere, they often lead to ones that are. Although political environments vary, none is such as to totally exclude some opportunities. By sharing ideas, municipalities can find comfortable ways to reach residents on this important issue.

36

Test Your Town's Trees

E. Thomas Smiley

DOES YOUR TOWN have healthy trees? If you are like most of us, you probably don't know the answer to that question. I hope this chapter will change all that. On your next walk around the block, take this test with you to check out the health of trees in your neighborhood. In the process, you'll improve your own health!

I will explain how to test trees in a small area of your community and how to use the information you gather to determine if your town's tree health is great, good, fair, poor, or not fit for a dog. The test is fun and can generate valuable information, which you may want to share with your community leaders.

Many cities have urban forestry programs that help maintain the health, longevity, and safety of street trees. Many others lack such programs. Experience indicates that the programs improve when citizens take an active interest in their community's trees. You may want to send your test results to community leaders or, better yet, take them to a public meeting and discuss them with everyone. The American Forestry Association will be keeping track of what you and people all across the country discover, so don't forget to send the association a copy of your completed data sheet. The address is P.O. Box 2000, Washington, D.C. 20013.

Tear out or photocopy the data sheet on page 256, and take it with you on your walk. All the necessary information can be collected in one walk, but concentrating on one factor per day and taking a week's worth of walks will make the test results more accurate—and make you healthier.

COURSE LENGTH

You should start by measuring a route of one or more miles along several different residential streets. The measurement can be made with a bicycle or car odometer or by walking with a pedometer. Several of the test's measurements are based on one-mile increments, so it's better if you end the course on a whole number. Look at trees on both sides of the street; you can walk up one side of the street and back on the other.

TREE AND TREE-SITE COUNT

Count all the trees on both sides of the street and all spaces that are wide enough and far enough from obstructions to safely accommodate a city-owned tree. Usually, the area between the sidewalk and street—the tree lawn—contains the city's trees. If your neighborhood does not have side-walks, look for utility poles, water-shutoff-valve covers, driveway aprons, or fence lines that indicate the public/private property line, and count only existing city trees and spaces where the city could plant a tree. When judging whether a space is suitable for a tree, remember that trees should be spaced forty feet apart, at least thirty-five feet from intersections and traffic signs, more than five feet from visible underground utilities, and ten feet from fire hydrants and driveways. To prevent sidewalk damage, the tree lawn should be three to eight feet wide.

MAINTENANCE NEEDS

The next step is to rate the trees' maintenance needs. There are many factors involved, but we will look for three conditions that are easy to spot: dead or dying trees; attached deadwood; and broken, hanging limbs.

Look in the upper portion of the trees for deadwood. If the wood is dead or dying in more than half the tree, count it as dead on the data sheet. If, however, the tree is between one-quarter and one-half deadwood, count it as deadwood. Consider it deadwood too if the dead limbs are greater than four inches in diameter.

Next is the hangers category. Hangers are dead branches that break off the tree and aren't removed or get caught in the tree's higher limbs on their way to the ground. They'll eventually fall, probably in a heavy wind. Whenever they come down, they're a potential hazard. For this test, enter a tree in the hangers category if the branches are more than two inches in diameter. A tree could have more than one hanger, but in this case, only one count per tree, please.

Every tree you encounter in your walk should be entered into only one of

Jan Smiley and baby daughter note deadwood in a tree on their walk around the block.

URBAN FORESTS

D   A   T   A   S   H   E   E   T

POINTS

1) COURSE LENGTH: _____ miles

2) TREE COUNT *(use hatch marks)* _____
Total Trees _____
Total Trees ÷ Course Length = _____ Trees/Mile

Trees Per Mile	Points	Trees Per Mile	Points
0- 50	1	151-175	8
51- 75	2	176-200	9
76-100	3	201-250	10
101-125	5	251-275	8
126-150	7	276-300	6

3) TREE AND TREE-SITE COUNT *(use hatch marks)*_____
Total Sites _____
Total Trees ÷ (Open Sites + Total Trees) × 100 = _____% Planted

% Sites Planted	Points	% Sites Planted	Points
0-30	1	61- 70	6
31-40	2	71- 80	8
41-50	3	81- 90	9
51-60	4	91-100	10

4) MAINTENANCE NEEDS
A) Dead Trees _____
B) Deadwood _____
C) Hangers _____
Total Hazard Trees (A + B + C) _____
(Hazards ÷ Total Trees) × 100% = _____% Hazardous Trees

% Hazard Trees	Points	% Hazardous Trees	Points
70	0	30	5
60	1	20	6
50	2	10	8
40	3	0	10

5) TYPES OF TREES _____
Types of Trees ÷ Course Length = _____ Species/Mile

Species Per Mile	Points	Species Per Mile	Points
1	0	4	6
2	2	5	8
3	4	6	10

6) TREE SIZES (DBH)
Less than 6 inches _____ ÷ Total Trees × 100% = _____%
6-12 inches _____ ÷ Total Trees × 100% = _____%
Greater than 12 inches _____ ÷ Total Trees × 100% = _____%

Less than 6"	6-18"	Greater than 18"	Points
Any category less than 10%			2
12	------------85------------		4
------------------85------------------		15	5
25	25	50	7
50	25	25	8
25	50	25	10

TOTAL POINTS _____

the three categories, even if it has more than one of these three conditions. The only exception is a nonhazardous healthy tree. If you have lots of healthy trees, you're in luck—not only is this a good preliminary indication of tree health in your neighborhood, but you'll also have less arithmetic to do when you get to the end of the test.

TYPES OF TREES

The mix of species in the urban forest is important because many insects and diseases attack only one genus or species of tree. If there is a lot of diversity in your town's trees, one catastrophic pest will eliminate only a small portion of the urban tree population. But don't panic: this test doesn't require that you identify each tree, only that you count the number of different species you encounter in the course of your walk. Enter it on the data sheet.

TREE SIZES

To assure that the urban forest will continue for generations to come, it is best to have a mixture of tree sizes. You will receive maximum benefits from large trees, especially those over eighteen inches in diameter. Studies have shown that urban trees live an average of thirty-two years. A half-inch of diameter growth per year is good for urban trees in temperate climates, so trees with an eighteen-inch diameter have lived longer than the average urban tree. But since urban trees tend to be short-lived, it is important always to have a supply of young, healthy trees on city streets.

Tree size can be measured in a number of different ways. Foresters often use a diameter tape or a Biltmore stick, but a regular tape measure wrapped around the tree's trunk at four and a half feet above the ground will do just as well. You just have to remember to divide the number you get by 3.14 to get what is called the diameter at breast height, or DBH. With a little practice, you should be able to classify a tree as less than six inches, between six and eighteen inches, or more than eighteen inches DBH just by eyeballing it.

DRUMROLL, PLEASE

When you are finished looking at these six factors, go back to the data sheet and assign points for each numbered item. If you come up with a total score of forty-five points or more, your city has a great program; call your city forester to offer congratulations. A good program will give you a score in the thirty-five to forty-four range; a little support and encouragement from citizens like you could make it a great program. A final score of twenty-five to thirty-four points means the program is working to some degree but needs much more support to make it active and efficient.

If your final score is in the fifteen to twenty-four range, your city's program (if it even has one) is plagued with numerous problems. Find out if there is a program, who is in charge, and what you need to do to get things rolling. If your score is less than fifteen points, your community probably has no active tree program and the present trees are—or very soon will be—in serious trouble. Contact the American Forestry Association for information on how you can get an urban forestry program started in your city.

No matter what your results, speak with your city's officials, and ask what you can do to help improve the program or make sure that a good program stays that way. As a taxpayer, you are a part-owner of your city's urban forest. As with most government-affected programs, urban forestry practices will not improve unless you and your neighbors insist on it. So take your findings, especially if they're poor, to your city forester, council representative, or administrator. And remember to send a copy of your data sheet to the American Forestry Association. It will let you know how your city rates.

37

A Ten-Step Citizens Action Program

American Forestry Association

STEP 1: CREATE PUBLIC AWARENESS OF TREES

Talk to People Before a community can get interested in starting a tree program, a foundation must be established on which to build. You can create an awareness and appreciation for the trees in and around people's backyards. Speak at the local civic and social functions. The Kiwanis, Lions, Rotary, JayCee's, League of Women Voters, garden club, chamber of commerce, local civic organizations, and other groups are likely to be willing to listen—and perhaps even contribute to the idea of improving the community's trees. Use this book and materials listed in the appendices as educational information for those interested in trees. Local newspapers may choose to use them as background for a feature on your efforts.

Identify the Issues Discuss the problems that are confronting your community's urban forest. Identify a specific need in the community, and use this need as a starting point. Some communities experience problems with a destructive pest or disease like Dutch elm disease, oak wilt, or gypsy moth. The destruction can actually be turned into positive action for the community. Many harmful insects and diseases can be controlled, thereby reducing the harm done to the trees. In other situations, poor pruning practices can be a problem. In newly established neighborhoods, tree planting may be the priority. Materials and information regarding all of these topics can be obtained through your county Extension Service. Small-scale projects, such as improving a community park or beautifying the downtown with assorted plantings, can be undertaken to demonstrate the need and the interest in community trees. Think of fundraising and consciousness-raising projects that will aid your cause. One community effort in Los Angeles managed to plant 1 million trees before the 1984 Olympics to improve air quality. Other community efforts in New York and Philadelphia have planted thousands of trees in neighborhoods. Small-scale projects like the beautifying of a railroad property in a suburb of Chicago helped to rally community support for a forestry program. Think of what you can do in your community.

Inform the Media The local newspaper may be interested in the development of your project. Let them know in advance of any meetings, presentations, or events relating to trees. Begin with press releases and follow up with letters of appreciation to those who respond. Articles in the newspaper will be helpful in increasing public awareness and also in educating people about trees. Local radio and television stations are sometimes interested in features or human interest stories that affect the community. Cable television programs also focus, at times, on local concerns. Let them know what your project is and how it is progressing.

Your municipal or county government may have a quarterly or monthly newsletter. Use this resource to get the word out to residents and to solicit help. Newsletters of local groups are another way to publicize your project and solicit members and interest.

Rally Support Keep your eyes and ears open for situations that present themselves, and take advantage of them. Creating awareness in the media is a good approach, and calls from concerned citizens to those in local government can be what is needed to start a community forestry effort. Obtain the names of people in municipal offices. Call them to express an interest in trees. Ask them for names of other residents who have an interest in trees. Start building a community trees constituency.

STEP 2: KNOW YOUR COMMUNITY'S MAKEUP

Gather Information How can your concern affect public policy and decision making? Every community has a process for making decisions. Learn enough about your community's decision-making process to become effective. Make a list of key people in the community such as councilmembers, business leaders, and community activists. Learn of their affiliation with environmental groups, government, business, industry, or the arts. When you are ready to select a committee to promote trees, try to find people with a variety of community concerns, and cultivate their interest in trees. Develop a network of key people who can advise you and who are willing to take action to improve the condition of their urban forest.

Branch Out Get to know the people who are active in community government. Learn the ropes of the community process. Who is in charge of the trees? Are park trees and street trees managed separately? Is there an existing environmental control commission or public works or parks committee? Will one need to be created? Learn the answers to these questions as you gather the information necessary to work within and outside the existing system.

STEP 3: FORM AN ACTION TEAM

Establish a Base After you have identified key people and learned their backgrounds and interests, select an action team from the group. The selection should be done after a thorough search of the community's human resources. Keep your core group small. Seven to ten people who are reliable and easy to reach will be a good base. People with a knowledge of trees and forestry are not necessarily those you will need for your action team. You will, however, need one person trained in urban forestry to act as your technical adviser. This person may be the county extension agent, state forester, or other person knowledgeable about trees. You may find that it is best to hire an urban forestry consultant to assist you with this part of the project.

Look for Specialists Choose your other members for their specific knowledge in an area. Each member should have a different specialty. Problems and opportunities that arise will vary, and by expanding your pool of resources, you will be better able to find needed solutions. Pick people who are respected in the community and within their own profession or business. Choose those who have a rapport or can develop contacts with the mayor, journalists, or councilmembers. Select people who live in the community and have or are willing to take an active role in community improvement.

Who exactly should you choose? The ideal mix may include a technical expert (an urban forester, arborist, nurseryman, or other professional tree person), a lawyer, a public relations specialist, a volunteer coordinator, a community business leader, a reporter/editor/writer, an engineer, legislators, councilmembers, and others. Try to find people who have experience in community activism and volunteer organizing.

Establish the Network Help develop communication within the action team by collecting addresses and phone numbers of members on a community directory form (see Appendix F). Each committee member should then receive a completed list. Set a definite and regular meeting date, time, and place for meetings.

STEP 4: TRAIN THE ACTION TEAM

Collection Sessions It may be useful to have training sessions prior to the collection of the data so that all members evaluate the trees the same way. The data collection is simple, but there are questions that may arise and it is best if everyone is consistent. A basic tree identification course that high-lights the major trees in your area will be useful. Sometimes the government body in charge of planting trees will have a list of trees planted over the years. This is a good place to begin. In addition to tree identification, the data collectors will need to know how and where to measure the trees and how to evaluate their condition. Your technical expert will be able to demonstrate how and where to measure trees. Usually trees are measured with DBH (diameter at breast height) tape at 4.5 feet above the ground. DBH is used as a standard measure for tree diameters.

Condition Rating The condition of a tree is a little tougher to evaluate. A tree must be examined from its root system up to its crown. Start with the root system. Although roots are underground, there are clues above-ground that can help to evaluate it. Is the area constricted? Does there appear to have been construction done in the area around the root system? Has the grade of the land changed? Do you see any signs of roots wrapping themselves around the base of the tree?

Next, move to the trunk of the tree. The trunk should be sound and free of holes or damage. If there are wounds on the trunk, check the size of the damage and note the amount of callous tissue that has formed over the wound. Healthy trees will callous over wounds over a period of growing seasons. Look for holes or hollowness in the trunk. Also examine the bark. Unhealthy trees will sometimes show atypical bark.

Last, but not least, thoroughly view the crown of the tree. Stand back and look at the overall shape of the tree. Is the crown symmetrical and balanced? Is there any deadwood? Can you see a pattern of dead or dying branches beginning from the outer branches to the inner ones or vice versa? Determine the amount of twig growth over the last few years. Has it stabilized, increased, or decreased? Are the leaves a typical color for the species of tree you're examining? Is there any yellowing or browning of the leaves? Are the leaves a consistent size or is there a lot of irregularity? Take all this into consideration when you are evaluating a tree's condition. Your technical expert will be invaluable at this stage.

STEP 5: CONDUCT A BASIC TREE SURVEY

Determine Needs The best way to determine the needs of a community's trees is to conduct a basic survey. In this survey, data concerning the number, size, species, and condition of the trees in the community will be collected. Appendix F includes survey forms which—in addition to the basic, single-neighborhood data gathered on the data sheet in Chapter 36—allows you to note species types and estimated values for trees in the community as a whole. If you are doing a one-person count, we recommend using the chart on p. 256; for a citywide, more comprehensive count, we recommend the forms in Appendix F. This more sophisticated survey will usually demand advice from a professional forester or arborist, and in this phase of the project your technical expert will be very active.

Choose one person to act as the group coordinator. This may be yourself or another qualified member of the group such as a forester or nurseryman. The committee members systematically go down the streets of the town, look at each tree, and record its condition (see Chapter 36). The group leader helps in identifying species and in evaluating the condition of trees in question. Collect only enough data to make a basic business decision. You will later have the option of doing a complete and detailed inventory, but for now, just collect the basic information needed.

The collection of the data will take a good deal of work by all on the committee, but regardless of the size of the community, it can be collected in one day. If the community is too large to count all the trees, work out a system to sample the area. A representative sample can give you a good foundation on which to base your decisions on the needs of the program. If you decide to do a sample survey in which only part of the community is surveyed, be sure that the sample area has a variety of tree species, sizes, and condition ratings that accurately represent the entire community.

If your community is not delineated into areas, you may want to consider developing a cooperative effort among the people on each street. Select one person per block to be the block captain, who is responsible for gathering data for the survey and dispersing information to others on the block. Use these people as your data collectors and information source for that particular street.

STEP 6: EVALUATE THE SURVEY DATA

Look at the Information Once the data is collected, it needs to be evaluated and turned into information that the community can use. An evaluation will contain items like the number, size, and location of trees and planting sites. The value of the urban forest can be determined by plugging these variables into the Tree Value Formula developed by the Council of Tree and

Landscape Appraisers (see Appendix F). The urban forester can evaluate the data and compile it into a presentable form.

A narrative can be written about the condition of the urban forest, and some general suggestions can be made about the action that is needed to improve the condition of the forest. For example, a trimming cycle might be suggested so that every tree in the community will be trimmed on a regular schedule. Yearly maintenance costs based on the trimming cycle can be estimated. To determine costs, choose a trimming cycle (three years) and divide the total maintenance needs into thirds.

You should also know what a minimum effort that removes safety hazards (like dead trees or large hanging limbs) will cost. Discuss this information with your action team. The action team should take the lead in presenting the results of the survey to community leaders and in developing political support for a community tree program. A management plan can be drawn up once the action team decides on a strategy.

STEP 7: DRAW UP A MANAGEMENT PLAN

Present a Clear Message If you have a forester or other technical expert working with you, a long-term management plan can be written that will enable you to evaluate and project the needs and value of your urban forest. The results of the survey and report should present a clear message of the need to properly manage the urban forest. Highlight the monetary, aesthetic, and ecological values of the forest, and present the findings in a straightforward report. The basic facts should include the value of the resource and the cost of maintaining its health. Put in these terms, the decision is no different from decisions on maintaining a building or a vehicle.

If you do not have a technical expert or urban forester, do the best you can to pull the information together. The action team will be able to take the information and make effective business presentations with this material if the data is properly organized. Talk with local sources like botanical garden or arboretum staff or your county extension agent to get the technical advice that you need. With this ammunition, participate in local neighborhood activities, and be prepared to give a formal presentation of the data to civic leaders and less formal presentations to local groups.

STEP 8: GET THE PLAN APPROVED

If your community is ready to move into a well-funded responsible urban forestry program—great! But if there is resistance to funding the program—wait! One of the biggest mistakes is to move beyond this stage before community leaders approve a program of tree maintenance or management with a budget. Until they decide to take on this responsibility, your efforts to begin a program within the existing structure may be wasted. They have to be willing to spend money and be committed to the long-term aspects of a tree care program. One of two things will happen at this point. Either the community government will support a tree care program or they won't. Assuming that they agree to a tree program, move on to step 9. If there is a problem convincing the community to initiate a community tree program, continue your tree awareness efforts and gather more support. If your community government is unable to provide the necessary assistance, the citizens will have to work independently of the government.

STEP 9: HIRE AN URBAN FORESTER

If the community has decided to go ahead with the forestry program, it will need to hire an expert, a professional urban forester to manage and coordinate the program. The urban forester should be a college graduate in urban forestry or a closely related field such as forestry, arboriculture, or urban horticulture. It is essential that the community take this step and hire a professional urban forester as this will ensure the proper and continuous management of the community forest. If the community is too small for a full-time urban forester, consider hiring someone part time or as a consultant. Try to remain involved in this part of the process to ensure that the needs of the trees are being addressed.

STEP 10: REMAIN ACTIVE AND INVOLVED

When your community decides it needs an urban forester on staff, a milestone has been reached. You have done your job well. Help establish strong ties between the new forester and the action team you've set up. Develop a relationship with the new forester so you can work together to increase the public's awareness of trees and forests.

At this point, your role as project coordinator can now be turned into that of a support person for the forestry program. Local maintenance problems and other day-to-day responsibilities now rest with the community forester. Direct questions on trees to the forester and be as supportive as possible.

The interaction between the forester and the community needs to be promoted as this is where the benefits and opportunities to improve the health of the community forest begin. Listed below are some activities that should help in developing a synergistic relationship:

1. Organize a pathway for delivering forestry information to the community, that is, newspapers, newsletters, block captains, etc.
2. Maintain an exchange of information on community tree conditions.

Create displays for city hall, write articles for the newspaper, start a community tree club, hold a community tree festival, etc.

3. Maintain regular communications so information on technical and managerial information can be exchanged. Encourage the community forester to get involved in urban forestry professional organizations and attend seminars and meetings.

4. Continue to work with the forester and others in the community to promote trees and tree improvement throughout the community.

38

Cultivating an Appreciation for Trees

*Adapted by Sara Ebenreck**

ALONG WITH PLANTING and maintaining trees, any successful urban forestry effort needs to keep one eye on education. Everyone from toddlers to centenarians notices trees. Fostering that appreciation and understanding of trees can help ensure that the urban forest will grow even healthier as it matures into the next century.

How does one build a communitywide educational program? The answers are as varied as the places and people who build them, but some models and resources can help. The following profiles may spark ideas about an overall program that fits your community's needs.

* The descriptions of Wisconsin tree walks, the Morton Arboretum field trip, the program at Spring Grove Cemetery, and the Camp Atwater summer program were adapted with permission from presentations by R. Bruce Allison, Charles A. Lewis, Thomas Smith, and Henry Thomas, respectively, at the Second and Third National Urban Forestry Conferences (1982, 1986), and published in the proceedings of those conferences. Arbor Day ideas are from an article by Deborah Gangloff in *American Forests* magazine (January 1985). The section "Kids Speak for Trees" appeared previously in *American Forests* magazine (July-August 1988).

Descriptions of the Philadelphia Urban Ranger program, the Cedar Crest Arboretum, the Trees for Tomorrow Resources Education Center, and the Lathrop E. Smith Center were adapted from material in the *National Urban Forest Forum*, March-April 1988, December 1985–January 1986, and February-March 1984, respectively.

AN ARBORIST PLANS TREE WALKS

Arborist R. Bruce Allison of the Allison Tree Care Company in Madison, Wisconsin, is committed to the public-spirited activity of cultivating tree appreciation. In 1981, Allison published a book called *Tree Walks of Madison and Dane Counties*. The book contains maps of several neighborhoods, with numbers locating interesting trees. Lines connect the tree numbers to form leisurely walking tours. A key in the book gives the tree species, common name, and specifics on the location. Also, interspersed throughout the book are short, informational, inspirational articles.

Tree Walks of Madison and Dane Counties was so successful that Allison then published *Tree Walks of Milwaukee County*, using the same format with fourteen walking tours through Milwaukee neighborhoods and parks. Newspapers in both cities were enthusiastic supporters, serializing the books and exposing a large number of the population to the idea of taking tree walks.

Following up on a winning idea, in 1982 Allison also revised his earlier look at champion trees, publishing a third book called *Wisconsin's Famous and Historic Trees*. This is a collection of stories gathered with the help of county historical societies, newspapers, and interested individuals. The tree histories and photographs ranged from Indian trailmarker trees to Civil War sign-up trees, from a soaring 160-foot white pine to a gnarled old "lynching" oak.

His ideal, says Allison, is to draw readers and those who take tree walks into using the same perspectives on a personal level, integrating trees into family and community events. (See a sample tree walk in Figure 38.1.)

FIELD TRIPS FOR INNER CITY TEENS

Charles A. Lewis, collections administrator at the Morton Arboretum in Lisle, Illinois, planned a tour of the grounds for a group of twelve teenage boys from Chicago's inner city. He had been thinking about ways to help them find some connections between their familiar urban environment and the natural place they were about to explore. At the beginning of the trip, the boys expressed fear at entering what for Lewis was a peaceful patch of woods. "Are there bears and tigers in there?" they wondered.

Perhaps, Lewis thought, the boys might understand the woods, pond, fields, and lake they were to visit if they could think of them as neighborhoods of another kind of city. Perhaps the tour would also go better if he made clear he was as interested in learning about their world as he thought they might be in the Morton Arboretum's world.

So Lewis started the tour with a handshake—the "soul-brother" one he had learned from inner city kids. And the meeting began with his inquiries about their city world. How did things work there? What is aboveground? Below the ground? Where did water come from and go? What about garbage? What made each neighborhood different?

Then he announced that the group was about to visit another sort of city: Nature City. First stop was a "pond neighborhood" where the boys caught sight of turtles, dragonflies, iris, cattails, and a frog. Excitement rose as the boys asked if they could catch the frog and take it home. Lewis's response to the first question was affirmative, but to the second, a comparison. How would they react if someone came into their neighborhood, took a look at someone in one of their houses, and decided to take that person away?

The impact of his question was powerful. The group established a rule: all things found in Nature City would stay in Nature City. The group could look at them, even pick them up and examine them, but everything had to go back.

On into the "woods neighborhood." What happened to the leaves of the oaks and maples when they fell? They did not pile up higher and higher. Who are the garbagepeople in Nature City that take away the leaves? Could they find them? Lewis led the boys in looking under leaves already on the ground until insects and bugs showed up. "Hey, look at that bug! Kill it, quick!" Lewis had to stop the execution with a question about what the insect was doing. The boys finally realized that the bug was eating holes in the leaf, working as one of the garbagepeople of Nature City by slowly converting forest debris into nutrient-rich soil.

As the boys looked through a hand lens at the miniature world of the forest floor, they started asking questions. The rest of the trip was an interplay between his queries and theirs. Did trees have pipes to get the water to the top? What was cooking in the woods as an onion smell came wafting through? Where did the seeds for flowers in the "field neighborhood" come from? What made neighborhoods different? What lived in them?

Lewis sums up the visit in various ways. "Perhaps the urban youngster who visits Nature City will not have learned the name of even one tree, flower, shrub, or animal, but he may have gained an idea of the organization and interplay of natural systems." One key to success that Lewis emphasizes: willingness to enter the world of the other person. An "interpreter" needs to understand other languages besides his own.

KIDS SPEAK FOR TREES

> I am the Lorax. I speak for trees.
> I speak for the trees, for the trees have no tongues.
> And I'm asking you, sir, at the top of my lungs, . . .
> Unless someone like you cares a whole awful lot,
> Nothing is going to get better. It's not.

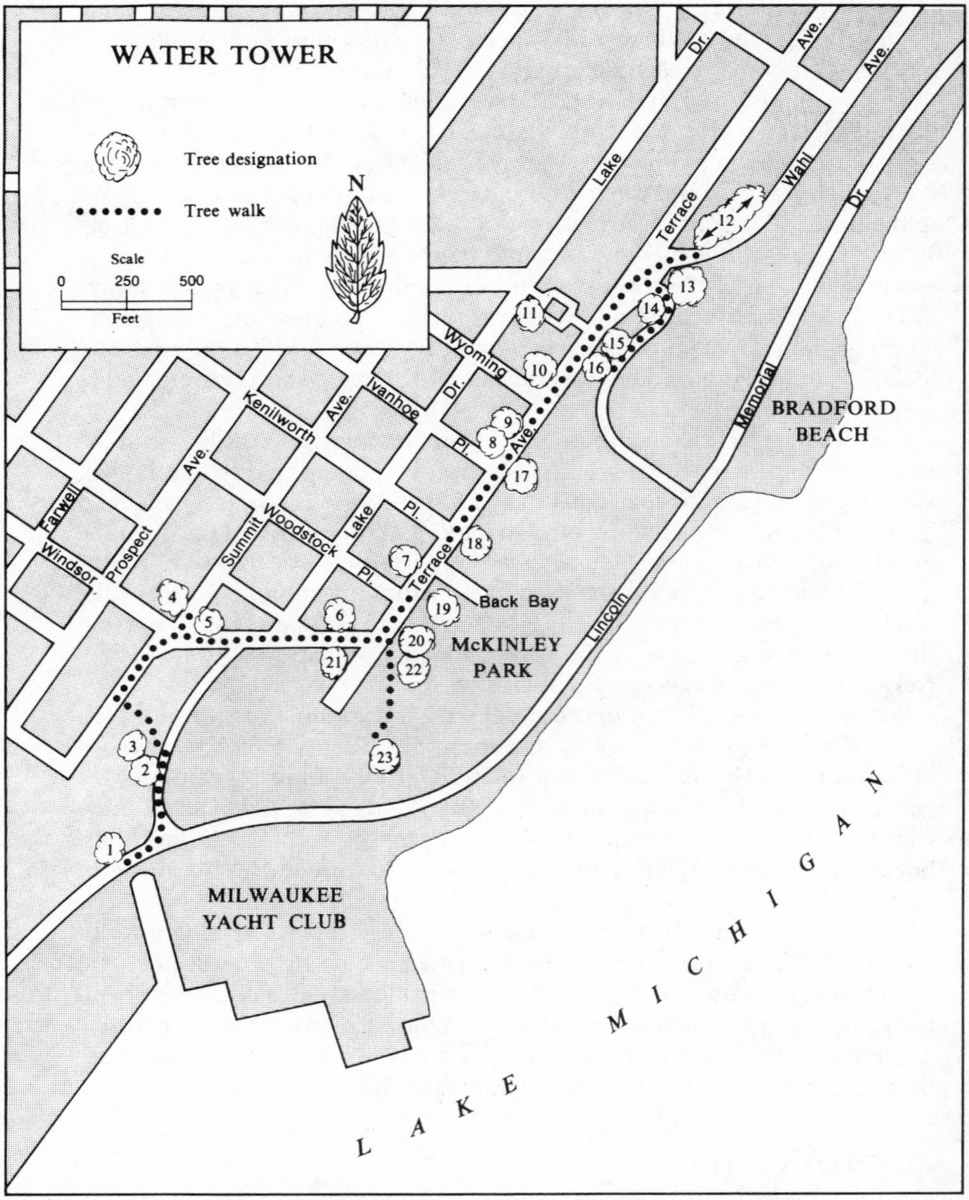

FIGURE 38.1. *Tree walks are fun and a healthy way to learn tree identification. This is one example of eleven walks in R. Bruce Allison's book,* Tree Walks of Milwaukee County.

Cartography by James M. Elliott

WATER TOWER

Park in the Milwaukee Yacht Club parking lot off Lincoln Memorial Drive. Find the maintenance building across Lincoln Memorial Drive on the corner and begin.

1. Ginkgo, *Ginkgo biloba*. Find a small grove of five ginkgos on the south side of the maintainance building close to the parkway. This tree is a member of the gymnosperms like our evergreens. Ginkgos are dioecious, that is, there are male and female trees. The largest of these trees is the third largest ginkgo in Wisconsin.
2. Eastern Cottonwood, *Populus deltoides*. This is a large tree with three main trunks and rough light gray bark just west of the sidewalk.
3. Black Locust, *Robinia pseudoacacia*. Walk about half way up the wooden stairs and turn to your left (south). There should be a tall, slender tree in front of you. Other black locusts can be found in the vicinity. This tree has exceptionally rot-resistant wood which is often used for fence posts.
4. White Poplar, *Populus alba*. On the north side of Lafayette. This tree is anchored in the ravine and is growing up over the metal railing and shading the sidewalk. The bark is whitish and the leaves have a silver sheen.
5. Japanese Yew, *Taxus cuspidata*. The small evergreen tree growing close to the south side of the house at 2006 Lafayette.
6. Ginkgo, *Ginkgo biloba*. In the front yard of 2128 Lafayette. This stately tree is probably quite old. At the same address, the street tree is a silver maple, *Acer saccharinum*. This huge tree shows the size that can be attained by silver maples.
7. American elm, *Ulmus americana*. Street tree at 2121 Terrace. Notice the old-fashioned bracing chains installed by an arborist years ago.
8. Horsechestnuts, *Aesculus hippocastanum*. A medium-sized tree in the southeast corner of 2229 Terrace. The fruit of horsechestnut, unlike chestnuts, is inedible.
9. White Ash, *Fraxinus americana*. Three tall trees between 2229 and 2239 Terrace about 20 feet west of the sidewalk. Baseball bats are made from white ash.
10. Northern Catalpa, *Catalpa speciosa*. Find two large catalpa trees in the southeast corner of the park approximately 50 feet apart. A horsechestnut is between and in front of these two catalpas. These are weak-wooded trees, and are continually dropping twigs, leaves, pods, or branches. They do, however, have very handsome white showy flowers in June and the wood is very resistant to decay. Walk to the north-western corner of this park square. Find a medium-sized tree with very white bark, the only white-barked tree in that part of the park.
11. Cutleaf European White Birch, *Betula pendula* 'Gracilis'. This is a very handsome tree when the leaves are present. But, to do well, European birch, like the American paper birch, need to have their roots in a cool, moist, preferably shaded site. Walk a short distance down Wahl Street.
12. White Ash, *Fraxinus americana*. Observe the ash street trees on both sides of Wahl Street. They extend to Grant Park. Wahl Street is an excellent example of what an older established street tree planting does to enhance the appearance of a neighborhood.
13. Sugar Maple, *Acer saccharum*. Return from Wahl Street by way of an asphalt path with a wooden fence to your left. The medium-sized tree just east of the wooden fence as you walk south is Wisconsin's state tree.
14. Austrian Pine, *Pinus nigra*. Find a picturesque, flat-topped pine standing alone on the grass penninsula overlooking the road down to the lake.
15. Weeping European Beech, *Fagus sylvatica* 'Pendula'. Find a peculiar-looking tree 50 feet east and a few feet north of the Terrace and North Street signs. This is the largest weeping beech in Wisconsin. Beech have interesting gray bark in winter, shiny green leaves as they unfold in spring, and red-bronze leaf color in autumn.
16. Norway Maple, *Acer platanoides*. Walk about 75 to 85 feet directly south of #15, and find a large, spreading tree with very little grass growing near the trunk. Norway maples are tolerant of city air pollution, soil salt, and heavy clay soil. Walk south down Terrace Avenue.
17. Common Horsechestnut, *Aesculus hippocastanum*. Find a medium-sized tree with large shiny buds overhanging the gate at 2220 Terrace Avenue. Horsechestnut, a European tree, is a close relative of our native Ohio buckeye, *Aesculus glabra*.
18. European Ash, *Fraxinus excelsior*. Walking past 2216 Terrace, locate a small tree with a green cast to the trunk and very dark buds in the grassy lot 15 feet east of the sidewalk, mixed in with other similiar-sized ash. European ash can be a handsome tree when grown on good sites, but it is much less hardy than both our native white and green ash.
19. Bur Oak, *Quercus macrocarpa*. Walk along the sidewalk in the park until you come to a white poplar (whitish bark in crown) just to your left. The poplar leans over and shades the sidewalk. Face the lake (east) and walk about 20 feet toward the lake until you are standing in front of a large, rough-barked tree. In spite of the fact that these trees have no fall color and lack showy flowers, bur oaks are almost universally loved by tree people. A tree native to southern Wisconsin.
20. Shagbark Hickory, *Carya ovata*. Walk south on the sidewalk a short distance past two sugar maples just east of the walk. About 15 feet east of the second sugar maple is a tall tree with rough light gray bark breaking off into plates.
21. European Beech, *Fagus sylvatica*. A medium-sized tree with smooth gray bark just east of the driveway at 2121 Lafayette and a few feet south of the walk. European beech is more widely used as an ornamental than our native American beech.
22. Red Oak, *Quercus rubra*. Find a large tree with twin leaders, 60 feet east of the fire hydrant at the end of Lafayette near the sidewalk. This is the largest tree in the general area. Red and black oak trees growing in forest situations can be killed in a matter of weeks if they contract Oak Wilt Disease. This disease is relatively rare in urban situations. It spreads by root grafts and wounds. The disease can be avoided by pruning these oaks during dormancy and severing the roots between infected and healthy trees. Find the wooden stairs leading down the bluff, just to the east of the termination of Terrace Avenue. At the bottom of the steps look both to your right and left and locate two young trees that are still heavily staked.
23. Honeylocust, *Gleditsia triacanthos*. The two small trees on either side at the bottom of the steps. Honeylocust trees grow rapidly.

This Dr. Seuss rhyme, printed on large orange tags, was placed on newly installed street trees by students in Columbus, Ohio. The students hope their efforts will stop tree vandalism.

The need for this project surfaced after nineteen out of 150 newly planted trees, the first phase of a $1 million effort, were destroyed. Local citizens groups and schools came up with the idea to "tag the trees." Middle-school students tied tags to the trees.

"The objectives," said Brad Shimp, executive director of the University Community Business Association, "are to show that both students and the community are concerned and to encourage people to take care of the gifts they are given."

The Ohio Division of Forestry demonstrated its support for this effort by presenting the Indianola Middle School with a special certificate of appreciation.

TIMBER HARVEST EDUCATION IN CINCINNATI

The Spring Grove Cemetery and Arboretum in Cincinnati, Ohio, sees its timber management program as an opportunity to educate urban people about timber harvest and woodland regeneration. Spring Grove is located on 733 acres just four miles from downtown Cincinnati, but it is not just convenience that draws people there. For 143 years, it has been widely recognized for the beauty of its landscaping and its welcome to visitors.

Since its founding in 1845, the cemetery's directors have been oriented toward conservation by the original premise of the founders, namely, to "employ some of the funds in rendering the place where our beloved friends repose, attractive and consoling at once to the eye and the heart not only for the present but also for the future." Applying this premise, the directors had always protected their 300 acres of woodlands by leaving them undisturbed.

In the early 1970s, the period of the energy crisis, the directors took a fresh look at the management of their woodlands. Recognizing that forests are a renewable natural resource, they began the selective harvesting of trees. They acted on the management principle that the solar energy stored in trees was best used by harvesting the trees at the point of maximum worth.

When visitors and local citizens raised concerns about the ecological soundness of the harvesting, the directors began to see an educational potential of their woodlands management program. Although only selected trees were harvested, the directors were often asked to explain the practices which temporarily disturbed the logged areas. Wisely, they saw this as an opportunity rather than a nuisance; and so they set aside a fifteen-acre parcel to be a kind of educational showroom where visitors could learn for themselves about the purpose of harvesting trees and the process of regeneration on timbered lands.

As a result, urban people, without leaving their own city, can experience what a well-managed timber harvest is like. Just as a child planting a tree can return to see its growth season after season and identify with the natural process, visitors to the harvested areas can return year after year and watch the process of regeneration.

In fact, hundreds of visitors, including forestry classes, garden clubs, and national conventions, do visit the cemetery specifically to see its logged areas. They can observe areas which have not been harvested since 1845 alongside others that have been logged at various times in the last decade and a half. The regeneration of areas timbered since 1974 is now obvious, and visitors have gained a new understanding of conservation practices that make intelligent use of resources.

ARBOR DAY IDEAS

Arbor Day events are popular with many communities and groups as ways of organizing tree planting. With some forethought, they can become ways to organize tree maintenance while providing ongoing education about trees for everyone, of every age, who is involved. For example:

- Organize a tree festival. South Austin, Texas, residents organized a Live Oak Fest to raise funds to pay for a fight against oak wilt disease, which was threatening the city's trees. The festival featured food booths, children's games, and a "wilderness" tour along with music and other lively activities.
- Have your group take a tree inventory of a specified neighborhood (see Chapter 36 and 37 for guidelines).
- Examine your city's tree ordinance and overall forestry program. The National Arbor Day Foundation has guidelines for nominating communities as a Tree City USA that provide standards for a sound city ordinance. (See Appendix D.)
- Develop an Adopt-a-Tree program that encourages residents to pledge to water, mulch, and report to authorities any problems signaling danger for their tree. Minneapolis, Minnesota, has such a program; it presents city residents with formal adoption papers for the tree of their choice.
- Sponsor a tree care workshop for your neighborhood, and hold a tree care tour to spot problems and talk about solutions. It's best to choose a public place and to notify responsible people before the event. Those same people may be the most likely leaders in such a tour. Invite businesspeople and legislators who are involved in creating budgets for public tree care. Invite local media to cover the tour.
- Revisit last year's Arbor Day plantings in your community and check the condition of the trees. Make plans to work on any needs.

ARBOR DAY IN NEBRASKA

The children of Elm Street
Elementary School have chosen
A site for a new tree, and file
Out like leaves on a walnut bough
For its planting now. Elm Street
Has long since seen the prairie
Elms die, but the new tree heaves
Shoulder-high among schoolchildren, promising
Life. Bantering its staff on an April
Wind, the starred flag flies; the State
And County on holiday stand by
With regalia. Nothing
Is launched at the sky for the crowd.
But something is given back
To the earth, something hunched down
In water and sod is settled with spades
In a welcome home, is raised
Like a flag for beatitudes
Of shade and birds, will green,
Will thrive, for a century to come
Will school our elementary lives.

Nancy G. Westerfield

PROJECT LEARNING TREE FOR SCHOOLS

Project Learning Tree (PLT) is an award-winning environmental education program for use in and out of the classroom with young people and their leaders and teachers, in kindergarten through grade twelve. The program is jointly sponsored by the American Forest Council and its foundation and the Western Regional Environmental Education Council, with the Society of American Foresters and the U.S. Forest Service as national associates.

Over 175 activities for grades K–12 use the forest as a window on the natural world. Activities include neighborhood tree walks, exercises to test noise abatement and air cleansing by trees, nature crafts, and even experiences to nurture appreciation for the quiet of the forest.

Teachers interested in participating attend workshops led by trained leaders to gain a hands-on experience in the activities. Since 1976, over 150,000 teachers in the United States, Canada, and Sweden have participated in such workshops, PLT organizers say, and most states now have official state coordinators for the program. For information, contact Project Learning Tree, 1250 Connecticut Ave., N.W., Suite 320, Washington D.C. 20036.

COMMUNITY ENVIRONMENTAL EDUCATION CENTERS

The Trees for Tomorrow Natural Resources Education Center in Eagle River, Wisconsin, has helped establish more than forty school forests in Wisconsin since 1944. The center was founded by the Wisconsin paper and power industries to help reforest overcut and burned private timberlands in Wisconsin and the Upper Peninsula of Michigan.

The chief work of the center is educating the public about the need for proper management and the wise use of all natural resources. More than 250,000 persons, mostly school students and teachers, have come to Trees for Tomorrow for multiday programs at actual resources management sites. Forestry, wildlife, and water management concepts are studied.

The center's full-time educational staff includes foresters and environmental educators. More than 100 resource management professionals from government agencies, universities, and businesses also serve as volunteer educators.

In Montgomery County, Maryland, the Lathrop E. Smith Environmental Education Center is located in Rock Creek Park, a forested area that provides outdoor learning experiences for students and teachers. This center is owned and operated by the school system.

Weeklong residential programs are given for sixth-graders and special education students. Topics include forest, pond, and stream study, local history, wildlife, map and compass work, geology, and ecology. Evening activities include astronomy, night hikes, and other recreation.

A high school intern program helps students explore environmental careers, build trails, survey timber, plant and care for trees, and take further field trips.

YOUTH CAMP EDUCATION

Camp Atwater is a national summer residential camp for youngsters between the age of six and sixteen. The camp itself, located in North Brookfield, Massachusetts, includes sixty-seven mainland and three island acres with facilities to accommodate up to 250 people at a time. The majority of campers are urban black youth from the Northeast, although participants have come from Los Angeles, Atlanta, and even several African countries.

Henry Thomas, president of the Urban League in Springfield, Massachusetts, has been active in the development of an environmental education program that includes forestry education at the camp. Thomas saw the importance of exposure to educational education for black youth. Like all other citizens, black people are responsible for environmental quality, but, as Thomas acknowledged, they are underrepresented in careers related to environmental and natural resources planning and management.

To meet that need for positive exposure, the Springfield Urban League worked with the State University of New York's College of Environmental Science and Forestry to implement and evaluate a pilot program in environmental education and natural resources management in the summer of 1981. The challenge, as Thomas puts it, was to develop environmental awareness in youths who may not have perceived any direct relationship between environmental values and their personal needs.

Over several years, Camp Atwater developed a sequence of activities that included study of decomposing trees, tree boring, soil sampling, bird watching, and pond exploration. Activities that involved active use of tools—microscopes, soil testing kits, compasses, field guides, maps— were enthusiastically received.

The camp developed a series of workshops and talks for camp counselors and staff that included career potentials for the youth. "We need to raise our consciousness and appreciation of the environment. At Camp Atwater," Thomas says, "we are a small part of the family, but a large part of the dream." Every summer camp should have a program that makes it part of that dream.

INTEGRATING TREES INTO A COLLEGE

Cedar Crest College in Allentown, Pennsylvania, has a unique match between students and trees: about one tree for each of its approximately 1,000 students. The trees are part of a registered arboretum and include ginkgos from China, weeping white birch from Europe, cryptomeria from Japan, and wild cherry from its home territory in the eastern United States. They weren't always there.

When Cedar Crest moved from downtown Allentown to what was then a fifty-acre cornfield on the outskirts of the town in 1915, only a single black walnut stood on the grounds. But its president, William Curtis, personally led the planting effort on the new grounds. The collection is now designated the William F. Curtis Arboretum.

Today visitors and students can travel a self-guided nature trail developed in 1982 by the student biology club. But the trees are an integral part of academic courses as well, serving as resources for students enrolled in botany, ecology, and other classes.

PHILADELPHIA URBAN PARK RANGERS

An educational experience that combines environmental appreciation, higher education, and job training for youth with maintenance of a major forested city park is the goal of the Philadelphia Ranger Corps training program. This innovative effort is a cooperative venture of the city of Philadelphia, Temple University, the city's Fairmount Park Commission, city schools, and the William Penn Foundation, which provided funds to get it started.

Recent graduates of city high schools apply for the positions as rangers in Fairmount Park by submitting high school grades, writing 300-word essays about why they want to be park rangers, and taking the Scholastic Aptitude Test. The corps pays for each ranger to complete an associate's degree at Temple University, specializing in liberal arts and park management. Each ranger is paid an annual salary of $14,000 plus scholarship money of $3,500 per year.

In 1988, about forty park rangers started work, directing visitors to park attractions, working on park maintenance, and traveling to city classrooms to offer students information about the park, which houses historic and cultural sites as well as naturally beautiful ones. The first-year youths include Hispanics, whites, blacks, and an Asian among its nineteen female and twenty-one male members.

Epilogue:
What Lies Ahead

*Gary Moll, R. Neil Sampson, and
Sara Ebenreck*

By GATHERING IN one place many independent voices from the urban forestry community, this volume has put forward a vision of a more ecologically sound future for our cities and towns, along with practical sketches of ways to achieve that goal. While minor differences in emphasis emerge from the many angles of view, what is overwhelmingly apparent is the overall harmony of vision: trees are vitally important to the future of our cities, and we must find more and better ways to integrate their living presence into our living places. If, as we think may be the case, we are in the early stages of experiencing the global greenhouse effect, that urban forestry agenda is made even more pressing.

To say that this agenda is pressing is not to say that its achievement is easy, however. The existing urban forest is complex, growing on lands held by a wide variety of owners, both public and private. It exists—or should exist—in old central city neighborhoods, in places already covered with concrete, in industrial parks, grimy riversides, affluent suburbs and poverty-stricken slums, in newly converted or about-to-be-converted farmlands and forests. Moreover, the mix of viewpoints and professions that contribute to urban forestry can sometimes make it difficult to tell who is in charge of the urban forest—and even what the best answers to particular planning problems really are.

But it is clearly a strength of the urban forestry community that the diversity of the forest's needs are matched, although not always evenly, by the broad diversity of people and groups concerned about the future of our urban trees. It is an asset that some of those groups are national, while others are local; that some are public while others are private; that some efforts represent broad coalitions of people while others are the outreach of a single person. And it is a benefit that multiple professions must come together if we are to achieve a more ecologically sound future for our cities and communities. Merging the orderly layout of a community with the complexity of the natural landscape and its ecological cycles requires a broad range of talent. The specific knowledge of foresters, landscape architects, arborists, horticulturalists, city managers, and others together creates the pool of skills needed for building healthy urban forests.

Despite these strengths, almost anyone involved in urban forestry knows that more is needed. On the local level, we need to increase the volume of voices that can articulate the ecological needs of communities. Even our very best models of urban forestry don't yet meet the vision we have set before ourselves, and in some cities, there is yet to be gathered even the beginnings of a voice of concern.

Urban forests are a long-range investment which need tree-by-tree maintenance on the level of yards, streets, parkways, and cities. They are an investment most visible and valuable to those for whom the trees are not simply numbers but friendly parts of a living community. So it is in the communities of their planting that the pride and commitment of owner-ship needs to be strongly fostered.

On regional, state, and national levels, needs also exist. Networking channels to assure the sharing of ideas, technical assistance, and useful tools such as workable tree ordinances are needed on all those levels. Public ignorance or apathy could be turned into enthusiastic support for forested cities if the right kind of public education and media attention could be marshaled.

Research on such matters as the positive health effects of urban forests and their ecological values needs more attention; state and national fund-ing would pay for itself. If we are moving into an era of global warming, much research will be needed on types of trees best prepared to survive amid climate changes. National community grant programs that recognize the important energy-saving contributions made by trees could spur pro-grams across the nation. And recognition for work done by citizens and groups of all sorts to help our urban forests is vital.

So while this book can give the reader an idea of the state and potential of urban forestry for our nation, it is ultimately not simply a sharing of vision but a call to action. With its publication, the American Forestry Association takes another step in its own commitment to support the better development and care of urban forests. In 1981, when the AFA sponsored the formation of the National Urban Forest Council, it envi-

sioned a national network of citizen activists and professionals committed
to the exchange of ideas and information about urban forestry. That network has grown to over 200 active council members, who reach out to
thousands more through the *Urban Forest Forum* newsletter. That newsletter and other information resources sponsored by the AFA with the council
are available to all interested groups and individuals (see Appendices A, B,
D, and G for some of these resources).

But what is needed is that many more concerned citizens and professionals find ways to take some, albeit small, steps toward turning around
the trends of urban forest decline now documented by portions of this
book and toward creating well-shaded cities whose beauty and environmental harmony are a regular cause for celebration. So that we may celebrate our success in the year 2000, it is essential that each of us find some
way to act now. It may be planting one tree; it may be contacting a county
commissioner or city councilmember and getting a tree survey under way;
it may be organizing a neighborhood group or a citywide greenway coalition; it may be contacting a member of Congress to support urban forestry
grants and research.

Whatever our choice of action, the time to invest in the future of our
cities is today. Whatever action you take, the American Forestry Association would like to hear about it. Write to us (P.O. Box 2000, Washington,
D.C. 20013) about your ideas, achievements, and comments. That
strengthening of our urban forestry network, in itself, can help us prepare
for the twenty-first century.

Books, Pamphlets, Newsletters, and Periodicals

BOOKS

Arboriculture: Care of Trees, Vines, and Shrubs (1983), by Richard W. Harris. Discusses overall benefits of landscaping, plant growth and forms, selection, planting, and long-term management. From Prentice-Hall, Inc., Englewood Cliffs, NJ 07632.

Diseases of Trees and Shrubs (1987), by Wayne A. Sinclair, Warren T. Johnson, and Howard H. Lyon. A comprehensive pictorial survey of disorders of forest and shade trees and woody ornamental plants in the United States and Canada. 574 pages, from Cornell University Press, 124 Roberts Place, Ithaca, NY 14850. Also from the American Forestry Association.*

The Earth Manual: How to Work on Wild Land Without Taming It (revised, 1985), by Malcolm Margolin. A guide for people who buy worn-out land, whether it is in a town or near the wilderness. The text explains planting trees, building trails, developing wildlife habitat, and stopping erosion. 237 pages, from Heyday Books, P.O. Box 9145, Berkeley, CA 94709.

Famous and Historic Trees, by Charles Randall and Henry Clepper. The stories of 268 well-known American trees from every state; trees associated with people, music, forestry, religion, conservation, education, and other special areas. 86 pages, from the American Forestry Association.*

The Granite Garden: Urban Nature and Human Design (1984), by Anne Whiston Spirn. A clear picture of the city's natural environment—its air and water, the land upon which it is built, and how a better knowledge of urban ecology may help create a healthier, safer, and better urban environment. 334 pages, from Basic Books, Inc., 10 East 53rd St., New York, NY 10022.

Homeowners Guide to Landscape Design (revised, 1986), by Timothy M. Michel. A step-by-step guide to landscaping from an experienced landscape architect. Including information on energy-saving shade trees, creating privacy, reducing noise, framing views, and defining special places. 176 pages, from The Countryman Press, P.O. Box 175, Woodstock, VT 05091.

Insects That Feed on Trees and Shrubs, by Wayne A. Sinclair, Howard H. Lyon, and Warren T. Johnson. A comprehensive handbook giving essential facts about more than 900 species of insects and other pests that injure woody ornamental plants in the United States. Beautifully illustrated with 241 color plates. From Cornell University Press, 124 Roberts Place, Ithaca, NY 14850. Also from the American Forestry Association.*

Inside Wood, by William M. Harlow. The wonders of wood as magnified and seen in all its intricate detail. Presented through prose and camera. 120 pages, from the American Forestry Association.*

Integrating Man and Nature in the Urban Environment (1987), edited by Lowell W. Adams and Daniel L. Leedy. Proceedings of a 1986 national symposium on urban wildlife. 249 pages, from the National Institute for Urban Wildlife, 10921 Trotting Ridge Way, Columbia, MD 21044.

Knowing Your Trees, by G. H. Collingwood, Warren Brush, and Devereaux Butcher. A practical guide to 182 species of trees through photographs and detailed text. Photos show the trees in summer and winter, along with closeups of leaves, bark, fruit, and flower. A map indicates places in the United States where the trees grow. 392 pages, from the American Forestry Association.*

Land Use and Forest Resources in a Changing Environment: The Urban Forest Interface (1984), edited by Gordon A. Bradley. 238 pages, from the University of Washington Press, P.O. Box 50096, Seattle, WA 98145.

Landscape Management (1988), by James R. Feucht and Jack D. Butler. From Van Nostrand Reinhold, Mail Order Dept., P.O. Box 668, Florence, KY 41042–9979.

Let There Be Forest (1986), by Arnold and Connie Krochmal. From Bernan-Unipub, 4611–F Assembly Drive, Lanham, MD 20706–4391.

A New Tree Biology (597 pages, hardcover) and *A New Tree Biology Dictionary* (132 pages, softcover) (1987) by Alex A. Shigo. *The New Tree Biology* has chapters on trees and microorganisms, roots, leaves, fruit, diseases, and management. The *Dictionary* lists terms from armillaria (a fungus) to pith and pathogens to yeasts and zone lines. Each is briefly defined in clear, laymen's language. From Shigo and Trees, Associates, 4 Denbow Road, Durham, NH 03824.

Proceedings of the Third National Urban Forestry Conference held in Orlando, Florida, December 1987. Contains all talks and lists of attendees. 272 pages from the American Forestry Association.*

This Green World (1988), by Rutherford Platt. A reprint of the 1942 award-winning description of forest botany, with brief additions to each chapter providing scientific updates for the material. 272 pages from Dodd & Mead, 71 Fifth Ave., New York, NY 10003.

Tree Walks of Milwaukee County (1981), by R. Bruce Allison. Eleven mapped tree walks interspersed with short articles on topics from identifying trees to tree ethics. 56 pages, from Wisconsin Books, 2025 Dunn Place, Madison, WI 53713.

The Tree Worker's Manual. From the Ohio Agricultural Education Curriculum Materials Service, Rm. 254, 2120 Fyffe Road, Ohio State University, Columbus, OH 43210–1099.

Trees in Urban Design (1980), by Henry F. Arnold. An approach to tree planting that advocates the collective use of trees in groves, rows, and symmetrical units. Explains the aesthetic principles used in grouping trees. Designed for architects and planners but interesting for the lay reader as well. 168 pages from Van Nostrand Reinhold Company, 135 West 50th St., New York, NY 10020.

Urban Forestry (2nd ed., 1986), by Gene W. Grey and Frederick Deneke. Covers the history and composition of the urban forest and its benefits and management. Scans the field of support organizations and programs. Designed as an overview for urban foresters. 299 pages, from John Wiley & Sons, Inc., One Wiley Drive, Somerset, NJ 08873.

Urban Forestry: Planning and Managing Urban Greenspaces (1988), by Robert W. Miller. A text for urban forestry students and a reference book for forestry professionals. Chapters cover the nature and history of the urban forest and assessing and managing its resources. Prentice-Hall, Inc., Englewood Cliffs, NJ 07632. Also from the American Forestry Association.*

Valuation of Landscape Trees, Shrubs, and Other Plants (1988). The seventh edition of the classic guide to appraising the dollar value of shade trees. From the International Society of Arboriculture, 303 W. University, P.O. Box 908, Urbana, IL 61801.

PAMPHLETS

Forestry: A Community Tradition (reprinted 1988). A 24-page overview of community forestry, its status and needs. Recommends expanding urban and community forestry programs. Published by the U.S.D.A. Forest Service and the National Association of State Foresters. Contact the NASF at Suite 526, Hall of States, 444 N. Capitol St., NW, Washington, DC 20001.

Growing Your Trees, by Wilbur Youngman and Charles Randall. A homeowner's guide to backyard trees with information on selecting, planting, and caring for the right tree, including protection from insects and blights. From the American Forestry Association.*

A Guide to Urban Wildlife Management (1984), by Daniel Leedy and Lowell Adams. A 42-page booklet showing how to incorporate wildlife habitat into urban settings, including homesites, parks, and whole communities. From the National Institute for Urban Wildlife, 10921 Trotting Ridge Way, Columbia, MD 21044.

A Gypsy Moth Handbook. A guide to help homeowners cope with this imported pest. From the American Forestry Association.*

Internship Directory. An annual listing of internships and summer jobs in
public gardens. Published by the American Association of Botanical
Gardens and Arboreta, P.O. Box 206, Swarthmore, PA 19081.

Land Development in Wooded Areas, by Gary Moll, with the U.S.D.A. Forest
Service and the Maryland Forest Service. A 20-page look at how to
incorporate sound forest management into a subdivision plan. Available
from the American Forestry Association.*

Managing Urban Woodlands for a Variety of Birds (1986). Publication no. NE-
INF-63-85 from the U.S.D.A. Forest Service, Publications Group, 359
Main Road, Delaware, OH 43015.

New Tree Health (1987), by Alex L. Shigo. A simple, well-illustrated, 10-page
guide to the care of trees. Shigo and Trees, Associates, 4 Denbow Road,
Durham, NH 03824.

Save Our Urban Trees: Citizen Action Guide. The AFA's 10-step citizen action
program with related tree survey materials. From the American Forestry
Association.*

So You Want to Be in Forestry (1988). Explains forestry and forestry careers
for young people thinking of their future. From the American Forestry
Association.*

Sources of Native Seeds and Plants. A 36-page booklet giving names,
addresses, and telephone numbers of approximately 250 growers and
suppliers of native vegetations in 38 states. From the Soil and Water Conservation Society, 7515 Northeast Ankeny Road, Ankeny, IA 50021–9764.

Tree Care Checklist. A helpful handout for Arbor Day or other community
awareness programs. Covers the process of planning, planting, and
maintaining urban trees. From the American Forestry Association.*

Trees Every Boy and Girl Should Know. A description of 91 most common
American trees. From the American Forestry Association.*

NEWSLETTERS

Arbor Day News, bimonthly publication of the National Arbor Day Foundation. Contact the NADF, 100 Arbor Avenue, Nebraska City, NE 68410.
(402) 474–5655.

Arborescence, quarterly newsletter with technical and membership information from the Minnesota Society of Arboriculture. Contact Mike Zins,
Editor, Minnesota Landscape Arboretum, 3675 Arboretum Drive, Box
39, Chanhasson, MN 55317. (612) 443–2460.

Communitree, quarterly newsletter for Nebraskans involved in community
forestry. Contact David Mooter, 8015 West Center, Omaha, NE 68124.
(402) 444–7804.

Georgia Tree Talks, triannual newsletter published by the Georgia Forestry
Commission. Promotes communication among professional urban foresters, city tree managers, and city officials. Carries success stories, tree

care information, and current events. Contact Sharon Dolliver, GFC, P.O. Box 819, Macon, GA 31298. (912) 744–3377.

The Metrian, biannual newsletter for members of the Metropolitan Tree Improvement Alliance. Contact METRIA, c/o Ohio Department of Natural Resources, Foundation Square, Building C, Columbus, OH 43224. (614) 265–6707.

Michigan Forestry and Park Association Newsletter, bimonthly newsletter to members. Contact Bob Cool, Editor, 1608 Kingswood Drive, Lansing MI 48912. (517) 483–4206.

Overstory, quarterly newsletter of the Minnesota Department of Agriculture. Covers tree selection and maintenance, public relations, success stories, programs, and policy updates. Contact Don Mueller, Minnesota Department of Agriculture, Plant Industry Division, 90 West Plato Blvd., St. Paul, MN 55107. (612) 296–6692.

Urban Forest Forum, bimonthly newsletter from the American Forestry Association in cooperation with the National Urban Forest Council. Covers success stories, legislation, events, technical information, and resources from across the country. From the American Forestry Association.*

Utility Arborist Association Newsletter, quarterly membership publication covering forestry and vegetation management on utility properties. $10 per year from the Utility Arborist Association, Bob Nosse, Treasurer, Ohio Edison Co., 76 S. Main Street., Akron, OH 44308. (216) 384–5713.

The Wisconsin Arborist, bimonthly newsletter of the Wiconsin Arborist Association with urban forestry information. Contact Dick Hass, 7300 Chestnut St., Wauwatosa, WI 53213. (414) 471–8420.

PERIODICALS

American Forests, bimonthly magazine of the American Forestry Association. Carries features on urban and community forestry in each issue along with articles on the national and global issues involving trees, forests, and forestry. From the American Forestry Association.*

Arboricultural Journal, a quarterly journal of urban forestry. Publishes research, management information, book reviews, and other notes for an international audience. From the Arboricultural Association, Ampfield House, Ampfield, Romsey, Hants, SO5 9PA, England.

Journal of Arboriculture, a monthly magazine of the International Society of Arboriculture. Publishes professional research papers, including many related to urban forestry. Contact the ISA, 303 W. University, P.O. Box 908, Urbana, IL 61801.

The Public Garden, quarterly journal of the American Association of Botanical Gardens and Arboreta. Includes some articles on urban forests and forestry. From the AABGA, P.O. Box 206, Swarthmore, PA 19081.

* See Appendix D for address.

Audio-Visual and Other Educational Aids

AUDIO-VISUAL AIDS

Avoidance of Construction Damage to Trees on Wooded Lots (VHS video). Discusses the necessary steps to preserve trees. From the International Society of Arboriculture, 303 W. University, P.O. Box 908, Urbana, IL 61801.

City of Seattle: Green City. A 12-minute film on the history of Seattle, Washington, which was once a forest and is trying to reinstate its forest cover. Contact Jerry Clark, City Arborist, Seattle Municipal Building, Room 704, Seattle, WA 98104.

Dead Trees: Sanctuaries for Wildlife. A 140-slide program explaining the importance of dead trees in forest ecosystems. Contact James Davis, Educational Director, Portland Audubon Society, NW Cornell Road, Portland, OR 97210.

Effect of Building Construction on Wooded Lots (1988 VHS video). Discusses the causes of tree decline following construction activity. From the International Society of Arboriculture Research Trust, 303 W. University, P.O. Box 908, Urbana, IL 61801.

Life, Death, and Rebirth of a Tree and *TLC for City Trees.* Slide-tape programs from the U.S.D.A. Forest Service, Audio-Visual Communications, 435 Crooked Lane, King of Prussia, PA 19406. (215) 272–8500.

On the Air. A set of seven catchy radio public service announcements. Contains messages about the importance of trees in our society, the importance of proper tree care, and whom to call about tree care needs. Designed for groups to add their own announcement at the end. From the International Society of Arboriculture, 303 W. University, P.O. Box 908, Urbana, IL 61801.

Preserving a Heritage: The American Elm. A film from the Elm Research Institute, Harrisville, NH 03450.

Pruning Standards for Shade Trees. A slide-tape show with standards booklet. Order from the National Arborist Association, Route 101, Box 1094, Amherst, NH 03031.

Replanting the Tree of Life. A 20-minute videotape for grades 7 through 12, plus adults, looks at trees and forests and what they mean to our well-being. That look starts with microscopic closeups of tree structure, shows the ecological functions of trees, and presents the diverse forest covers of the globe. A stewardship and sustainable use message is given. From Bullfrog Films, Olney, PA 19547.

This Is Urban Forestry (1988). Available in VHS or Beta from the American Forestry Association.*

Urban Forestry Public Service Announcement for TV. Designed for national distribution with open space at the end of 60- or 30-second spots for any logo. Contact Terry Johnson, Mills/James Productions, 4555 N. High St., Columbus, OH 43214.

EDUCATIONAL AIDS

Adopt-a-Woods. A forest curriculum for grades K–6 developed for Minnesota's Forest Resource Center but adaptable to other wooded areas whereby children can "adopt" a tree for the duration of the study. The kit outlines specific activities to do in the woods, then provides follow-up exercises for the classroom. Contact the Forest Resource Center, Route 2, Box 156A, Lanesboro, MN 55949.

Gypsy Moth Workbook. An 8-page book with 25 projects that will challenge children while teaching them about the gypsy moth. Projects are coded into three age levels. From the American Forestry Association.*

Project Learning Tree. A national environmental education program that uses the forest as a window into the natural world. The program has activities in different areas of study (language, science, etc.) for grades K–12. Developed by classroom teachers with technical assistance from foresters and others. Contains over 175 activities for a wide variety of learning styles. Participants also receive a subscription to PLT's newsletter, filled with updates on teaching ideas and activities. Six-hour workshops on PLT are held in all areas of the country, where teachers participate in learning activities and receive the PLT guide free of charge. For information, contact Project Learning Tree, American Forest Council, 1250 Connecticut Ave., NW, Suite 320, Washington, DC 20036.

Wildlife Habitat Conservation Teacher's Pac Series. Eight educational packets from the National Institute for Urban Wildlife, 10921 Trotting Ridge Way, Columbia, MD 21044. $5 each. Write for information and order form.

POSTERS

Famous and Historic Trees, Is There a Forest in Your Future? and *Arbor Day.* From the American Forestry Association.*

* See Appendix D for address.

Computer Software for Urban Forest Management: A Buyer's Guide

E. Thomas Smiley

As MICROCOMPUTER PRICES have fallen and become affordable for mid-sized cities, many urban forestry departments have computerized their tree information systems. When a department purchases a computer, it must decide which software to use. Different software functions serve different forestry needs.

Urban forestry software systems designed for municipalities have six major functions: the first three are data files and the last three are ways the files can be manipulated.

DATA FILES

The first data file manages tree inventory data. The information on individual trees must be easily updatable as the condition of the tree or planting site changes. There must be provision for adding newly planted trees and deleting trees that are removed. In order to keep the inventory current, data must be added regularly. Prior to purchasing a system, assess the ease of changing individual tree information.

The second capability of most systems is the ability to record work conducted on trees. This work history file should keep records of what work has been completed, when, by whom, what equipment was used, how many hours were required, and what materials were used. These factors can be summarized and used to help with budget preparation, species selection, comparison of crew/contractor efficiency, and determination of equipment requirements. It can also be valuable in tree-related legal disputes.

The third data file is for service requests. Most municipal forestry departments are deluged with requests for tree work from citizens who notice problems. Hand recording and keeping track of inspection cards can be a monumental task during the spring and summer months. Computerizing service requests greatly simplifies matters and allows the inspection orders, tree inventory data, and work histories to be linked together.

MANIPULATING FILES

The fourth system capability is that of numerically summarizing tree inventory data, work history data, and service request data. For example, if you need to know how many dead trees there are in the inventory database with a DBH (diameter at breast height) greater than twelve inches, the computer should be able to display that number. This type of numerical information can then be used to prepare annual and/or monthly reports on the condition of municipal trees, how much work has been completed, and how many service requests have been received.

The fifth capability of most systems is the ability to generate listings of trees. This allows foresters to pinpoint the location of problem trees or to produce a work order. For day-to-day operations, it's best to have listings based on maintenance requirements. If you need to schedule the removal of all dead trees greater than twelve inches DBH, the computer can list the address or location of each tree in this category. Listings of trees on which work has been completed and listings of service requests are also available in many systems.

Computer mapping of tree locations can be an integral part of a computer system. Computer-generated maps are a valuable aid in locating park and boulevard trees. If the database includes underground and overhead utilities as well as building setback distances, computer maps can be a valuable aid in selecting the right species for a given location.

Prior to purchasing a system, look at these six capabilities and decide which you require. Systems should also be assessed for "friendliness," or general ease of use. If you have special needs, make sure they can be added to the system.

The majority of these systems were developed for IBM personal computers or compatible systems (see Table C.1). One has been developed for the Apple IIe and three for minicomputers.

System capabilities vary among the programs (see Tables C.2 and C.3). Most appear to store and manipulate tree inventory data in similar ways and can generate tree listings, work orders, and numerical summaries. Work histories can be recorded in nine of the systems, and maps can be generated by one system. The UTIP (Urban Tree Inventory Program) system is intended for use in a "windshield"-type partial inventory. UTIP provides information to make decisions on the needs of a city forestry department, but it is not intended for daily operations.

TABLE C.1

Software Packages: Who Produces Them, What Computers Do They Work On, and How Many Trees Can They Handle?

Package Code	System Name	Developer/ Organization	Hardware/Software Required	Capacity	
				Floppy	10mb Hard Disk
CFIP	Community Forestry Inventory Program	Helburg, Hoefer/CO State University	IBM PC/Word Proc. Apple IIe/Word Proc.	?	?
CTI	Central Tree Inventory	Reidel/Nat'l Park Serv.	Unify/Unix	100K	
CT	Compu-Tree (TM)	?/Systemics	IBM PC/MSDOS	1,800	50K
dT	dTree	Jones, Dossin/dTree	IBM PC/MSDOS	1,500	30K
GCTM	Golden Coast Tree Mgmt. Software System	Giedraitis, York/Golden Coast Env. Services	IBM PC/MSDOS Unix/Rel DB Mgr.	?	30K
OUF	Oakland U.F. Data Mgmt. System	?/USFS, Oakland, CA	IBM PC/dBase III	500+	50K
SMUF	Santa Maria U.F. Data Mgmt. System	?/USFS, Santa Maria, CA	HP3000/IMAGE	?	?
TB	Trebase	Miller, Andrews/Univ. of Wisconsin	IBM PC/dBase III	4,000	?
TI	Tree Inventory	?/Michigan State Univ.	IBM PC/MSDOS	2,500	75K
TIMS	Tree Inventory and Mgmt. System	Maggio/Texas A&M	IBM PC/DOS, Lotus	10,000	?
TIS	Tree Inventory System	McCarter, Baker/Utah State University	IBM PC/MSDOS	6,800	200K
TM	Tree Manager (TM)	Joehlin/ACRT, Inc.	IBM PC/dBase III	1,300	50K
UTIP	Urban Tree Inventory Prog.	?/OK Forestry Division	IBM PC/MSDOS	?	?

The costs of systems vary greatly (see Table C.4). Off-the-shelf software systems tend to be less expensive. Due to the high cost of customization, systems that are adapted to existing management needs are more expensive. Some systems include installation, which consists of an expert visiting the municipality to make sure the software works on its computers. Training of personnel who will use the system is also included in the installation expense. Support costs are for the right to call the software provider and have them solve problems that arise during the use of the software. This is helpful for departments without staff knowledgeable about computers.

To find out more about computer systems, contact the organizations that provide software or software developers listed in Table C.5.

TABLE C.2
System Capabilities: What Do They Do?

| Package Code | Tree Inventory Data | | | | | Work Order (WO) Generated by | | Work History (WH) Record by | | Numerical Summaries | | |
| | Updated | | Location System | | | | | | | | | |
	Daily	Batch	Address	Grid	Other	Block	Tree	Block	Tree	Inventory	WO	WH
CFIP	X	X	X	X	X	X				X	X	
CTI	X	X		X		X	X	X	X	X	X	X
CT	X	X	X	X	X	X	X	X	X	X	X	X
dT	X	X	X	X		X	X			X	X	
GCTM	X	X	X		X	X	X	X	X	X	X	X
OUF	X	X	X			X	X	X	X	X	X	X
SMUF	X	X	X			X	X	X	X	X	X	X
TB	X		X		X			X	X	X	X	X
TI	X		X			X	X			X		
TIMS	X	X	X		X	X	X	X		X		
TIS	X		X	X		X	X	X	X	X		
TM	X	X	X	X		X	X		X	X	X	
UTIP		X			X					X	X	X

TABLE C.3
Software Packages: What Do They Do?

| Package Code | Tree Listings by | | | Maps |
	Location	Maintenance Requirements	Other	
CFIP	X	X		
CTI	X	X	X	
CT	X	X	X	
dT	X	X	X	
GCTM	X	X	X	
OUF	X		X	
SMUF	X	X	X	
TB	X	X	X	
TI	X	X	X	
TIMS	X	X	X	X
TIS	X	X	X	
TM	X	X	X	
UTIP				

TABLE C.4
Software Packages: Who Is Using Them and How Much Do They Cost?

| Package Code | No. of Cities Using System | Approximate Costs | | |
		Software	Installation	Support
CFIP	3	?	?	?
CTI	0	?	?	?
CT	5+	$10,500		
dT	0	$200	–	–
GCTM	4	$3,500	$600	$600[a]
OUF	1	?	?	?
SMUF	1	?	?	?
TB	11	$175	?	NC[b]
TI	1	$300	$300+	$30/call
TIMS	1	$9,000	$2,500	$500[a]
TIS	1	$100	?	NC[b]
TM	5+	$3,500	$600	$600[a]
UTIP	28	NC	NC	NC

[a] Installation costs do not include travel expenses or hardware.
[b] No charge.

TABLE C.5

Providers of Tree Management Computer Software

Organization	Contact Person	Address	Phone
Commercial			
ACRT, Inc.	Beth Buchanan	P.O. Box 219 Kent, OH 44240	(216) 673–8272
dTree	Dan Dossin	8601 Roberts Dr., Suite 4–1 Dunwoody, GA 30338	(404) 993–0831
Golden Coast Env. Service	Thomas Pehrson	2736 W. Orangethorpe Ave., Suite 5 Fullerton, CA 92633	(714) 441–1308
Michigan State University	J. James Kielbaso	Department of Forestry, MSU E. Lansing, MI 48824	(517) 355–7533
Systemics	Arthur Costonis	43 Green St. Foxborough, MA 02035	(617) 543–4557
Texas A&M	Robert Magio	Department of Forest Science College Station, TX 77843	(409) 845–5069
Utah State University	Fred Baker	Department of Forest Resources Logan, UT 84322	(801) 750–2550
University of Wisconsin	Robert Miller	College of Natural Resources Stevens Point, WI 54481	(715) 346–4189
Noncommercial			
Colorado State University	Larry Helburg	Fort Collins, CO 80523	(303) 491–6303
Oklahoma Forestry Division	Rob Doye	2800 N. Lincoln Blvd. Oklahoma City, OK	(405) 521–3864
U.S. Forest Service	Philip Barker	P.O. Box 245 Berkeley, CA 94701	(415) 486–3927

Organizations with Resources

American Association of Botanical Gardens and Arboreta, Inc.
P.O. Box 206
Swarthmore, PA 19081

Nonprofit membership organization serving North American botanical gardens and arboreta, their professional staffs, and their work on behalf of the public and the profession. It publishes a quarterly journal, *The Public Garden*, and a directory of internships and summer jobs at public gardens.

American Association of Nurserymen
1240 I Street, NW, Suite 500
Washington, DC 20005
(202) 789–2900

Network of organizations representing garden centers, landscaping, and horticultural research. Publishes various magazines and newsletters. Catalog available.

American Chestnut Foundation
c/o Dr. David French
Department of Plant Pathology
University of Minnesota
St. Paul, MN 55108

Established in 1983 to bring back the American chestnut. Supports research and breeding efforts, has a journal, and gives advice on growing chestnuts.

American Forest Council
Suite 320, 1250 Connecticut
    Avenue, NW
Washington, DC 20036
(202) 463–2459

Information and education organization supported by forest products industries. Publishes a quarterly magazine, *American Tree Farmer*, and a biannual newsletter, *Branch*. Sponsors *Project Learning Tree*, a K–12 education program.

American Forestry Association
1516 P Street, NW
Washington, DC 20005
(202) 667–3300

Citizens organization to advance proper management of forests and other interrelated natural resources of soil, water, and wildlife. See Appendix G for multiple resources.

American Horticultural Society
7931 East Boulevard Drive
Alexandria, VA 22308
(703) 768–5700

Serves the needs of American gardeners through membership program. Provides catalog of free seeds, gardeners information hotline, and travel services. Publishes a monthly magazine, *American Horticulturist*.

American Planning Association
1313 East 60th Street
Chicago, IL 60637
(312) 955–9100

National organization of people working for better-planned communities. Provides professional aid to community planners, current information, and advice to all. Publishes a quarterly magazine, *APA Journal*, and a monthly magazine, *Planning*.

American Rivers
801 Pennsylvania Avenue, SE, Suite 303
Washington, DC 20003
(202) 547–6900

Provides policy work and technical assistance related to saving free-flowing rivers, community rivers, and associated greenways. Publishes a quarterly newsletter, *American Rivers.*

American Society of Consulting Arborists
700 Canterbury Road
Clearwater, FL 34624
(813) 446–3356

Professional society providing landscaping and arboricultural services. Publishes a bimonthly newsletter, *Arboriculture Consultant.*

American Society of Landscape Architects
4401 Connecticut Avenue, NW
Washington, DC 20007
(202) 686–2752

Dedicated to the advancement of knowledge, education, and skill in the art and science of landscape architecture. Publishes *Landscape Architecture* and *Landscape Architecture News Digest.*

American Trails
1400 16th Street, NW
Washington, DC 20036
(202) 797–5418
Nonprofit membership organization providing information on trail issues at federal, state, and local levels. Publishes a bimonthly newsletter, *Trail Tracks.*

Associated Landscape Contractors of America
405 North Washington Street
Falls Church, VA 22046
(703) 241–4004

Professional association dedicated to improving the landscape industry. Publishes a monthly newsletter, *ALCA Action.*

Center for Environmental Information
99 Court Street
Rochester, NY 14604
(716) 546–3796

Provides on-call references and referrals on air pollution, urban forestry, and other issues related to greenhouse effect. Publishes monthly bulletins on acid precipitation and global climate change.

Elm Research Institute
Harrisville, NH 03450
(603) 827–3048

Provides information on elms and Dutch elm disease. Publishes a quarterly newsletter, *The ERI News.*

Greenways for America Program
The Conservation Fund
1800 North Kent Street, Suite 1120
Arlington, VA 22209
(703) 525–6300

Provides an umbrella of services and guidance for building greenway systems in local communities across America. Publishes a quarterly newsletter.

Holly Society of America, Inc.
304 Northwind Road
Baltimore, MD 21204
(301) 825–8133

National organization that promotes use
of holly in landscaping. Publishes a
quarterly journal, *Holly Society Journal.*

Human Environment Center
1001 Connecticut Avenue, NW,
  Suite 827
Washington, DC 20036
(202) 331–8387

Provides information and technical assistance on conservation and service
corps employment programs for youths
and minorities. Publishes a quarterly
newsletter, *Human Environment Center
News,* and other reports.

International Society of Arboriculture
P.O. Box 908, 303 W. University
Urbana, IL 61801
(217) 328–2032

Professional affiliation of commercial,
educational, municipal, research, and
utility arborists dedicated to the care
and preservation of shade and ornamental trees. Publishes a monthly magazine, *Journal of Arboriculture,* and
various guides: *Establishing the Values of
Trees and Other Plants, A Standard Municipal Tree Ordinance,* and *Tree and Shrub
Transplanting Manual.* Offers select vid-
eos on tree care and preservation.

Land Trust Exchange
1017 Duke Street
Alexandria, VA 22314
(703) 683–7778

National network center for groups involved in gaining conservation easements and other forms of land
preservation. Publishes directory of local and regional land conservation organizations.

**Metropolitan Tree Improvement
  Alliance (METRIA)**
c/o Ohio Department of Natural
  Resources
Fountain Square, Building C
Columbus, OH 43224
(614) 265–6707

Professional organization dedicated to
developing better trees for metropolitan
and urban landscapes. Publishes a biannual newsletter, *The Metrian.*

**Municipal Arborist and Urban
  Foresters Society**
17 Lafayette Place
P.O. Box 1255
Freehold, NJ 07728
(201) 431–7903

Professional society of arborists, urban
foresters, and park managers. Publishes a bimonthly newsletter.

National Arbor Day Foundation
100 Arbor Avenue
Nebraska City, NE 68410
(402) 474–5655

Nonprofit education organization dedi-
cated to tree planting and conservation.
Sponsors National Arbor Day, Tree City
USA, and conservation trees programs.
Publishes a bimonthly newsletter, *Arbor
Day News.*

National Arborist Association
Route 101, Box 1094
Amherst, NH 03031
(603) 673–3311

A national trade association committed
to serving the management needs of
tree service firms. Publishes two
monthly newsletters: *NAA Reporter* and
Tree Worker.

National Association of Conservation Districts
509 Capitol Court, NE
Washington, DC 20002
(202) 547–6223

National organization of local conservation districts charged with carrying out comprehensive natural resource management programs. Publishes a catalog of environmental films and publications.

National Association of State Foresters
Hall of the States, Suite 526
444 N. Capitol Street, NW
Washington, DC 20001
(202) 624–5415

Includes the 50 state forestry program directors. Publishes a monthly newsletter, *Washington Update.*

National Association of Towns and Townships
1522 K Street, NW, Suite 730
Washington, DC 20005
(202) 737–5200

National organization comprised of small cities and townships. Provides training programs for local government officials, policy research, and lobbying for small government interests. Publishes a monthly, *NATAT's Reporter,* and three quarterly newsletters: *Town Crier, Insider's Report,* and *NATAT Perspective.*

National Environmental Health Association
720 South Colorado Boulevard, Suite Tower, 970
Denver, CO 80222
(303) 756–9090

Professional society of environmental health practitioners. Publishes the annual *Environmental Health Trends Report,* a quarterly newsletter, and the bimonthly *Journal of Environmental Health.*

National Institute for Urban Wildlife
10921 Trotting Ridge Way
Columbia, MD 21044
(301) 596–3311

Provides research and information on wildlife in urban areas. Publishes two quarterly newsletters: *Urban Wildlife News* with supplement and *Urban Wildlife Manager's Notebook.*

National League of Cities
1801 Pennsylvania Avenue, NW
Washington, DC 20004
(202) 626–3000

Public-interest group lobbying for federal policies that reflect the needs of cities, towns, and municipalities. Publishes a weekly newsletter, *Nation's Cities Weekly,* and a monthly magazine, *Resource Recovery.*

National Parks and Conservation Association
1015 31st Street, NW
Washington, DC 20007
(202) 944–8530

Membership organization concerned with preservation, promotion, and improvement of the nation's park system. Publishes *National Parks* magazine.

National Recreation and Parks Association
3101 Park Center Drive
Alexandria, VA 22302
(703) 820–4940

Nonprofit education and research organization dedicated to improving park and recreation leadership and facilities. Publishes *Parks and Recreation Magazine, Recreation and Parks Law Reporter,* and *Park Practice Program.*

National Trust for Historic Preservation
1785 Massachusetts Avenue, NW
Washington, DC 20036
(202) 673–4000

Provides information and technical assistance on historic preservation, including natural environments. Publishes *Historic Preservation* magazine and numerous newsletters.

National Urban Forest Council
c/o American Forestry Association
P.O. Box 2000
Washington, DC 20013
(202) 667–3300

Coalition of citizens and professionals dedicated to the development and management of trees in urban areas. Publishes a bimonthly newsletter, *Urban Forest Forum*, in cooperation with the American Forestry Association.

National Urban Forestry Program
State and Private Forestry
U.S. Department of Agriculture Forest Service
P.O. Box 96090
Washington, DC 20090–6090
(202) 447–6657

This office of the federal government is responsible for administering the federal grants to state urban forestry programs and for coordinating efforts between federal and state governments.

National Wildlife Federation
1400 16th Street, NW
Washington, DC 20036
(202) 797–6800

Provides conservation education with focus on wildlife. Conducts yearly wildlife program, which includes educational packets, posters, audio-visual materials. Publishes multiple magazines for all ages.

New Jersey Shade Tree Federation
P.O. Box 231
Cook College
New Brunswick, NJ 08903
(201) 246–3210

Coordinates the efforts of public agencies in selecting, planting, and maintaining trees for public areas. Publishes a monthly newsletter, *The Shade Tree*— ten issues per year covering timely topics in the arboriculture industry.

Partners for Livable Places
1429 21st Street, NW
Washington, DC 20036
(202) 887–5990

Works with community planning departments to promote urban landscape design, waterfront protection, urban parks, and general conservation of natural and man-made environments. Publishes a weekly newsletter, *Amenities*.

Professional Grounds Management Society
7 Church Lane
Pikesville, MD 21208
(301) 667–1833

Professional society of grounds managers and others in the greens industry. Publishes a monthly newsletter, *Grounds Management Forum*. Membership includes subscriptions to four magazines: *Grounds Maintenance*, *Landscapes*, *Sports Turf*, and *Sports, Recreation and Leisure*.

Rails-to-Trails Conservancy
1400 16th Street, NW, Suite 300
Washington, DC 20036
(202) 797–5400

National, nonprofit membership organization working with citizens groups and public agencies to preserve abandoned railroad corridors for transportation, conservation, and recreational use. Publishes a quarterly newsletter, *Trailblazer*.

Small Towns Institute
P.O. Box 517
Ellensburg, WA 98926
(509) 925–1830

Devoted to addressing the problems and potentials of the small community. Publishes *Small Town*, a bimonthly magazine covering case studies of communities that have engaged in innovative projects to better the quality of life in their towns.

Society of American Foresters
5400 Grosvenor Lane
Bethesda, MD 20814
(301) 897–8720

National organization representing professional foresters; publishes the *Journal of Forestry*, *Forest Sciences*, and numerous brochures. It also supports other educational and research activities. Coordinates 28 forestry working groups, including one on urban forestry.

Society of Municipal Arborists
975 Pennsylvania Avenue
University City, MO 63130
(314) 862–6767

Professional society of city arborists and landscapers. Publishes a bimonthly newsletter, *CityTrees*.

Soil and Water Conservation Society
7515 Northeast Ankeny Road
Ankeny, IA 50021–9764
(515) 289–2331

Society of professionals advancing proper land and water use worldwide. Publishes professional journal and educational materials related to soil and water conservation.

The Trust for Public Land
116 New Montgomery
San Francisco, CA 94105
(415) 495–4014

Helps groups to acquire scenic, recreational, urban, and rural lands for conservation. Publishes a quarterly newsletter, *The Update*.

Urban Land Institute
1090 Vermont Avenue, NW, Suite 300
Washington, DC 20005

Nonprofit organization dedicated to improving the quality and standards of urban land use. Publishes a monthly magazine, *Urban Land*, a monthly newsletter, *Land Use Digest*, and a quarterly member newsletter, *Inside ULI*.

Utility Arborist Association

Contact the International Society of Arboriculture.

The Waterfront Center
1536 44th Street, NW
Washington, DC 20077
(202) 337–0356

Offers community consulting services. Sponsors annual conference on urban waterfronts and annual awards program, "Excellence on the Waterfront." Publishes conference summary documents and a bimonthly magazine, *Waterfront World*.

More on Tree Ordinances

Municipal tree ordinances generally fall into three broad categories:

1. A *preservation ordinance* regulates the cutting of trees within a given jurisdiction. Most come with some sort of diameter or height specification. For example, a municipality might require a citizen to obtain a permit before cutting a tree of twelve inches or more in diameter. Some regulate only public property, while others regulate both public and private property.
2. A *development ordinance* regulates the impact of construction and development upon the area landscape. Builders might be required to leave a number of trees per acre or to replant trees cleared for construction. Some ordinances require the builder to submit an overall landscaping plan for city approval.
3. A *street tree ordinance* ensures that proper tree species are planted in a given location. Different tree species have different soil, air, light, and moisture requirements. Some species might grow too large for a given location, causing cracks in sidewalks, interference with utility lines, or other problems. Street tree ordinances often assign lists of acceptable species for given locations.

Many municipalities incorporate these three principles into an overall landscaping plan for their area. The length and complexity of these plans often range from highly intricate and detailed documents to simple, one-page statements of purpose. Assess the needs of your community and create your ordinance accordingly. The following publications may be helpful.

A Municipal Tree Ordinance Manual: Contains introductory ordinance information, a discussion of different types of ordinance sections, and two sample ordinances—one brief and one comprehensive. Also includes a sample description of arboricultural specifications and practices, a list of further references, and five sample tree work permit forms. Contact the International Society of Arboriculturists, P.O. Box 908, 303 W. University, Urbana, IL 61801. (217) 328–2032

Analysis of Tree Ordinances: Gives information about different types of ordinance sections, and provides examples drawn from actual city tree ordinances. Contact the Michigan Municipal League, 1675 Green Road, P.O. Box 1487, Ann Arbor, MI 48106. (313) 662–3246

Tree Survey Forms

TREE SURVEY INSTRUCTIONS

COMMUNITY:_____ DATE:_____

SPECIES	DIAMETER BREAST HEIGHT												
	0-3	4	6	8	10	12	14	16	18	20	22	24	26+

TREE SURVEY INSTRUCTIONS

The survey should be kept as simple as possible. It is a tool used to help your community visualize the value and condition of the urban forest. A more complete inventory can be compiled in the future.

1. Use the sheet titled "Tree Survey." Make several copies of the Tree Survey sheet. Fill in the community, name, and date at the top of the page.

2. Take four sheets of the Tree Survey page and fill out the condition class at the bottom of the page using the categories of good, fair, poor, or dead. The condition class of the tree should be identified according to the definitions listed at the bottom of the Suggested Abbreviations for Tree Species.

3. Fill in common species on each page. Only one species of tree should be listed per line. After a tree species is identified, the species code should be listed in this column. (See Suggested Abbreviations for Tree Species.)

4. The data collection process begins with the identification of the tree condition.
　　　a) Use the appropriate condition page for the tree you are evaluating. Keep all trees of each defined class on the same page. Do not mix the poor trees with the good trees, etc.
　　　b) Identify the tree species and locate the name on your sheet.
　　　c) Measure the diameter with a diameter tape at 4.5 feet above the ground.
　　　d) Fill in a square for each tree found in the appropriate sized categories. The 0-3 inch category includes all trees under 3.5 inches in diameter. The 4 inch category includes trees between 3.5 and 5.5 inches in diameter. Be consistent when categorizing diameter classes.

Remember, this is a quick survey. If there is a problem, make a note of it and move on. Your technical expert should be able to assist you with any difficulties.

CONDITION CLASS: _____

TREE SURVEY

COMMUNITY:_____ DATE:_____

SPECIES	DIAMETER BREAST HEIGHT												
	0-3	4	6	8	10	12	14	16	18	20	22	24	26+

CONDITION CLASS: _____

COMMUNITY TREES -- SURVEY SUMMARY

COMMUNITY: _____ DATE: _____

SPECIES	NO. TREES	AVERAGE DIAMETER	PERCENT OF SPECIES TOTAL				% OF TOTAL TREES	VALUE (OPTIONAL)
			GOOD	FAIR	POOR	DEAD		

SUGGESTED ABBREVIATIONS FOR TREE SPECIES

CODE	SPECIES	CODE	SPECIES
001	Ash, Green	031	Mulberry (Sp.)
002	Ash, White	032	Oak, Sawtooth
003	Baldcypress	033	Oak, Southern Red
004	Basswood	034	Oak, Scarlet
005	Birch (SP.)	035	Oak, Pin
006	Boxelder	036	Oak, Northern Red
007	Bradford Pear	037	Oak, Willow
008	Black Gum	038	Oak, White
009	Catalpa	039	Persimmon
010	Dogwood	040	Pine, Austrian
011	Elm, American	041	Pine, Loblolly
012	Elm, Red	042	Pine, Scotch
013	Elm, Siberian	043	Pine, White
014	Flowering Crab (var.)	044	Poplar, Lombardy
015	Fruit (Sp.)	045	Poplar (Sp.)
016	Gingko	046	Purpleleaf Plum
017	Goldenraintree	047	Redbud
018	Hackberry	048	Redcedar
019	Hawthorn (Sp.)	049	Serviceberry
020	Hickory (Sp.)	050	Spruce (Sp.)
021	Honeylocust	051	Sweetgum
022	Japanese Pagodatree	052	Sycamore-Plane Tree
023	Linden (Sp.)	053	Tree of Heaven
024	Locust, Black	054	Tulip Poplar
025	Magnolia	055	Walnut, Black
026	Maple, Norway	056	Willow (Sp.)
027	Maple, Red	057	Zelkova
028	Maple, Silver	058	
029	Maple, Sugar	059	
030	Mountain Ash	060	

CONDITION CLASSES

Good: Health vigorous tree. No apparent signs of insect, disease or mecahnical injury. Little or no corrective work required. Form is representative of species.

Fair: Average condition and vigor for area. May be in need of some corrective pruning or repair. May lack desirable form characteristic of species. May show minor insect injury, disease or physiological problem.

Poor: General state of decline. May show sever mechanical, insect or disease damage, but death not imminent. May require major repair or renovation.

Dead or Dying: Dead, or death imminent from Dutch elm disease or other causes.

TREE VALUE FORMULA

(developed by the Council of Tree and Landscape Appraisers)

FORMULA

$V = B \times S \times L \times C$

V = estimated value
B = basic value in dollars per square inch of basal area (subject to change with inflation)
S = species value in percent (see next page)
L = locational value in percent (street trees valued at 70%)
C = condition value in percent (Good = 80%; Fair = 50%; Poor = 30%; Dead = 10%)

TABLE		
Trunk Caliper or diameter-inches (cm)	Cross-section or area-square inches (cm²)	Basic value in dollars (at $27/in²)
8 (20.32)	50.3 (324.5)	1378
9 (22.86)	63.6 (410.3)	1717
10 (25.4)	78.5 (506.4)	2120
11 (27.94)	95.0 (612.9)	2565
12 (30.48)	113.1 (729.7)	3054
13 (33.02)	132.7 (856.1)	3583
14 (35.56)	153.9 (992.9)	4155
15 (38.1)	176.7 (1140.0)	4771
16 (40.64)	201.1 (1297.4)	5430
17 (43.18)	227.0 (1464.5)	6129
18 (45.72)	254.5 (1641.9)	6872
19 (48.26)	283.5 (1829.0)	7655
20 (50.8)	314.2 (2027.0)	8483
21 (53.34)	346.4 (2234.8)	9353
22 (55.88)	380.1 (2452.3)	10263
23 (58.42)	415.5 (2680.6)	11219
24 (60.96)	452.5 (2919.3)	12218
25 (63.5)	490.9 (3167.1)	13254
26 (66.04)	530.9 (3425.2)	14334
27 (68.58)	572.6 (3694.2)	15460
28 (71.12)	615.8 (3972.9)	16627
29 (73.66)	660.5 (4261.3)	17834
30 (76.2)	706.9 (4560.6)	19086
31 (78.74)	754.8 (4869.7)	20380
32 (81.28)	804.2 (5188.4)	21713
33 (83.82)	855.3 (5518.1)	23093
34 (86.36)	907.9 (5857.4)	24513
35 (88.9)	962.1 (6207.1)	25977
36 (91.44)	1017.9 (6567.1)	27483
37 (93.98)	1075.2 (6936.8)	29030
38 (96.52)	1134.1 (7316.8)	30621
39 (99.06)	1194.6 (7707.1)	32254
40 (101.6)	1256.6 (8107.1)	33928

TREE VALUE BY SPECIES

Listed below is a sample of tree value percentages by species. In order to accurately assess your trees, the appropriate percentage value must be used. Values change for the same species of tree from one location to another. The American Forestry Association (AFA) can provide this information to those using this Community Tree Management Package. Clip the coupon at the bottom of the page, fill in the information, and send it to AFA for your location's specific data. We will work with you in order to determine your area's specific values.

EXAMPLE OF TREE VALUE PERCENT BY SPECIES

Norway & Red Maple	70-80%
Green Ash	60-70%
Dogwood	60-75%
Honeylocust	60-70%
Sweetgum	70-80%
Walnut	55-65%
Black Gum	80-90%
Callery Pear	70-85%
White Oak	80-90%
Red Oak	80-90%
Willow Oak	80-90%
Littleleaf Linden	70-80%
Sycamore	50-60%
London Plane	60-70%

COMMUNITY DIRECTORY

Community: _____

NAME	ADDRESS	PHONE	BEST TIME TO CONTACT

American Forestry
Association Resources

The American Forestry Association, founded in 1875, is the citizens organization for trees, forests, and forestry. The AFA is a strong voice for tree planting, maintenance, and care. Its objective is to bring Americans closer to forest resources through action-oriented programs, information, and communication. Its members include professional foresters and arborists, businesspeople, lawyers, educators, researchers, administrators, and interested citizens. In becoming a member, you are helping to promote forest conservation and stewardship, tree planting, legislative action, and forest education.

Membership brings you physical benefits, as well. Along with supporting the goals and objectives of the AFA, members can receive and contribute to the following publications and activities:

American Forests magazine is a bimonthly publication that has brought inspiration, images, and insight to the field of forest conservation since 1894. It represents the main voice of the AFA and consistently reflects the association's goal of promoting an enlightened public appreciation of natural resources.

Urban Forest Forum is a bimonthly newsletter, published since 1980, which serves as a source of information and national cheerleader for urban forest professionals and citizen activists in the rapidly expanding field of urban forestry.

Resource Hotline is a biweekly policy and legislative publication of the AFA, which serves to inform politically active members of current proposals and AFA activities on Capitol Hill to promote forest resource conservation.

Global ReLeaf Report is an action newsletter containing up-to-date information on local, national, and international developments in urban, rural, and tropical forestation.

Forests for Us is an AFA clearinghouse for media information and educational materials on National Forests.

The National Register of Big Trees has been maintained by the AFA since 1940 in an effort to seek out and preserve our nation's largest tree specimens.

Famous and Historic Trees is the AFA's program to collect and plant the seeds of trees old enough to have witnessed the historic events of our nation's birth.

Friends of the National For__ts is a support program for local Friends chapters formed to protect and enhance our national forests.

National Urban Forest Council is a coalition of individuals from many professions dedicated to the development and management of trees in our cities and towns for the benefit of people.

National Urban Tree Network (TreeNet) is a computer-based communications network, established in 1986, to provide electronic mail exchange, weekly bulletins on urban forest activities and a library for urban forestry information.

American Forest Adventures, originally Trail Riders of the Wilderness, are educational wilderness trips sponsored by the AFA.

Awards are presented annually to five citizens and professionals for their efforts to promote the conservation of trees and forests on both a local and national level; two of these awards are dedicated to urban forestry.

Urban Forestry conferences are organized and sponsored by the AFA every three years in an effort to strengthen and keep abreast of the rapidly expanding science and profession of urban forestry; workshops are held to promote citizen action and involvement as well as new scientific achievement.

White Papers are research reports by the AFA staff to address specific problems and solutions of national import, such as the effects on forests of air pollution.

Discounts are provided to members for AFA publications, tree-related gifts, car rentals, and more.

A one-year subscribing membership costs $24 and brings you six issues of *American Forests* magazine. A one-year plus membership, $45, includes a one-year subscription to most AFA publications. For more information on membership options and costs, please write to the American Forestry Association, P.O. Box 2000, Washington, DC 20013.

State Foresters

State forestry organizations are a source of information on urban forestry, and many of the states have state urban forestry coordinators as well. This list contains the name and address of each State Forester. They can be used as the first point of contact for information in your state.

C. W. Moody, State Forester
Alabama Forestry Commission
513 Madison Ave.
Montgomery, AL 36130

Tom Hawkins, Acting State Forester
Division of Forestry
400 Willoughbury Ave.
Juneau, AK 99801

T. Michael Hart, State Forester
State Land Department
1616 W. Adams
Phoenix AZ 85007

Edwin E. Waddell, State Forester
Arkansas Forestry Commission
P.O. Box 4523, Asher Sta.
Little Rock, AR 72214

Gerald Partain, Director
Department of Forestry and Fire Protection
    Resources
P.O. Box 94246
Sacramento, CA 94244–2460

James E. Hubbard, State Forester
Colorado State Forest Service
203 Forestry Building
Colorado State University
Fort Collins, CO 80523

Peter Babcock, State Forester
Bureau of Forestry
Department of Environmental Protection
165 Capitol Ave.
Hartford, CT 06106

Walter F. Gabel, State Forester
State of Delaware
Department of Agriculture
2320 South Dupont Highway
Dover, DE 19901

Harold Mikell, Director
Division of Forestry
3125 Conner Blvd.
Tallahassee, FL 32399–1650

John W. Mixon, Director
Georgia Forestry Commission
P.O. Box 819
Macon, GA 31298–4599

Carlos L. T. Noquez, Chief
Forestry and Soil Resources Division
P.O. Box 2950
Agana, GU 96910

Dr. Calvin W. S. Lum, DVM, Administrator
Division of Forestry and Wildlife
1151 Punchbowl St.
Honolulu, HI 96813

Stanley F. Hamilton, Director
Idaho Department of Lands
State Capitol Building #121
Boise, ID 83720

Allan S. Mickelson, State Forester
Division of Forest Resources
Northwest Office Plaza
600 N. Grand Ave. West
Springfield, IL 62706

John F. Datena, State Forester
Department of Natural Resources
Division of Forestry
613 State Office Building
Indianapolis, IN 46204

William Farris, State Forester
Iowa Department of Natural Resources
Wallace State Office Building
Des Moines, IA 50319

Lester R. Pinkerton, State Forester and
    Department Head
Department of Forestry
2610 Claflin Road
Manhattan, KS 66502

Donald A. Hamm, Director
Kentucky Division of Forestry
627 Comanche Trail
Frankfort, KY 40601

Carlton Hurst, Acting Asst. Comm.
Department of Agriculture
Office of Forestry
P.O. Box 1628
Baton Rouge, LA 70821

John H. Cashwell, State Forester
Department of Conservation
Bureau of Forestry
State House Station #22
Augusta, ME 04333

James B. Roberts, State Forester
Maryland Forest Park and Wildlife Service
Tawes State Office Building
580 Taylor Ave.
Annapolis, MD 21401

Thomas F. Quink, Chief Forester
Division of Forests and Parks
100 Cambridge St.
Boston, MA 02202

Henry H. Webster, Chief and State Forester
Forest Management Division
MI DNR, Stevens T. Mason Building
Box 30028
Lansing, MI 48909

Gerald A. Rose, Director
Division of Forestry
500 Lafayette Road
St. Paul, MN 55155-4044

Robert S. "Sid" Moss, State Forester
Mississippi Forestry Commission
Suite 300, 301 Building
Jackson, MS 39201

Gerald Ross, State Forester
Missouri Department of Conservation
2901 West Truman Blvd.
P.O. Box 180
Jefferson City, MO 65102

Gary G. Brown, State Forester
Division of Forestry
Department of State Lands
2705 Spurgin Road
Missoula, MT 59801

Dr. Gary L. Hergenrader, Head and State
    Forester
Department of Forestry, Fish, and Wildlife
Rm. 101, Plant Ind. Bldg.
Lincoln, NE 68583

Lowell V. Smith, State Forester
Division of Forestry
201 South Fall St.
Carson City, NV 89710

John E. Sargent, Director
Division of Forests and Lands
Box 856, Prescott Park
105 Loudon Road
Concord, NH 03301-0856

Olin D. White, Jr., State Forester
State Forestry
CN 404, 501 E. State St.
Station Plaza #5
Trenton, NJ 08625

William Chapel, State Forester
Forestry Division
P.O. Box 2167
Santa Fe, NM 87504–2167

Robert H. Bathrick, Director
Division of Lands and Forests
Department of Environmental Conservation
50 Wolf Road
Albany, NY 12233–4250

Harry Layman, Director
Div. of Forest Resources
P.O. Box 27687
Raleigh, NC 27611–7687

Larry A. Kotchman, State Forester
North Dakota Forest Service
First and Brander
Bottineau, ND 58318

John Dorka, Acting State Forester
Division of Forestry
Fountain Square
Columbus, OH 43224

Roger L. Davis, Director
Department of Agriculture
Forestry Division
2800 N. Lincoln Blvd.
Oklahoma City, OK 73105

James E. Brown, State Forester
Oregon Department of Forestry
2600 State St.
Salem, OR 97310

James Nelson, Acting Director
Bureau of Forestry
P.O. Box 1467
Harrisburg, PA 17120

Jorge Ivan Sanchez, State Forester
Director of the Forest Service Department
   of Natural Resources
POB 5887 Puerto de Tierra

San Juan, PR 00906
Thomas A. Dupree, State Forester
Division of Forest Environment
1037 Hartford Pike
North Scituate, RI 02857

Leonard A. Kilian, Jr., State Forester
South Carolina Forestry Commission
P.O. Box 21707
Columbia, SC 29221

Frank Davis, Director
Division of Forestry
Sigurd Anderson Building
445 East Capitol
Pierre, SD 57501

Roy C. Ashley, State Forester
Tennessee Department of Conservation
Division of Forestry
701 Broadway
Nashville, TN 37219–5237

Bruce R. Miles, Director
Texas Forest Service
College Station, TX 77843–2136

Richard P. Klason, State Forester
Division of State Lands and Forestry
3 Triad Center, Suite 400
Salt Lake City, UT 84180–1204

Conrad M. Motyka, State Forester
Division of Forests
Agency of Environmental Conservation
103 S. Main St., 10 South
Waterbury, VT 05676

James W. Garner, State Forester
Virginia Division of Forestry
Department of Forestry
P.O. Box 3758
Charlottesville, VA 22903

Eric L. Bough, Assistant Commissioner
King Field Post Office
St. Croix, VI 00851

James A. "Art" Stearns, Supervisor
Department of Natural Resources
201 John A. Cherberg Building
Mail Stop QW-21
Olympia, WA 98504

Ralph Glover, Acting State Forester
Department of Agriculture
Forestry Division
State Capitol
Charleston, WV 25305

Joseph M. Frank, Chief State Forester
P.O. Box 7921
Madison, WI 53707

Carl E. Johnson, State Forester
Wyoming State Forestry Division
1100 West 22nd St.
Cheyenne, WY 82002

Contributors

R. Bruce Allison is a forester and writer and the owner of Allison Tree Care Company in Madison, Wisconsin.

Steven J. Anlian, a vice president with HOH Associates in Virginia, is a landscape architect and urban planner who designs entire communities.

B. Bruce Bare is a professor at the College of Forest Resources, University of Washington, Seattle, Washington.

Gordon A. Bradley is an associate professor at the College of Forest Resources, University of Washington, Seattle, Washington.

Susan Cerulean is the supervisor of Florida's Nongame Wildlife Program in Tallahassee, Florida.

Nancy A. Dawe is a writer/photojournalist from Decatur, Georgia, whose work has appeared in numerous regional and national publications.

David F. DeVoto is director of forestry for the Minneapolis Park and Recreation Board, Minneapolis, Minnesota.

Robert Dyke is an assistant editor at the American Forestry Association.

Sara Ebenreck, former executive editor of *American Land Forum*, is a Maryland writer, editor, and teacher.

Jan Goldstein is a horticulturalist-turned-landscape architect currently practicing with the Arlington County, Virginia, government.

Gene W. Grey, formerly Extension Forester in Kansas, is director of member services for the Society of American Foresters in Bethesda, Maryland.

Peter A. Grove, who for five years was director of the Norris Square Neighborhood Project, currently teaches lower school science at Friends Central School in Philadelphia.

Gary Hennen is a science writer and anthropologist from Virginia.

Robert A. Herberger, Jr., is an associate forester with the New York Department of Environmental Conservation, in Wappingers Falls, New York.

Deborah B. Hill is an associate extension professor with the Department of Forestry at the University of Kentucky in Lexington.

Clyde M. Hunt is a forester with the U.S. Department of Agriculture Forest Service in Broomall, Pennsylvania.

Joseph M. Keyser is a conservation writer and advertising director at the American Forestry Association.

J. James Kielbaso is professor of forestry at Michigan State University in East Lansing, Michigan.

316   SHADING OUR CITIES

Charles E. Little is a Maryland author and editor of numerous books and articles on land use and conservation, most recently *Louis Bromfield at Malabar Farm* (1988).

Edward A. Macie is senior arborist in Fulton County, Georgia.

Robert W. Miller is professor of forestry at the University of Wisconsin, Stevens Point, and author of *Urban Forestry: Planning and Managing Urban Greenspaces* (1988).

Gary Moll is a vice president and the director of programs and urban forestry at the American Forestry Association.

James J. Nighswonger is urban and community forestry program leader at Kansas State University, Manhattan, Kansas.

James Patterson is a soil scientist with the National Park Service, Ecological Services Laboratory, in Washington, D.C.

Thomas O. Perry is a professor of forestry recently retired from North Carolina State University, Raleigh.

F. Dale Robertson is chief of the U.S.D.A. Forest Service.

Josephine Robertson is a writer from Boulder, Colorado, with a special interest in gardens and trees.

Robert L. Rose is a Washington, D.C.-based news correspondent who reports on the environment.

Thomas R. Ryan is a landscape architect from Watertown, Massachusetts, who has spent fifteen years designing and building projects in the eastern and midwestern United States.

R. Neil Sampson is executive vice president of the American Forestry Association and the author of numerous conservation books and articles.

Alex A. Shigo is a retired forest researcher from the U.S. Forest Service who now directs Shigo and Trees, Associates, in Durham, New Hampshire.

Ralph C. Sievert, Jr., is the city forester in Cleveland, Ohio.

E. Thomas Smiley is a plant pathologist, soil scientist, and arboriculture consultant at the Bartlett Tree Research Lab in Charlotte, North Carolina.

David R. Smith, formerly a planner in Dayton, Ohio, is a consultant on urban forestry and greenspace management systems in Virginia.

Charles Stewart is president of Urban Forest Management, Inc., an urban forestry consulting firm with fifteen years experience in development on wooded sites.

Steven Teske is a Washington, D.C.-area journalist.

David Tylka is a freelance writer/photographer and professional urban biologist.

James Urban is a landscape architect based in Annapolis, Maryland, who is researching new techniques for growing trees in difficult city spaces.

Charles C. Weber was urban forester for the Northeast Alabama District of the Alabama Forestry Commission for seven years before becoming Huntsville's city arborist in 1985.

Nancy G. Westerfield, an Episcopal chaplain and journalist, was Nebraska's first Fellow in Literature under the National Endowment for the Arts.

Donald C. Willeke, an attorney and urban environmentalist from Minneapolis, Minnesota, is a director of the American Forestry Association.

Grateful acknowledgment is made for permission to reprint the following work: "The History of Trees in the City," from *Urban Forestry: Planning and Managing Urban Greenspaces,* by Robert W. Miller. © 1988 by Prentice-Hall, Inc., reprinted by permission of Prentice-Hall, Inc., Englewood Cliffs, N.J. "The Imperative Forest," by Donald C. Willeke, © 1987, appeared in the July-August 1987 issue of *American Forests* and is reprinted here with permission of Donald C. Willeke. "Who Owns the Trees," from *Tree Walks of Milwaukee County,* by R. Bruce Allison, © 1981, is reprinted by permission of R. Bruce Allison. "Planning for Wildlife," by Susan Cerulean, is excerpted from "Planting a Refuge for Wildlife," published by the Florida Game and Fresh Water Fish Commission; it is reprinted here by permission of the author. "Resolving Conflicts in the Urban/ Rural Forest Interface," by Gordon A. Bradley and B. Bruce Bare, is part of a forthcoming work and is used here by permission of the authors. "Planting the Campus," and "Arbor Day in Nebraska," by Nancy G. Westerfield, are reprinted by permission of the author; the latter poem first appeared in *Modern Maturity,* the magazine of the National Retired Teachers' Association. "Greenways and the City," by Charles E. Little, will be part of his forthcoming book from Johns Hopkins University Press, and all rights to its use are reserved by Charles E. Little. "Public Awareness and Urban Forestry in Ohio," by Ralph C. Sievert, Jr., is adapted with permission of the author from an article which first appeared in the *Journal of Arboriculture* 14 (2) (February 1988): 48–51.

The following chapters first appeared as articles in *American Forests* magazine and are reprinted here by permission of their authors: "Journey to the Center of a Tree," by Alex A. Shigo; "A Blueprint for Tomorrow: Getting Trees into Urban Design," by James Urban with Ralph C. Sievert, Jr., and James Patterson; "The Green Team: Who's Working on Trees?" by Jan Goldstein and Steven Teske; "Critters in the City," by David Tylka; "Improving the Health of the Urban Forest," "Branches and Wires: The Conflict Above," and "Construction That Fits the Forest," by Gary Moll; "Timber Cutting and the Law," by Robert A. Herberger, Jr.; "Reforesting the Campus," by Josephine Robertson; "Restoring Urban and Historic Parks," by Joseph M. Keyser; "Andrea's Tree," by Peter A. Grove; "Creating a Backyard Orchard," by Gene W. Grey; "Living Fences," by Deborah B. Hill; "Citizens with a Vision," by Nancy A. Dawe; "Kids and Trees for a Cleaner Chesapeake," by Robert L. Rose; and "Test Your Town's Trees," by E. Thomas Smiley.

"Developing a Successful Urban Tree Ordinance," by Charles C. Weber, was adapted from the Proceedings of the Second National Urban Forestry Conference (American Forestry Association, 1982) and is reprinted with permission of the author.

The following were adapted from the Proceedings of the Third National Urban Forestry Conference (American Forestry Association, 1986) and are reprinted with permission of their authors: "From Nursery to Planting," by David F. DeVoto; "On-Site Protection for Large Construction Projects," by Thomas R. Ryan and Charles Stewart; "Computer Software for Urban Forest Management: A Buyer's Guide," by E. Thomas Smiley; and "The Urban Forest Balance Sheet," by David R. Smith.

Index

Page numbers in *italics* refer to illustrations.

322 INDEX

Fairfax County, Va., 155, 156, 159
Fairmount Park, 195
Fairmount Park Commission, 277
falcons, 114
farmers, 33, 207, 236
farms, 25, 207
Federal Highway Administration, 96
fedges, 223
feeder roots, 82, 83–84, *84*
Feith, John, 195
fertilizer, 26, 88, 174, 219–220, 225
fibers, 75–76
fibrous roots, 83
field trips, 268–269
fir trees, 192
fish, 53
Fish and Wildlife Service, U.S., 115
flood plains, 85, 88, 164
floods, 204, 209
flowers, 55, 113–114, 249
forest fires, 9, 175, 234
forests, 9, 10
   community, 179–184, 206–210
   old growth, 52
   rural, 14, 17, 27, 66, 88, 155, 160, 208
   tropical, 9, 11, 12
   see also rural development; urban forests
Forest Service, U.S., 49, 50, 56, 66, 234, 274
fossil fuels, 12
Foster, Eugene, 239
foxes, 112, 113, 117, 208
France, 32
freeze-thaw cycle, 190
Friends of Conservation, 230
Friends of the Urban Forest, 232, 242–243
frogs, 113
frost, 84, 85
fruit trees, 216–221, *218*, 234
fuel sources, 12
Fulton County, Ga., 155, 156, 157–158, 159
fungus, 7, 76, 78, 82, 83, 192

Gallaher, Joanne, 19, 20
Gangloff, Deborah, 267*n*
Garden of Eden, 61
gardens, 233
   baroque, 32, 33, 109
Gardescu, P., 34
geese, 52, 64, 65, 69, 112, 114–115, *115*
General Sherman trees, 73
General Telephone, 241
George, Henry, 65
George Washington Memorial Parkway, 109
geotextile cloth, 99, 163
geotropism, 80
germ plasm, 124

ginala trees, 192
ginkgo trees, 28, 192, 276
Global ReLeaf, 12
global temperature, 8, 9
Glover-Archbold Park, 193
Goetz, Steve, 96, 97
Golden Gate Park, 195
Goldstein, Jan, article by, 102–105
golf courses, 113
Gould, Stephen Jay, 13, 24
graft incompatibility, 120, 124
Granite Garden, The (Spirn), 52
grapes, 27
grass:
   city, 29, 50, 51, 190, 191
   prairie, 28
   sea, 53
gravel, 99, 100, 133, 134, 163
gravity, 80, 81, 83
Great Britain, 33, 123, 225
Greeks, ancient, 55
Green, Tom, 195
greenbelts, 229
greenhouse effect, 8–12, 38, 57, 211, 278
Green Shores program, 237, 238, 239
greenways, 6, 10, 16, 17, 18, 22–23, 109, 166, 199, 200–205
   definition of, 200
   development of, 200–205
Grey, Gene W., articles by, 179–184, 216–221
ground covers, 191
Grove, Peter A., 197
growing season, 25
growth regulators, 140
growth rings, 74, 76, 83
gum trees, 27, 50, 85, 102, 192
Guthrie, Mike, 187, 192
gutters, 20
gypsy moths, 7, 29, 147

habitat, 4, 6, 12
hackberry trees, 106–107, 222
Haeckel, Ernest, 13
Halloween Haunted Trail, 56
Haney, Dennis, 187
Hansen, James, 8
hardwood trees, 7, 75, 109, 156, 198
hawks, 114
hawthorn trees, 191, 225
hazelnut trees, 225
Hazel-Peterson, 164
health, 52, 54
heart rot, 187
heartwood, 74
heat islands, 4, 5, 7, 10, 20, 22, 51
hedges, 222–225

Olympic Games of 1984, 231, 240, 241
onions, 74
orchards, 110
  backyard, 216–21
Oriental planetrees, 123
ornamental trees, 107, 113
Osage orange trees, 74, 222
O'Toole, William, 136
Owen, Wilfred, 46
owls, 113
Oxford (England), 123
oxygen, 10
  in soil, 26, 28, 81, 83, 84, 85, 87, 88, 89,
    97, 101, 134
  in water, 53
ozone, 6, 12

palm trees, 55, 60
palo verde trees, 19
pansies, 82
Paradise, Pa., 30
Paris (France), 32, 109
parks, 6, 16–17, 88, 113, 193–199
  decline of, 195
  maintenance programs for, 197–199
  philosophy of, 34, 194–195, 199
  preservation policy and, 193–195, 196,
    198–199
  wildlife of, 113
pastures, 9, 191
Patterson, James, 97
  article by, 93–101
paulownia trees, 17–18
Paxtang, Pa., 31
peace, 62–63
peach trees, 216
pear trees, 110
pecan trees, 27, 28, 217
Peck, Gregory, 241
Penn, William, 33, 233
Pennsylvania Horticultural Society,
  233
pepper, 28
Perry, Thomas O., article by, 80–89
pesticides, 26, 30
pH, 26, 101
phenols, 78
Philadelphia, Pa., 33, 195, 196–197, 233,
  276–277
Philadelphia Flower Show, 233
Philadelphia Green, 233
Philadelphia Ranger Corps, 276–277
phloem, 74, 75, 78
phosphorus, 237
photosynthesis, 10, 81
pigeons, 87, 114
Pinchot, Gifford, 194–195, 199

pine trees, 27, 28, 66, 83, 85, 110, 136, 192,
  195, 198, 206, 208, 213, 222, 225, 229
pin oak trees, 27, 88, 120
pith, 74
"Planting the Campus" (Westerfield), 191
Platte River Greenway, 204
pleaching, 109–110
poison ivy, 27
politicians, 5, 55, 58
pollination, 219
pollution:
  air, 4, 5, 6, 7, 12, 26, 38, 49, 50, 52, 54,
    57, 123, 133, 193, 210, 211, 214
  particulate, 52, 241
  water, 7, 53
poplar trees, 83, 88, 140, 164
population distribution, 3–4, 208
Portland, Ore., 96–97, 202
Post, Buckley, Schuh, and Jernigan, Inc.,
  201
"Potential Effects of Global Climate
  Changes on the United States, The," 28
poverty, 6, 54
prairie, 188, 189
privet shrubs, 27
Progress and Poverty (George), 65
Project Learning Tree, 274–275
property values, 38, 49–50
Proposition 13, 232
pruning, 78–79, 120, 128–129, 129, 140,
  217, 220, 225, 249
publications, 281–285
PVC pipes, 163

quality of life, 4–5, 6, 18
Quality of the Urban Environment, The
  (Owen), 46
Queens, N.Y., 245

rabbits, 28, 113, 117
raccoons, 113, 114, 115, 117
Raffel, Andrea, 196–197
rain, 7, 26, 49, 51, 52–53, 85
raspberries, 25
rats, 16
recreational activities, 112–113, 115, 176,
  191, 193, 194, 195, 198, 199, 208–209
redbud trees, 27, 140, 191
red maple trees, 123–124
Reed-Keppler Park, 195
reservoirs, 209
resource organizations, 294–299
respiration, 75
"Return of the Natives, The," 28
rivers, 51
roadrunners, 117
Robbinsdale, Minn., 231

Also Available from Island Press

The Challenge of Global Warming
Edited by Dean Edwin Abrahamson
Foreword by Senator Timothy E. Wirth
In cooperation with The Natural Resources Defense Council
1989, 350 pp., tables, graphs, bibliography, index
Cloth: $34.95 ISBN: 0-933280-87-4
Paper: $19.95 ISBN: 0-933280-86-6

The Complete Guide to Environmental Careers
By the CEIP Fund
1989, 300 pp., photographs, case studies, bibliography, index
Cloth: $24.95 ISBN: 0-933280-85-8
Paper: $14.95 ISBN: 0-933280-84-X

Creating Successful Communities: A Guidebook to Growth Management Strategies
By Michael A. Mantell, Stephen F. Harper, Luther Propst
In cooperation with The Conservation Foundation
1989, 350 pp., appendixes, index
Cloth: $39.95 ISBN: 1-55963-030-2
Paper: $24.95 ISBN: 1-55963-014-0

Resource Guide for Creating Successful Communities
By Michael A. Mantell, Stephen F. Harper, Luther Propst
In cooperation with The Conservation Foundation
1989, 275 pp., charts, graphs, illustrations
Cloth: $39.95 ISBN: 1-55963-031-0
Paper: $24.95 ISBN: 1-55963-015-9

Natural Resources for the 21st Century
Edited by R. Neil Sampson and Dwight Hair
In cooperation with the American Forestry Association
1989, 350 pp., charts, index
Cloth: $39.95 ISBN: 1-55963-003-5
Paper: $24.95 ISBN: 1-55963-002-7

The Poisoned Well: New Strategies for Groundwater Protection
By the Sierra Club Legal Defense Fund
1989, 400 pp., glossary, charts, appendixes, bibliography, index
Cloth: $31.95 ISBN: 0-933280-56-4
Paper: $24.95 ISBN: 0-933280-55-6

Reopening the Western Frontier
Edited by Ed Marston
From *High Country News*
1989, 350 pp., illustrations, photographs, maps, index
Cloth: $24.95 ISBN: 1-55963-011-6
Paper: $15.95 ISBN: 1-55963-010-8

Rivers at Risk: The Concerned Citizen's Guide to Hydropower
By John D. Echeverria, Pope Barrow, and Richard Roos-Collins
Foreword by Stewart L. Udall
In cooperation with American Rivers
1989, 220 pp., photographs, appendixes, index
Cloth: $29.95 ISBN: 0-933280-83-1
Paper: $17.95 ISBN: 0-933280-82-3

Rush to Burn
From *Newsday*
Winner of the Worth Bingham Award
1989, 276 pp., illustrations, photographs, graphs, index
Cloth: $29.95 ISBN: 1-55963-001-9
Paper: $14.95 ISBN: 1-55963-000-0

War on Waste: Can America Win Its Battle with Garbage?
By Louis Blumberg and Robert Gottlieb
1989, 325 pp., charts, graphs, index
Cloth: $34.95 ISBN: 0-933280-92-0
Paper: $19.95 ISBN: 0-933280-91-2

These titles are available from Island Press, Box 7, Covelo, CA 95428. Please enclose $2.00 shipping and handling for the first book and $1.00 for each additional book. California and Washington, DC, residents add 6% sales tax. A catalog of current and forthcoming titles is available free of charge.